The Childlike Kingdom

The Childlike Kingdom

An Alphabet for all Ages

JAY J. ANDERSON

RESOURCE *Publications* • Eugene, Oregon

THE CHILDLIKE KINGDOM
An Alphabet for all Ages

Copyright © 2025 Jay J. Anderson. All rights reserved. Except for brief quotations in critical publications or reviews, no part of this book may be reproduced in any manner without prior written permission from the publisher. Write: Permissions, Wipf and Stock Publishers, 199 W. 8th Ave., Suite 3, Eugene, OR 97401.

Resource Publications
An Imprint of Wipf and Stock Publishers
199 W. 8th Ave., Suite 3
Eugene, OR 97401

www.wipfandstock.com

PAPERBACK ISBN: 979-8-3852-3678-7
HARDCOVER ISBN: 979-8-3852-3679-4
EBOOK ISBN: 979-8-3852-3680-0

VERSION NUMBER 02/21/25

Unless otherwise noted all Scripture quotations not otherwise noted were taken from the Holy Bible, New Living Translation 1996, 2004, 2007, 2013, 2015, by Tyndale House Foundation. Used by permission of Tyndale House Publishers, Inc., Carol Stream, Illinois 60188. All rights reserved.

Scriptural quotations marked NIV are from the Holy Bible, New International Version. 1973, 1978, 1984, 2011 by Biblica, Inc. Used by used by permission of Zondervan. All rights reserved worldwide. www.Zondervan.com. The "NIV" and "New International Version" are trademarks registered in the United States Patent and Trademark Office by Biblica, Inc.

Scriptural quotations noted MSG are from THE MESSAGE. Copyright 1993, 1994, 1995, 1996, 2000, 2001, 2002 by Eugene H. Peterson. Used by permission of NavPress. All rights reserved. Represented by Tyndale House Publishers.

Scriptural quotations marked ESV are from the ESV BIBLE (The Holy Bible, English Standard Version). Copyright 2001 by Crossway, a publishing ministry of Good News Publishers. Used by permission.

Scriptural quotations marked BSB are from The Holy Bible, Berean Standard Bible. BSB is produced in cooperation with BibleHub, OpenBible.com, Discovery-Bible, and the Berean Bible Translation Committee. This text of God's Word has been dedicated to the public domain.

All original images are © Jay J. Anderson and may not be republished without permission.

For Kyle & Calvin

My favorite childlike kids

Jesus did not just forgive sinners. He gave them a new world to live in.

(WALTER WINK)

This, then, is how you should pray: "Our Father in heaven, hallowed be your name, your kingdom come, your will be done, on earth as it is in heaven."

(JESUS)

Contents

Foreword by Leonard Sweet | ix
In Gratitude | xiii
Introduction | xv

The First Bridge | 1

Kingdom 1, 2, 3's | 5

The Alphabet Bridge | 41

Kingdom A, B, C's | 43

The Final Bridge | 253

Appendix: CLK Main Takeaways | 259
About the Author | 263
Bibliography | 265

Foreword

In the shadow of Christmas lies a darker tale—that still echoes in remarkable traditions across the Christian world. The biblical account of King Herod's massacre of firstborn children has left such an enduring mark that even today, on December 28th, the Feast of the Holy Innocents, many Christians observe a custom born of that ancient trauma: they refuse to wash or hang clothes outside their homes. This practice, stemming from a haunting historical logic, recalls how hanging laundry could betray the presence of children during Herod's murderous search. Known as "Dia dos Innocents" in Latin America, this tradition persists across Portugal, Spain, Italy, and parts of Eastern Europe, carrying forward a memory of protection and sacrifice that reached its height in medieval times but continued to shape folk religious practices through the 19th century.

This profound historical wound appears to have shaped not just cultural memory but the very heart of Christian spirituality through Jesus's own ministry. In a time when children under six were often regarded with emotional distance—a protective response to devastating mortality rates and the economic burden of childrearing—Jesus took a revolutionary stance. His fierce defense of children emerged as one of his most distinctive characteristics, marked by some of his strongest language. He declared the following about those who would harm children, words that rang with the force of divine protection:

> *Better for you that a millstone be wrapped around your neck and you be dropped into the depths of the sea. (Matthew 18:6; Mark 9:42; Luke 17:2)*

Perhaps Jesus's extraordinary emphasis on children stemmed from a deep awareness that his very existence had cost innocent lives in Bethlehem. This personal connection to the Massacre of the Innocents might explain why he not only welcomed children into his movement but actively championed their worth, elevating them as models of authentic faith. In a culture that routinely overlooked the young, Jesus's approach to spiritual formation—what we would later call sanctification—centered on a radical premise: childhood represents the ideal state of faith.

> "Unless you change and become like little children," Jesus declared, "you will never enter the kingdom of heaven." (Matthew 18:3)

This stunning reversal suggests that childhood, with its inherent capacity for trust, wonder, and unfiltered love, is not a stage to outgrow but rather a state to aspire to. In this light, the Massacre of the Innocents takes on even deeper significance: those first martyrs were not just victims but exemplars of the very state of being that Jesus would later declare essential for entering God's kingdom. True discipleship formation, then, becomes a process of recovering childhood—of cultivating again that original openness to grace and capacity for holy wonder.

It is in this context that Jay Anderson's The Childlike Kingdom emerges as such a vital contribution to contemporary discipleship formation. At a time when childhood is increasingly compressed and faith formation often reduced to mere information transfer, Anderson's work reclaims Jesus's radical vision of childhood as a spiritual ideal. This remarkable book speaks to the "child" in all of us, offering wisdom that transcends not only age categories but spans of time as well. It is truly an alphabet for all *ages*.

Through masterfully crafted narratives, Anderson brings abstract theological concepts into vivid life. When young Jay learns to trust despite his fear of the dark woods surrounding him, or captures the joy of the wonder years, or considers the transformation of a caterpillar into a butterfly, readers encounter the essence of childlike faith in action. The book weaves together biblical insights, contemporary stories, and interactive exercises that invite readers—young and old—into a deeper experience of trust, wonder, and divine love.

Anderson's writing adopts the very qualities it celebrates: simplicity without simplification, wonder without naïveté, and wisdom without pretense. Each chapter builds upon the last, creating a comprehensive approach to faith formation that serves multiple audiences: children seeking to understand their relationship with God, parents and caregivers hoping to nurture spiritual growth, educators designing faith-based curricula, and any adult willing to rediscover the sacred art of becoming like a child.

In a world that often seems to have forgotten Jesus's revolutionary elevation of childhood as a spiritual ideal, The Childlike Kingdom arrives as both reminder and guide. It helps us understand why Jesus could point to children as our teachers in faith, and why the memory of those first martyred innocents continues to shape Christian practice today. This book isn't just about children's spiritual formation—it's about the recovery of childhood as the very path to God's kingdom.

Leonard Sweet
Orcas Island, WA
www.leonardsweet.com

In Gratitude

Everyone who finishes a book seems to have a large army to thank. Me? I have a small family. Family *all*. Let me introduce you to a few:

Marshall & Lesley Snider. Our besties. Marshall was *huge* in the development, editing, and graphics of this book. Thanks buddy. And we all have Lesley to thank for the name The Childlike Kingdom. So blessed to be living life with you both!

Heath Hollensbe. This is the second book my incredibly talented cohort mate has helped me with. I don't deserve you. I can't afford you. I can't live without you!

Kyle & Calvin Anderson. This book is dedicated to my two boys. Your challenges, encouragement, and examples were indispensable in bringing The Childlike Kingdom to life. And the life you bring to me is pure joy!

Stacie Anderson. My bride has stuck it out with me in the good times and especially the hard times, the healthy times and especially the sick times, at the top of the mountain and especially in the deep valleys. You're my best friend. Thanks for never giving up on me and for thinking of me much higher than will ever be justified. You are my love and my life!

Dr. Donald & Marriane Anderson. Your support not just for my writing ventures but for my entire life has been indispensable and overwhelmingly generous. Without you both this project doesn't happen and our quality of life plummets. We could never repay. Thank you.

In Gratitude

Father. The greatest revelation of God is not as king but as Father. My greatest peace, hope, and love is found in your arms.

Son. I am first and I am last a *Jesus guy*. You are all in all. The great I Am. My everything. My King.

Holy Spirit. I have never felt closer to you than when I was writing this book. Thank you for guiding me into truth, and for allowing me to *feel* your presence with a pen in my hand. Anything of lasting value in this book came from you.

Introduction

*Children have one kind of silliness, as you know,
and grown-ups have another kind.*[1]

(C.S. Lewis)

The priest took the small child from his mother, and then returned to the front of the sanctuary. He looked to the audience and simply said, "This is all God really wants from you." Then, in the hushed silence, he slowly returned the child to his mother's lap, and then to his seat on the front pew. After a long, pregnant pause, the service resumed.

The young priest wasn't the only one in a robe on this occasion. His was the only black one, however, in a sea of red and white mortar caps and gowns. It was the Baccalaureate service for the Central High School Class of 1986, in Independence, Oregon. *My* Baccalaureate. A service I had helped plan. A service where I was one of five student speakers. A service highlighted by the young priest who was highly recommended to us, both as a speaker and a host. But, quite honestly, I was surprised, confused, and disappointed by his brief homily. If you want to call it that. *I'm sure glad the student speakers will be able to carry the occasion,* I thought to myself. Especially the tall one. It would be more than three decades before I'd realize how wrong I was, and how truly profound his words were.

This book, crayons and cartoons notwithstanding, really isn't a children's book. Yet, at its heart, that's *exactly* what it is. It's kind of hard to

---

1. Lewis, *The Magician's Nephew*.

explain, which is probably why I use so many colors and pictures, though that's not the only reason. As a starting point, let's agree it's a book for kids of all ages, especially those who have experienced a few more birthday parties and Christmas mornings. And for my first word *play* it is also a book filled with truth that is for all times, all places, and all people . . . all *ages*. After all, the eternal words of Jesus will be front and center from start to finish.

This book is about change—not through political campaigns or religious rites—but through a total transformation of our thinking, loving, and living. In Scripture, this is called repentance. Repent, in our day, most often refers to a change of behavior, taking a 180-degree turn from our evil ways (sin). But there is so much more to it! True repentance, which Jesus has called all of us to, is the Greek word *metanoia*, which literally means to "change your thinking." But not just about sin. About *everything*. Jesus said it in his first recorded sermon:

> *Repent, for the kingdom of heaven has come near. (Matthew 3:2, NIV)*

But let the reader be warned this change of thinking is no small endeavor, and the conclusions are nothing short of revolutionary. We are talking about Jesus, after all. When Jesus said these words, those walking with and listening to him had *no idea* what he really meant. And neither do we . . . *yet*.

In that day everyone understood the reality of kingdom. They, and their ancestors before, had known nothing else. A powerful, singular ruler was in charge, and if you did what you were told, paid your taxes, and stayed within the borders, you would be protected and live in peace and prosperity. Well, that was how it was *supposed* to be, when there was a capable, good-hearted and generous king (or queen) in the castle. But, most unfortunately, it was most often not the case. Kingdom didn't, and doesn't, usually carry a positive connotation.

This was especially true in the days when Jesus was walking the dusty roads of the Middle East in sandals. There were several kings and other rulers in the picture, but they all answered to the not so benevolent Caesar. The empire of the day, based in Rome, was at its zenith with territory, power, and influence unmatched in the history of the world. But it was a worst-case scenario for many, including the nation of Israel. Which is still how most people react when they hear the word kingdom. Caste. Control. Colonialism. But, again, there is so much more to it! There must

Introduction

be, otherwise Jesus wouldn't have talked about it so much, and declared nothing else is more significant! He did?

> *What you should want most is God's kingdom and doing what he wants you to do. (Matthew 6:33, ERV)*

That's a resounding *yes* (!) in the red letters of Jesus, or any color you choose. And not just Jesus. In fact, the Kingdom of God is the central theme of the New Testament, and the phrase is used 126 times in the gospel accounts alone. The kingdom Jesus is announcing, and offering, is different. *Entirely different.* This is good news for those who have suffered under the yoke of slavery. This is good news for those who have been suppressed and oppressed in their life quests (hey, that's pretty good!). This is the *best news* for all who feel disillusioned by the systems, values, and governing philosophies of this world. In the end, I hope you'll find this primary metaphor as helpful, illuminating, and *fun* as I have.

Yet, it is perfectly understandable that some, and perhaps many, are starting with a negative, or even hostile, view of kingdom. It is amazing you've picked up this book and gotten this far. Bravo! I hope I can even change your kingdom outlook, or at least soften it a bit. Because I love it! Disney's Magic Kingdom anyone?

I often believe I was born in the wrong era and live in the wrong part of the country. I've got more than a bit of stuffy formal in me and think it perfectly reasonable to be required to change from a black coat to white tails at dinner time. Yes, Downton Abbey is my all-time favorite television show. But I live in the beautifully casual Pacific Northwest, so my bow ties and coats are rather dusty in my closet.

Now, before you throw down this book in disgust, I'm perfectly aware of the issues. *Significant* issues. But so was the creator of Downton, Julian Fellowes, who depicted the necessary and long overdue "changing of the guard" of this unfortunate (for most people), reality. I'm a strong believer that *all people* are created in the image of God and have incalculable value. So good riddance to the days of Downton. But I still said, "God Save the Queen," when I visited merry old England, and I still think *Lord Anderson* has a wonderfully noble ring to it!

Perhaps you have already discovered the Kingdom of God is almost always at odds with the empires and so-called wisdom of our world, both religious and secular. Scripture states:

> *For the wisdom of this world is foolishness in God's sight. (1 Corinthians 3:19, NIV)*

Read that again. Do we really believe this as followers of Jesus, or are we chasing the same *"vain philosophies, lust of the flesh and eyes, and pride of life" (See Colossians 2:8* and *1 John 2:16)* as everyone else? It is a fair question, and one we must ask ourselves continually.

If we desire to enter and experience God's kingdom, there is one requirement that is non-negotiable for Jesus. He said it, and he also *showed* it. And to say that it shocked the early listeners and followers of Jesus is an understatement. It still surprises the unsuspecting today. Here it is:

> *I tell you the truth, anyone who doesn't receive the Kingdom of God like a child will never enter it. (Mark 10:15)*

Jesus gives a clarion call, to *all*, to be *childlike*. Some of you already knew where this was going from the main title. Clever kids. However, there is a big difference between being child-*ish* and child-*like*. As big as the difference between the perpetually childish *Peter Pan* and his adventures in Neverland, and, well, *Jesus* and his adventures in the Promised Land! Scripture certainly doesn't celebrate immaturity, and neither does Jesus. God-willing, we will have our own grand adventure discovering and celebrating the difference as we pursue *childlike maturity* in each letter and every number waiting for us just ahead. And, God-willing, The Childlike Kingdom will be more than a book, but a series of books. Have I said how much I love the Kingdom of God? You might hear it once or twice . . . or even *five times* over.

Childlike is the whole idea. The very words of Jesus spell out his Father's intentions rather clearly:

> *O Father, Lord of heaven and earth, thank you for hiding these things from those who think themselves wise and clever, and for revealing them to the childlike. (Matthew 11:25)*

Here's the bottom line of what I'm saying, and showing:

> **If we are to enter and experience the Kingdom of God offered by Jesus, it will require us to change our thinking about everything, not just some things. It will require us to become, and live, childlike.**

Introduction

This book is a *primer* and makes no claims otherwise. The dictionary defines a primer as "an elementary book for teaching children to read and any book of elementary principles."[2] Both of these describe what is intended here. It is not the whole story, not by a long shot! It is simply an introductory guide to kingdom thinking, living, and loving. The first task in the schoolhouse is to learn to read. Literacy opens the door to all manner of learning and the world itself. Learning to read must be an intentional priority, both in the schoolhouse and in the kingdom. We need help with this, even more than the alphabet banner at the front of the classroom can provide. This is exactly why Jesus came and why the Holy Spirit remains. And why I use letters and numbers. And colors and crayons. And pictures. Lots of pictures. It will be up to *you*, by the way, to bring the pictures and headings to full color. So get yourself some new kingdom crayons (*gold, emerald, royal, sapphire, ruby, citrine*), and have fun kids! Don't worry if you go outside the lines.

The following pages are a labor of love for me. It is also my story. Because even though I have been a pastor and teacher for over three decades and have three rather impressive degrees (please refer to the words of Jesus above), my thinking has been *dramatically* changed in recent years. This has often been like a match being struck in a pitch-black cave. Have you ever experienced that? I can't wait to tell you all about it.

But for now, is that the bell ringing? Everyone grab a seat. Actually, grab your backpack, compass, and hiking boots. It's time to start our kingdom adventures!

2. Dictionary.com.

The First Bridge

Portland Oregon's Hawthorne Bridge (1910)

In Portland as it is in Heaven.
(BRIDGETOWN CHURCH VISION, PORTLAND, OREGON)

Before we start our journey into the ABC's, there is so much more to introduce! Perhaps the most important things... hence: 1, 2, 3's. They are also my favorite things to talk about. So if I have my way, I'll be starting each of these Childlike Kingdom (CLK) books with a few of my favorite things. Cue the Sound of Music soundtrack. To truly believe, live, and love in the Kingdom of God, we must first cross a bridge. This bridge is a fitting metaphor, especially for me, as I live in Portland, Oregon, often called "Bridgetown" for the eleven bridges spanning the Willamette River downtown. The Hawthorne Bridge, pictured above, is the oldest working lift bridge in the United States.

But in this context, I want to introduce the ideas of *orthodoxy* and *orthopraxy*. These concepts, and fancy religious words, denote two crucial aspects of following Jesus deep into kingdom territory. *Orthodoxy*, in simplest terms, means "right beliefs," and *orthopraxy* "right behavior." Now, certainly, there is much more to following Jesus than just believing all the right things and behaving appropriately at all times. However, it is a good place to start, because Jesus isn't calling us to just be his "BE-lievers," but as his followers to be kingdom "be-LIVE-rs!" And it follows that before we can truly follow, we must first consider *how* we should follow (say that fast three times), as well as the *why*, the *what*, and the *where*. But most important is the *who*.

This is where orthodoxy comes in. It spans the river of unbelief with sure footing to get to the other side. In modern religious terms, we most often refer to orthodoxy as theology. For many, that's not helping you want to keep reading, but stick with me, because just like Portland's, some of these bridges of belief are *beautiful!* (And say *that* fast . . . never mind).

At this point, I think it's fair for you to know I'm kind of a nerd. But I'm a *particular kind* of nerd thank you very much, and likely you are too (do I sound defensive?). No, not the science & engineering kind, with the pocket protector full of instruments, who design the bridge. And no, not the numbers whiz kind, who make sure the bridge reaches the other side and remains intact through weather, weight, and time. By the way, I learned the world doesn't want me building their bridges while I was in Mrs. Jobe's Physics class my senior year at Central High. Our hardest assignment (at least for me) was to build a bridge out of light balsa wood that could withstand twenty pounds of weight. It was pass or fail and I passed, so there! But the condition of my bridge at the end of the test, was, let's just say, less than road worthy. Some of my classmates' bridges were truly amazing and could withstand much more than the required weight and even looked like beautiful bridges. *Nerds!*

My particular brand of nerdiness is of the bookish kind. The librarian who shushes people. The kid who stays inside reading instead of being

The First Bridge

outside climbing trees. The kind of kid for whom the school system was designed. But particularly a *letters* kind of student. Jaybird was my name and Language Arts was my game. Some things will never change, because you don't want me doing your taxes or fixing things around your house. Thus, you'll see that this first book includes the whole alphabet, but only the first three numbers. *Perfect*. As the sign reads which hangs over my dad's wood stove, "I cannot live without books." (Thomas Jefferson) Or letters. A-men.

And a-men to a little bit of theology. But *just a little bit*. That's all it takes, actually. It is the smallest part that is often the most *essential*, like yeast in a loaf of bread, a U-bolt on a rocket ship, or a math equation in constructing a bridge. I promise to do my best to make it a sturdy and *tasty* bridge that will get off the theological launchpad! I'm also good at mixing metaphors.

Are you ready to cross the bridge and dive into the deeper theological waters? Or at least into the deep end of the pool? Don't forget your duckie ring!

Kingdom 1, 2, 3's

Kingdom 1,2,3's

1 Jesus

The central question of the gospel is not how can I be saved, but who is Jesus?[1]

(SCOT MCKNIGHT)

Jesus is a socialist.

(BUMPER STICKER)

Announcing the Kingdom

It matters where you start, because this largely determines how and where you finish. Our theology, our life, and the Kingdom of God begins and ends with Jesus, because he is the beginning and end, the first (alpha) and last (omega). Therefore, it is only appropriate we consider the teaching and example of Jesus first and most. Jesus said of his teaching:

---

1. McKnight, *Kingdom Conspiracy*.

> *Come to me, all of you who are weary and carry heavy burdens, and I will give you rest. Take my yoke upon you. Let me teach you, because I am humble and gentle at heart, and you will find rest for your souls. For my yoke is easy to bear, and the burden I give you is light. (Matthew 11:28–30)*

This sure beats the heavy yokes our theological constructs often fit us with, which are anything but easy or light. Better every day and twice on Sunday!

Countless books have been written, movies have been made, sermons have been preached, songs have been sung. Yet, how is it we haven't fully captured a theology of Jesus (Christology)? We can't. His story is so much *bigger*. His glory is so much *greater*. *He* is so much more than we can possibly understand, imagine, or even write about. Which lead John the Apostle to say:

> *Jesus did many other things as well. If every one of them were written down, I suppose that even the whole world would not have room for the books that would be written. (John 21:23, NIV)*

Nothing has changed, despite our digital advances and storage capacities. Yes, I suppose if every one of them were written down, not a single *chip* or the entire *cloud* could contain what has and could be written!

It shouldn't keep us from trying, however, to fill the earth and clouds with the words, deeds, and glory of Jesus. This will be my feeble attempt, which I'll repeat in each of the CLK books, with a slight twist in each one, of course.

1 Jesus

This is What I Believe About Jesus

Believe it or not, there are just a few religious doctrines I would pound my fist on the table over, take a bullet for, or stake my eternal life on. In fact, I've boiled it down to a single paragraph. I'm not saying these are the *only* beliefs I possess with conviction. I'm a trained preacher, after all. In fact, my Bible college preaching professor, dear Dr. Braddy, said preachers are too often guilty of "pontificating the unknowable." Guilty. However, we *should* pontificate the knowable. Here's a summary of what I know to be true:

> Jesus came from heaven to earth (his creation) to seek and save the lost, to offer and make possible eternal life in the Kingdom of God to all. He remained fully God while becoming fully man. Because of his great love for a harassed and helpless mankind, he died on a cruel Roman cross and on the third day rose again to life, victorious over death, sin, and the forces of evil. He will come again so that his children, created in the image of God, can experience new creation and live with him forever. I know all this because of the witness of Scripture, the witness of the saints before, and the witness of the Father (Almighty God), the Son (Jesus, the living Word of God), and the Holy Spirit (the very present breath of God).

Now, I know what you're thinking; *This sounds like a pretty fancy theological construct, Dr. Jay.* Guilty again. But let's take another look:

> Eternal Life Through Jesus [Only Him]
> The Divinity of Jesus [He's God]
> The Incarnation of Jesus [Fully God. Fully Man.]
> The Crucifixion of Jesus [He Died]
> The Resurrection of Jesus [He Rose From the Dead]
> The Return of Jesus [He's Coming Again to Earth]
> The Image of Jesus [The Imago Dei]
> The Inspired Word of God [The Scriptures]
> The Bride of Jesus [The Divine Community]
> The Trinity [One God ... Three Persons.]

Did that help? Yeah, me too. But do you notice what gets repeated over and over? Clever kids. Again, it's not what but *who*. If we're to have a proper orthodoxy, Jesus must be at the very center. Can we agree to *agree* on this?

Throughout this book, you'll find the *Kingdom Announcements* of each section will be written in a super cool old-world font. If this book were full color, they would also be in purple (my favorite color). But you can underline them in purple from your box of kingdom crayons, or with your e-reader highlighter. Most are shorter than the paragraph above, but when it comes to Jesus I can get totally carried away. As further proof:

This is Who Jesus is to Me

Jesus Is ... The Headline and the Bottom Line of the Kingdom

There is *nothing*. There is *nowhere*. There is *no one* who will *ever* approach the glory, majesty, and power of King Jesus. No movie marquis could ever have enough lights chasing around his name. No newsprint could ever make his name big enough or bold enough, nor could any posting fully capture his story. No prophet, priest, teacher, general, president, minister, or king is worthy to be mentioned in the same breath as *Jesus*.

1 Jesus

> *Therefore, God elevated him to the place of highest honor and gave him the name that is above all other names, that at the name of Jesus every knee should bow, in heaven and on earth and under the earth . . . (Philippians 2:9–10)*

Jesus is . . . a Person

Don't ever forget this: We are called to follow a *person*, not a road map, owner's manual, organization, tradition, or specific theological system (religion). Everybody has a message and a cause. We can have him!

Christmas is the perfect place to start our theological journey. Jesus, the king of the wooden feed box, came to earth as fully God and fully *a man* (not a myth or a legend). It's the doctrine of the incarnation: Jesus is God come in the flesh. And I'll fight you for it! This is why the Christmas story, and the first Account of Jesus (Matthew), starts with his genealogy. Before you skip over it, realize it is there so there will be no doubt the Son of God is also the Son of Man, and a real historical person. Go ahead and check it out. So put that in your pipe and smoke it, Santa! If we get this, *really* get this, it changes *everything*.

Jesus Is . . . The Gospel

Historically, a "gospel" was issued whenever kings conquered a territory, city, and people. It began something like, "Now hear this!" Then came the "good news" declaring who was their new ruler, and what was immediately expected. It wasn't always good news for the conquered, but nonetheless it was "the gospel" of the conqueror. Scripture announces "The Gospel" that King Jesus is the conqueror of death, sin, and hell, and it was (and is) good news indeed! Full surrender is still required, but the king himself will take care of the required terms. No more bloodshed is needed. It is finished.

But wait, there's one more thing. Jesus not only announced the good news; *He is* the good news! The gospel is not just a message *about* Jesus; The gospel *is* Jesus.

Jesus Is . . . The Focus of All Scripture

In Scripture, the Accounts of Jesus (Matthew, Mark, Luke and John) are in the center. This is helpful because the center of our theology must be the words and person of Jesus. "According to Jesus" must always be our default. One teacher, a former university professor, has a clever way of presenting this idea. He holds up the Scriptures by the spine of the book, the spine representing the Accounts of Jesus, noting they are:

> . . . the spine or backbone of the narrative, the climax and focal point toward which the Old Testament points and ascends and the peak from which the vigor and vitality of the New Testament flows. This is how Jesus can be seen . . . as the supreme and ultimate revelation of God, with the Old and New Testaments pointing to him like dual spotlights.[2]

What a great picture! Everything and everybody in all the scriptural account is wildly waving, pointing, and shouting; "It's him! It's *him!!*"

Jesus is . . . The King

Jesus Christ is *not* the crown prince of the kingdom. He is not the first in line to assume the throne. Unlike the newly crowned King Charles III of England, he hasn't been waiting in the wings to become sovereign. His rule and reign were announced and secured before the foundation of the earth. His reign *is* the very foundation of the earth. The very words of the Father declare:

> But about the Son he says, "Your throne, O God, will last for ever and ever, and righteousness will be the scepter of your kingdom." (Hebrews 1:8, NIV)

Isaiah the prophet, hundreds of years prior, announced Jesus to Israel and the whole world. It is perhaps the greatest prophetic utterance in all of Scripture, so stand up and read it out loud (I'm serious):

> For to us a child is born, to us a son is given, and the government will be on his shoulders. And he will be called Wonderful Counselor, Mighty God, Everlasting Father, Prince of Peace. Of the increase of his government and peace there will be no end. He will reign on David's throne and over his kingdom, establishing

---

2. McLaren, *A New Kind of Christianity*, 678–79.

and upholding it with justice and righteousness from that time on and forever. The zeal of the LORD Almighty will accomplish this. (Isaiah 9:6–7)

Sit down if you can. But don't get too comfortable. It's rather impossible, not to mention inappropriate, to sit in the presence of a king. Let alone *The King!* Stand in awe? *Yes.* Fall to your knees and cover your head? *Good idea.* Fall flat on your face prostrate, trembling and unmoving. *Most likely.* Isaiah himself experienced this:

In the year that King Uzziah died, I saw the LORD seated on a throne, high and exalted; and the train of his robe filled the temple . . . "Woe to me!" I cried. "I am ruined! Because I am a man of unclean lips . . . and my eyes have seen the King, the LORD Almighty." (Isaiah 6:1,5, NIV)

The prophet Isaiah had a rough go of it in life. So did all the prophets, including Jesus. *Rough.* The vision God gave to Isaiah was *terrifying.* The message God entrusted him to share with rebellious Israel was too. And the nation of Israel did not take it sitting down. The way he was treated by the people he was sent to warn and encourage was, like the others, *shameful.* The calling God gave Isaiah was impossible, and not the first *mission impossible* given to one of his prophets. Therefore, this summons to the throne room was a gift that no doubt sustained Isaiah in the darkness and suffering to come.

We, too, can be encouraged in our own darkness and suffering. We will likely have to wait awhile to be ushered into the very throne room of God. Yet there is no waiting required to experience the presence, rule, and reign of King Jesus. We simply need to respond as Isaiah: *"Here am I."*

Jesus is . . . So Much More!

What would *you* add to this royal list? Because the greatest question of all, for each one of us, is the same one asked of the first followers:

But what about you? Who do you say I am? (Mark 8:29, NIV)

Picturing the Kingdom

How do you picture Jesus? If you were given an empty canvas, like Leonardo da Vinci, or a block of marble, like Michelangelo, where would your imagination take you? What would you emphasize? What colors would you use? What features of his body and face would be unforgettable? Before you pick up your brush or chisel, you'd better listen to the prophet Isaiah one more time:

> *He had no stately form or majesty to attract us, no beauty that we should desire Him. He was despised and rejected by men, a man of sorrows, acquainted with grief. Like one from whom men hide their faces, He was despised, and we esteemed Him not. (Isaiah 53:2–3, BSB)*

Alright, artists, you may begin.

Yet, the world is full of priceless and exquisite pieces of art, from the scores who have tried. Thank God they did! But the fair skin, perfect proportions, and well-trimmed beards fall far short, as do our books and sermons.

I do have a favorite, however, and I imagine you do, too. Here is mine. I love it! Why this one? It captures his childlike side, of course. In fact, Jesus serves as our *greatest* example of childlike. And as the priest from Independence said, "This is all God expects from you."

1 Jesus

Life in the Kingdom

We are first called to believe. It is not passive, but is our first work: *"The work of God is this: to believe in the one he has sent." (John 6:29, NIV)*

It goes beyond proper orthodoxy, however. We don't just believe the right things. We believe the right *person*. And make no mistake, as Isaiah's life demonstrates, it is *work* to believe Jesus in the midst of darkness and suffering. But as one of my boys' most influential athletic coaches used to urge, "Do the work!" (Scott Olson) Then we follow. We *exercise* proper orthopraxy. What? When? Where? How? We'll get to these in due course. But we begin, and end, our journey with *who*:

I am the way and the truth and the life. No one comes to the Father except through me. (John 14:6, NIV)

That's more than enough for now. Jesus himself is more than enough.

2 The Kingdom of God

No teaching in the New Testament has been more vigorously debated than this. However, the Kingdom of God was the central message of our LORD's ministry.[1]

(George Eldon Ladd)

Announcing the Kingdom

What do I really mean by the Kingdom of God? Most importantly, what did Jesus mean when he announced the kingdom? If you want the best theological answer, I recommend Professor George Ladd. His short book, The Gospel of the Kingdom, published in 1959, is still *the* textbook on the subject. In fact, I just talked to a professor who said it is still required reading for each new student at his school. Perhaps that should be true for all my new readers, too? But whether you take me up on this or not, you'll be hearing from Dr. Ladd frequently on our journey. So buckle up kingdom scholars.

In the introduction to Ladd's kingdom opus, Oswald Smith gives a fantastic summary, which will give us a great kick-start:

---

1. Ladd, *The Gospel of the Kingdom*, Forward.

2 The Kingdom of God

> The Kingdom of God is basically the rule of God. It is God's reign, the divine sovereignty in action. God's reign, however, is manifested in several realms, and the Gospels speak of entering into the Kingdom of God both today and tomorrow. God's reign manifests itself both in the future and in the present and thereby creates both a future realm and a present realm in which man may experience the blessings of His reign.[2]

It will take us awhile to unpack this so we'd better get started, don't you think? Oh, what great fun we're going to have!

This is What I Believe About the Kingdom

The Kingdom of God is . . . The Rule and Reign of Jesus

Speaking of, I just made a fun discovery (nerd alert!). As I was meditating on Ladd's theology, I found myself wondering if God's rule and reign are the same thing. Not exactly, but close enough for our purposes now. However, when I looked up both words in the Oxford Dictionary, I noticed that both can either be a noun or a verb. I think this might be something to dig in to:

Divine sovereignty in action (verb). Can you think of anything more awesome than this? No, not how we kids often misuse awesome. I mean in the truest sense of the word: *Awe-inspiring! Breathtaking!! Cool!!! Divine!!!! Extraordinary!!!!!* And that's just the first 5 letters of the alphabet. We should probably stop right there. But, of course, I can't . . .

F is for Frightening. Yes, this too. Sorry. Scripture often touts the value of a healthy fear of God. But this can be overblown, and preachers are the worst culprits. However, when it comes right down to it, it really *can't* be overblown. It is the omnipresent (all-present), omniscient (all-knowing), and omnipotent (all-powerful) God we're talking about after all. Yes, he calls us his friends. Yes, he calls us his children. Yes, he moved into the neighborhood. But we can't let this *awesome* reality cause us to forget . . . this is *God* we're talking about!

Scripture is clear and consistent: When God is moving and active . . . saints *be glad!* But when God is moving and active . . . saints (and sinners) *beware!* Both are true at the same time. Because his sovereignty in action is both a *cleansing* and *consuming* fire. His presence in its fullness will cause us to both *wonder* and *weep* (remember Isaiah?). His very

---

2. Smith in Ladd, *The Gospel of the Kingdom*, 11.

nature is both love and truth in action . . . which must cause us to *rejoice* and *repent*.

His sovereignty in action is the perfect description of the rule and reign of Jesus. One of many perfect descriptions. Here's another one:

> *The people walking in darkness have seen a great light; on those living in the land of the shadow of death a light has dawned. (Isaiah 9:2, NIV)*

Isaiah, like many of the other prophets, foretold of the coming calamities due to the unfaithfulness of the people of God. Yet, Isaiah, like most of the other prophets, also foretold the coming *Day of the LORD*, when all wrongs will be made right, when death will be swallowed up in life, and when darkness will give way to the kingdom of *light*. Matthew repeated the words of Isaiah, as he recounted the beginning of Jesus's preaching ministry, declaring the fulfillment of the prophet's words. Let the sermon begin:

> *Repent, for the kingdom of heaven is near. (Matthew 4:17, NIV)*

A new day was dawning. The dawning of the Day of the LORD. The Day Jesus said the prophets waited for with bated breath. The Day of the fresh dawning of the Kingdom of God, embodied in the Son of Man and the Son of God, released on the dawning of the first Easter Sunday. The Day of resurrection and life. The sonrise that would never set. On that day, the kingdom of light shone brightly on a dark world . . . light never to be extinguished. An empty tomb . . . never be filled again. A divine rule come to earth . . . never to depart. A divine reign made available to man . . . never to be taken away. The divine sovereignty of God active on earth in Jesus . . . never to cease. *Awe-inspiring! Breathtaking!! Cool!!! Divine!!!! Extraordinary!!!!! Frightening!!!!!!*

Awesome.

The Kingdom of God is . . . The Realm of Now and Not Yet

Here is where we add to rule and reign the idea of *realm*. It certainly makes sense that a sovereign must have a realm to reign and rule over. For most of the kings of the earth this realm was passed down, one king to another, royal subjects included. And, unfortunately, for most this realm also included territory recently conquered. Yes, kings most often were at war. It was just part of the job description. Aren't you glad that has changed? Never mind.

2 The Kingdom of God

Going back to our friends George and Oswald, they record several statements relating to God's realm:

> God's reign, however, is manifested in several realms, and the Gospels speak of entering into the Kingdom of God both today and tomorrow. God's reign manifests itself both in the future and in the present and thereby creates both a future realm and a present realm in which man may experience the blessings of His reign.[3]

The heading above is one of my favorite descriptions of the Kingdom of God. *The Realm of Now and Not Yet.* Smith uses *today and tomorrow, present and future.* Take your pick because the truth of each is good news! It helps all the pieces fall into place. The prophets have a now and not yet aspect, as well. The poets, too, rejoice in the today and tomorrow of the kingdom. And the historical narratives tell the current story and point to the future. If we're to understand the Scriptures, and follow their divine author, we must keep this in focus.

There is a story of a strange funeral request which perfectly illustrates this reality. A woman who knew she was soon to die met with her pastor, who would be officiating her service, to confirm her wishes. One of these was the strangest he'd ever heard. She wanted to be viewed, and buried, with a fork in her right hand. Surely the pastor had a befuddled look on his face as he asked the question for all of us, "Why in the world?" We'll let her explain:

> In all my years of attending church socials and potluck dinners, I always remember that when the dishes of the main course were being cleared, someone would inevitably lean over and say, "Keep your fork." It was my favorite part because I knew that something better was coming.[4]

So the next time, and every time, you eat your dessert with a fork remember the best dessert (and everything else) is still to come.

---

3. Smith in Ladd, 11.
4. http://www.llerrah.com/keepthefork.htm.

Divine sovereignty on earth as in heaven (noun). However, as Jesus spoke of the Kingdom of God, he most often focused on its present reality. It was a kingdom whose time had come. He came to usher in the kingdom (noun), on earth just as in heaven. He planted a flag on earth, as American astronauts did on the moon, but in the form of a cross. And if you look closely, you'll see a four-letter word written on each nail. And he longs to tattoo the same word on each and every heart on earth (just as in heaven).

Not only does Jesus plant flags on earth, he plants gardens. And cities. Eden was simply the first garden, but just wait until the last one! If you turn to the last two chapters in Scripture, you'll read a breathtaking description of what our master gardener has in store:

- *The New Jerusalem . . . It shone with the glory of God, and its brilliance was like that of a very precious jewel, like a jasper, clear as crystal.*

- *The River of the Water of Life . . . As clear as crystal, flowing from the throne of God . . . Down the middle of the great street of the city. On each side of the river stood . . .*

- *The Tree of Life . . . Bearing twelve crops of fruit, yielding its fruit every month. And the leaves of the tree are for the healing of the nations.* (See Revelation 21 & 22)

2 The Kingdom of God

The heavens and earth becoming one. The people of God *fully* in the presence of God, forever. And written on the streets, in the sky, and on every heart . . . *MINE!*

Yep, realm is surely one of my favorite *Nown's* . . . and *not yet's*.

The Kingdom of God is . . . Upside Down and Backwards

One of my favorite children's books, written by my hero and his wife, Josh & Dottie McDowell, is titled The Topsy Turvy Kingdom. It humorously illustrates what happens to a kingdom when people don't live and base their life on truth. "What if up became down, and cold became hot, and night was no different than day?"[5] It's a brilliant fairy tale, that, like all fairy tales, communicates a profound truth. In this case, the confusion and despair when truth is ignored, and people live however they want.

Now stick with me here, because I want this *image* to stick with you. The kingdom Jesus was making possible on earth is also upside-down and backwards. But unlike in the McDowell's story, it isn't upside-down and backwards from the way that it should be. It is upside-down and backwards from the misguided empires of this world which are totally contrary to the thinking, living, and loving of the Kingdom of God.

Jesus also used stories *(parables)* to illustrate the Kingdom of God. They, too, were fictional, but also brief, memorable, and *profound*. Whenever Jesus uttered the words, *the Kingdom of God is like . . .* everyone sat up and listened. Are you sitting up? Because along the kingdom road we do *best* to consider each story and each word of Jesus.

But Jesus did more than tell stories. He *re-wrote* the stories and teachings of the day, introduced by his oft repeated words, *you have heard it said . . . but I tell you . . .* And if the audience wasn't sitting up by this point, they surely were now. Why? Because the kingdom Jesus was announcing was not only different but completely upside-down and backwards. *Topsy-turvy!* Like the McDowell's describe, "Something is topsy-turvy when it is totally different from the way you would expect it to be."[6] And how true this is of the Kingdom of God. Thus, did most of the crowd *totally* miss it. And so can we.

So what was Jesus doing? He was *(re)signing* the Kingdom of God. Huh? Another literary hero of mine is my doctoral professor (and sage),

---

5. McDowell, McDowell, and Weiss, *The Topsy Turvy Kingdom*.
6. McDowell, McDowell, and Weiss.

renowned author Leonard Sweet. If ever there is a person who embodies the Dos Equis Most Interesting Man in the World, it is Dr. Sweet. What an honor to have his signature on my diploma, and on the Forward of this book. Part of Len's life mission is helping students of all stripes understand *the signs of the times.* The fancy higher-ed term for this is Semiotics.

The Tribe of Issachar was known as *"men who understood the times and knew what Israel should do." (See 1 Chronicles 12)* Our dear professor, after drilling and grilling us for three years, welcomed us into this tribe. We dare not miss the signs of *our* times all around us. We just need to learn how to look, interpret, and know what to do. Just like the Tribe of Issachar. *Just like Jesus.*

Jesus was a master semiotician. Part of the job of the semiotician is to take the familiar signs of the day and give new meanings to these images. Literally *re-signing*. The first book Dr. Sweet introduced us to was written by another smartie professor. She uses the primary metaphor of a coin (special state edition quarter) standing on edge and rolling through culture (with you doing a balancing act on the top). From here you can see both sides of the coin, one side which remains constant (George's face) and the other which is (re)signed for each state. This profoundly illustrates the delicate balance of tradition and change:

> This is the position of (re)signing truth: resigned to the headship of Jesus Christ, you maintain trust in the sign to the right, where the words 'In God We Trust' still appear. But your position on the edge also enables you to look to the left, where you can enjoy and celebrate the re-signing of the coin. Just as each state of the union determines its own sign on the quarter, so each new era or state of culture determines new signs for the faith.[7]

Brilliant! This is the special quarter for my home state of Oregon, with me balancing as it rolls. I had the most talented cohort mates.

So how did Jesus (re)sign the kingdom? He did it with words and stories, but, like any master teacher, it went far beyond this. I talked specifically in my dissertation about how Jesus re-*image*d (read that word again) signs, bringing new meaning to the

---

7. Downing, *Changing Signs of Truth,* 57.

foot-washing *basin*. You say you want to be great in the Kingdom of God? Then do as he did and serve like a slave would. Really? And gross! There is also the re-imaged *table of showbread* that became the table of the Eucharist (Communion), with Jesus himself being the bread (of life). And how about King Jesus riding into Jerusalem on a humble *donkey* (sign of the tribe of Issachar), instead of an impressive and imposing war horse, like Pilate did? This was not what was expected from the long-awaited Messiah. Just wait.

The cross is, of course, the best (re)sign of Jesus. Jesus, on one Good Friday, re-imaged the cross from the greatest symbol of terror and torture to the greatest symbol of love and forgiveness. New Testament scholar N.T. Wright has said:

> . . . it is because he is the Son of God that Jesus must go to the cross, that he must stay there, that he must drink the cup to the dregs. And he must do so not in order to rescue people from this world for a faraway heaven, but in order that God's kingdom may be established on earth as in heaven.[8]

Umm . . . *wow*.

Picturing the Kingdom

Connect the Dots

I've already brought up several powerful kingdom images Jesus and others have used. But to further help us with the concept of semiotics, picture the child's game of Connect the Dots. Actually, you won't have to. I've done it for you below. Yes, you must stop reading and connect them . . .

---

8. Wright, *Simply Jesus*, 184.

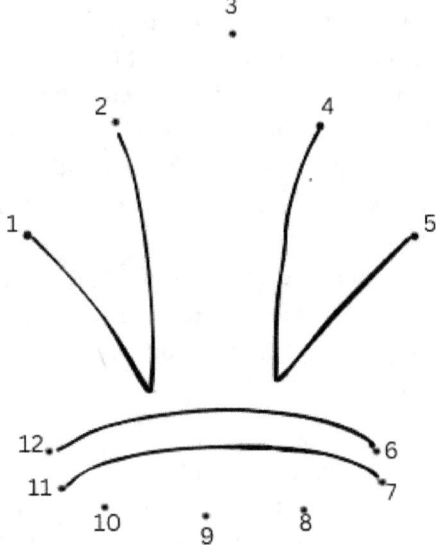

Once the dots are connected the image becomes clear. But first the dots must be *seen* (keen observation), *connected* (wisely interpreted), and the resulting image *understood* (in proper context). Easy-peasy. Welcome to the Tribe of Issachar. *Hee-Haw!*

In the pages to come, we'll be spending ample time (in every letter) considering our *Life in the Kingdom*. Jesus has always been about the *living* not just the hearing:

- *Therefore everyone who hears these words of mine and puts them into practice is like a wise man who built his house on the rock.* (Jesus, preaching on the Mount)
- *LORD, I am ready to go with you to prison and to death.* (Peter, at the Last Supper)
- *I preached that they should repent and turn to God and demonstrate their repentance by their deeds.* (Paul, before King Agrippa)
- *Do whatever He tells you.* (Mary, at a wedding in Cana)
- *Now that you know these things, you will be blessed if you do them.*[9] (Jesus, after washing his first followers' feet)

---

9. Matthew 7:24; Luke 22:33; Acts 26:20; John 2:5; John 13:17 (All NIV).

2 The Kingdom of God

The Scriptures are abundantly clear from start to finish (A to Z); God really does care how we live. Why? So he can slap the back of our hand with a ruler when we don't obey? No. He wants us to live life to the full in the kingdom he has prepared for us. He wants us to live . . . *really live!*

But first . . .

Life in the Kingdom

Full Surrender

Love the LORD your God with all your heart and with all your soul and with all your mind. This is the first and greatest commandment. (Matthew 22:37–38, NIV)

In warfare, when a commander is ready to surrender, he sends for the "terms of peace" from the enemy. It is the conquering king who has the right to set the requirements. Sometimes the demands are acceptable, but other times they decide to fight on. The Old Testament story where Saul rescues the city of Jabesh-Gilead is a great example. The Ammonites had surrounded the city and were preparing to siege and sack it, as was their custom. So what were the terms of peace to stop the destruction and carnage? The Ammonites demanded gouging out the right eye of each fighting man. Not good. Fortunately, it was Saul to the rescue!

How wonderful it is that the king and commander of the armies of heaven isn't an evil tyrant who is only satisfied, in Shakespearian terms, with a "pound of flesh," or right eye. His character is love and his expressions benevolent. But as our conquering king, should we choose to surrender, his terms are nonetheless demanding. *All.* Everything. Only then can we know peace. But some choose to fight on. Someday the fighting will be over, and the outcome is already sure. But should we have the good sense to come to terms with our Creator, peace will cost us everything. *It cost him everything, too.*

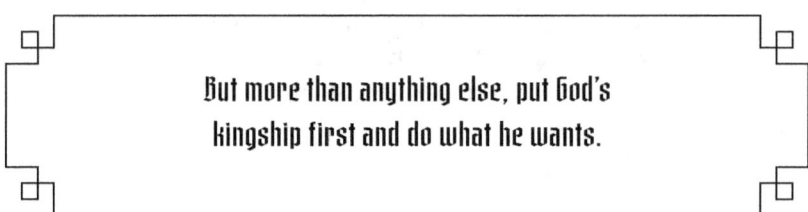

But more than anything else, put God's kingship first and do what he wants.

First Priority. First Pursuit.

Full surrender doesn't stop after we've put down our sword. It has just begun. Because fully surrendered living equals abundant life in the kingdom. When we *"seek first his kingdom and his righteousness,"* the upside-down and backwards kingdom kicks in. We no longer need to *"run after all these things"* (life, food, drink, body clothes), like everyone else. Because *"your heavenly Father knows that you need them. Therefore do not worry about tomorrow, because all these things will be given to you as well."* (See Matthew 6, NIV)

Full surrender doesn't stop with all our heart, soul, and mind. Jesus was quoting the law from Deuteronomy 6, just one chapter after the Ten Commandments. By the way, you realize that as a Rabbi he had all five books of the law memorized, right? Thus, he knew exactly what he was doing, though sometimes there was an unexpected twist. This is one of those times, because Jesus changed one of the words from the original *Shema* as he declared the most important commandment. The law calls us to:

> *Love the LORD your God with all your heart and with all your soul and with all your strength . . . Tie them as symbols on your hands and bind them on your foreheads. (Deuteronomy 6:5,8, NIV)*

And they did, literally, though God ultimately wants his commandments written on our hearts. Fully surrendered living involves our head, our heart, and our hands . . . all of us. It is not just a decision of will or warm affection. It is the engagement of all of our strength, too. Jesus knew that the teachers and experts of the law had that much figured out. But they had stopped before *all*. The kingdom, and the king, must continue to be our *first* priority, and *first* pursuit.

For me, this concept truly came to life in a conversation with a mentor right after losing a dream job due to budget cuts. I was devastated. After receiving the news, we immediately sold our home with a view, moved out of my corner office, and said goodbye to beloved friends and colleagues. Fortunately, we did very well in the sale of our home and were able to bank a significant "nest egg" for a future home purchase. Six months later, and still without a job, the conversation ensued, as I recounted all we had "lost." Not only was I convinced I was willing to give all, but actually believed I had. Then I mentioned *our* nest egg. My mentor pounced. Uh-oh.

2 The Kingdom of God

"So you're saying the nest egg is yours?" The tears flowed as a fresh realization of the terms of peace hit.

"You mean after all we've given up, Jesus still wants more?"

"He simply wants *all*."

Have you put down your sword and fully surrendered? Good! Just don't pick it up again, despite what the commanders in this world are shouting. Do you remember what *The Commander* shouted to Peter after he had cut off an ear in the garden?

> *Put your sword away! Shall I not drink the cup the Father has given me? (John 18:11, NIV)*

Jesus could have called on legions of angels who were just itching for him to say the word. He did. But it wasn't the word anyone was expecting. He said, *enough!* Then he held out his wrists for the cuffs (nails). *Fully surrendered.*

God has a cup (will) for each of us, as well. We don't get to choose the cup. But, as with the Eucharist, we choose to follow Jesus and drink. And as the Roman Catholic parish signs near my house say, we become God's *Walking Eucharist*. And from death springs *life!* Abundant. Eternal. Unimaginable.

You won't miss your sword a bit.

3 Childlike

My faith is getting more simple, more childlike ... while my theology is getting more complex, more adult, and mature.[1]

(LEONARD SWEET)

A childlike faith is often challenged.

(VICAR JOHNNY HUGHES)

God can do anything, you know—far more than you could ever imagine or guess or request in your wildest dreams! (Ephesians 3, MSG)

Kids have the craziest imaginations. Especially Calvin. In Bill Watterson's comic strip, he and his fuzzy side-kick Hobbes live life on a wild ride, by wagon, sled, and spaceship! Most people only see a stuffed tiger when they come across Hobbes, but Calvin knows the truth. Hobbes is actually a ferocious tiger waiting to pounce and have fantastic adventures. Oh, and he is full of sage wisdom and a wicked sense of humor. Calvin & Hobbes is the comic pages GOAT (Greatest of All Time). Thanks, Bill, for the childlike world you created.

---

1. Sweet, *Jesus Human*, 378.

3 Childlike

God created a childlike world, as well. It's called the Kingdom of God. Sadly, most don't picture God's kingdom this way. Perhaps it's because of our *under* active imaginations. Or because we stopped watching cartoons. Or playing with Legos. But I think there is something much more sinister afoot. It's time to call in Scooby Doo and his team in the Mystery Machine.

When the lead dog and his gang of sleuths piled out of their green van it was monsters and ghouls beware! Sure, the villains had them on the run in the beginning, but it always ended up with the great unveiling and the suddenly not so menacing bad guy in the creepy costume. "And let's see who it is . . . *Mr. Murphy!*" And they always would've gotten away with it if it wasn't for "you meddling kids!" Take him away, sheriff. Another mystery solved and another castle no longer haunted.

But then we grow up, only to realize, as in later episodes when Scooby and Shaggy hit the big screen, sometimes the monsters are real. Right? Then it's not so fun anymore. It's a sad day when we finally put down our magnifying glass, only to pick up some not so childish fears. These days they call it *adulting*. We're now old enough to realize sometimes there really is danger around the next bend. We're experienced enough to know our terror is sometimes justified. We've seen enough of life to know it really can be a horror show with a bad ending. And we've read enough of Scripture to know we have a very real adversary who is *not* wearing a costume! Well, sometimes he does.

Sorry, it got a little dark there. But you all know what I'm talking about. So what's the answer for everything that goes bump in the night? More importantly, what's the answer when it also bumps during the day? As always, the answer is *who*. And what is his answer to all that scares us, all the ails us, and all that so easily confuses us? *Childlike*. This again? Yes. Sherlock Holmes was right; it simply *is* elementary.

I mentioned earlier Jesus has called us, and pointed us, to childlike living. Again, this is not Peter Pan being pulled back to Neverland for another epic sword fight with Captain Hook. This is not an imaginary world of our creation where our elderly task master teacher (Miss Wormwood) becomes an evil space alien. This is the very real realm called the Kingdom of God, where love, joy, and peace rule and reign supreme. Where we lay down our sword and embrace our enemy. Where the lion lays down with the lamb, and we don't have to get a new lamb in the morning! It is the Childlike Kingdom, where twenty-four-hour adulting is no longer required. Where we're never alone and there are no monsters under the bed.

Thus, the answer, it seems to me, is to have a properly orthodox theology of childlike. Have you ever imagined such a thing? Yeah, me neither. Until the words of that Independence priest finally sunk in. "This is all God really wants from you." Okay, but what does that really mean? Perhaps we should ask Calvin.[2]

Classic! Can you see why we named one of our boys Calvin? I tried to name the other Hobbes, but my wife Stacie got out the veto stamp. She's the president, you know. She's also a bit more of a grown-up than me (was that a compliment?). And significantly more spiritual (or is she?). She would say put down the comics, if you really want to know what childlike means, and go ask Jesus. Because as fantastic as the above strip is, Calvin got it exactly backwards. It is *maturity* that is temporary (in all of its forms). Childlike is forever!

Before we go any further, it's important we understand what Jesus thinks about kids. It was rather unexpected. Jesus was famous for that. But not just unexpected, *shockingly* unexpected! Jesus was *most* famous for that. It's true. Such as how he treated women. We'll get to that later, but it is surprisingly similar to how he treated the kids, in a culture that, well, hang on a minute . . .

Culture is an important part of our lives on earth. We are social. We are tribal. We create and we cultivate. We were designed this way. In the next book we'll take a deep dive into culture, because our understanding of it is critical *(Hee-Haw!)*. For now, however, I want us to get used to looking to Jesus *first, last,* and *most.* This is our way forward in the Kingdom of God. What did Jesus teach? What did Jesus command? What did Jesus demonstrate? We must hang on every word, every deed, every verse.

---

2. CALVIN AND HOBBES © 1989 Watterson. Reprinted with permission of ANDREWS MCMEEL SYNDICATION. All rights reserved.

3 Childlike

Jesus Demonstrated We Should *Notice* the Children

> *You see this child . . . ? (See Mark 10)*

Can you just picture the bewildered looks when Jesus said this? Perhaps not, because in our culture kids are highly visible. In the culture where Jesus was living, kids were essentially invisible. So when he asked this simple question, for most the answer was, "Wait, what?" Or, "Nope." Including his first followers.

Jesus Taught We Should *Value* the Children

They meant well, but Jesus's original gang of twelve were a product of their culture. So are we. It's not all bad. But in this case, Jesus wasn't having it. He rebuked his boys right in front of God and everybody:

> *Let the children come to me! Don't try to stop them.*

Talk about confused and befuddled. They were just trying to manage the crowd so people could hear his teaching. But with Jesus, these meddling kids *were* his message. He told the *adults* to stop meddling!

The adults of that day had quite different values than we do today. A big part of this was a pronounced "survival mentality." Life was hard. Resources were scarce. The Romans were cruel. And kids were *expensive*. That's true of every culture. But they were also *expendable*. Because of disease, malnutrition, and abounding danger, way too many kids died way too early. Early mortality was the norm. Losing a child along the way was expected. The idea of a children's hospital wouldn't have crossed their minds. Wait, what is a hospital?

But Jesus valued the children. And he didn't just call them forward, from the back of the crowd, to sit at his feet. He welcomed them into his arms. Like the Independence priest, how many times do you think Jesus taught with a child in his arms or in his lap? If we can picture *that* then we're well on our way to understanding and embracing the Kingdom of God.

But not just that . . .

Jesus Commanded We Should Be *Like* Them

People who are like these children belong to the Kingdom of God.

Sorry to use a fancy theological word again, but this is scandalous! Even in our day. Yep, Jesus again. Then and now. Some of them got more than confused or befuddled. They got mad. Most of these were the religious types. Some others were the political types (Jesus had a revolutionary on his staff after all). Jesus was an equal opportunity offender. He wasn't always meaning to offend (which means sometimes he was). It was just the natural response to a supernatural person with a supernatural message. Beliefs were being questioned. Traditions were being challenged. Power was being threatened.

Jesus responded by pointing to the children. You want real power? Go to the back. You want to protect your precious traditions? Give them up, because something greater is here. The kids surely saw it. You believe the law and the prophets? Good! Because they all speak of me. You want to get God's attention? Then stop trying to impress people and start serving them. You want to make God smile? Become like this little child.

So what did Jesus mean? What was he pointing to as he pointed to Johnny and Jenny? Ah, now we're getting somewhere.

Brand New Values

Humility

Sometimes Jesus got a little cagey with his listeners. Especially the religious elites. In fact, Scripture says he didn't teach the crowds without telling a story (parable). That sounds childlike. Yep. We'll find all along the way that Jesus is our greatest example of childlike. *"No one has ever taught this way,"* the crowds gasped, when Jesus finished his most famous sermon. No one ever lived this way, either. But if we follow Jesus, we can too.

Fortunately, sometimes Jesus just came right out with it:

> *So anyone who becomes as humble as this little child is the greatest in the Kingdom of Heaven. (Matthew 18:4)*

For a culture that had little value for children, it had *zero* value for humility. So even though the words of Jesus are clear the concept was completely foreign. It was the gladiators and the gilded who were celebrated.

3 Childlike

The rulers. The rugged. The successful. The senators. The few, the proud, the powerful! The Roman and Greek gods weren't wimps, either. Why are people still afraid of being struck by lightning when they do wrong, after all?

So the people looked around wondering what in the world Jesus was talking about. "Humility? Do you get that in a hospital? Wait, what is a hospital? And why would you ever want *that*? Anything but that! I fought the odds and made it to adulthood, Jesus. Why would I want to go back?" But Jesus, with a sly smile, doubled down:

> *But those who exalt themselves will be humbled, and those who humble themselves will be exalted. (Matthew 23:12)*

Now more than a few were mad. Except for the slaves, who made up around half of the population. Little wonder why they flocked to Jesus with the kids, leaving the adults to say:

"I can't sign my artwork? But I'm a master!"

"I can't Lord my authority over others? But I've worked my whole life for this!"

"I can't walk around in flowing robes, expensive jewelry, or ride into the city on a stallion? What kind of gibberish is this Jew spouting? This is madness!"

Fortunately, Jesus did more than simply go about Galilee introducing the Childlike Kingdom. He showed what it was like. "Today I've brought a basin and a towel." And he did it with an attitude:

> *You must have the same attitude that Christ Jesus had. Though he was God, he did not think of equality with God as something to cling to. Instead, he gave up his divine privileges, he took the humble position of a slave and was born as a human being. When he appeared in human form, he humbled himself in obedience to God and died a criminal's death on a cross.*

Talk about the universe's ultimate Show & Tell. But the Almighty didn't stop there:

> *Therefore, God elevated him to the place of highest honor and gave him the name above all other names, that at the name of Jesus every knee should bow, in heaven and on earth and under the earth, and every tongue declare that Jesus Christ is LORD, to the glory of God the Father. (Philippians 2:5–11)*

Now go and do likewise . . . kids.

Trust

Everyone has trust issues. Even the most powerful kings on earth were always watching their backs. Except Julius Caesar. And that didn't turn out so well. In fact, one of the greatest literary geniuses in history made a very good living chronicling tragedy and treachery amongst the royals. Even the comedies were tragic. This is none other than William Shakespeare, of course, whose writings have confused and befuddled school kids for generations. But I can help. The greatest takeaway for those on the throne, or those who aspired to be, is "Don't trust *anybody!*" Oops, I said that wrong. "Thou shan't trusteth a mortal soul!" That's better.

Into this reality came a bearded nobody from backwater nowhere. Jesus of Nazareth. Who? Where? Exactly. And his ragtag band of miscreants and misfits he seemingly scooped up from the ditches and dregs of civilization along the way. And he had the audacity to say:

> *Trust in God, and trust also in me. (John 14:1)*

Little wonder the mobs who followed Jesus initially, thinned out substantially as time went on. "Trust me? We've heard *that* before." Over and over and over, and that hasn't turned out so well, either. Most turned away disappointed. "We thought this one was different." They had no idea how right they were. Those who stuck around for another day were *rewarded* by hearing:

- *If any of you wants to be my follower, you must give up your own way, take up your cross, and follow me. (Matthew 16:24)*
- *But anyone who eats my flesh and drinks my blood has eternal life. (John 6:54)*
- *Yes, now go and do the same. (Luke 10:37)*

"No more miracles? Well, the bread and the fish weren't that good anyway."

"Eat flesh and drink blood? Nope."

"We're not taking over? We're outta here."

As I'm writing this, I'm reclining in my beloved Central Oregon, where I spent most of my childhood. Less than fifty miles away from the house where we're staying is Crane Prairie Reservoir. When I was around ten, my family went camping there. The mosquitos were memorable. So was the upright piling I about ran our boat into. But what I remember,

3 Childlike

more than anything, was the radio program we listened to in our tent one night. You know, those old radio cinemas with the sound effects and organ flourishes? Never mind.

I've blocked the plot out of my memory, but I remember the terror I was left with. Suddenly the darkness all around us was darker. The shadows dancing all around our tent from the night breeze were shadowier. The animals that had us surrounded were closer and hungrier. And I even caught a brief sighting of Scooby and Shaggy running *away* from our camp sight!

We've all been there, frozen in our sleeping bags, certain the tiniest movement or sound will be our last. Unable to slow down the pounding of our heart we know is giving our location away. Our breathing becomes shallow and quick, and we can't help when a stifled cry or moan escapes our mouths. Until . . .

"Jay, we are right here." Five simple words that calmed the storm and sent the monsters and carnivores running. My parents were right there all along, in the same tent as me. So was my sister, but she was no help. What was the secret sauce, silver bullet, or fresh garlic that immediately calmed fear, released peace, and sent the werewolves running? It was *trust*. As long as mom and dad were there, no danger or creature would dare cross over the line into our tent.

The first followers also had a terrifying experience on another lake in another time. Jesus was asleep on the boat, manned by experienced fishermen, who were certain they were going to perish in a squalor on Lake Galilee. But Jesus had such a childlike trust in his Father that he was surprised, and perhaps even annoyed, when they woke him up. He remarked on their lack of faith, and then spoke only three words to the storm: *"Peace! Be still!" (Mark 4:39, ESV)*

It's not recorded in any of the Accounts of Jesus, but I picture him turning to his gasping and gawking groupies from Galilee and reminding them: "I said you could trust me." He would have to tell them again and again and again. Just like me. I so easily trust when the water is smooth, and the fish are biting. I'm not so trusting in ten-foot swells and relentless winds with the shore nowhere in sight. I know Jesus has the power to calm any storm, but sometimes he makes me keep paddling while he is seemingly asleep in the stern. But just as at Crane Prairie in the dark, I am never alone. All it took was being reminded of the nearness of my father and mother. "Jay, we are right here." And all it takes for us is a simple reminder from our king: "I am right here. You can trust me. Now go to sleep."

And I did.

A Brand-New Vision

If it's not obvious by now, Jesus has a brand-new vision of childlike living, whether we're ten, twenty, forty, or eighty. I recently read a short account of the life of Royce Saltzman, someone you have no doubt ever heard of. He is approaching the finish line of his life journey, at ninety-four, and wrote a short memoir from the perspective of a ten-year-old, which he refers to as "That perfect age . . . before the anxiety, insecurity, attitude kick in."[3] Right? What a fun read. And what a fun (and fruitful) life.

Most would never refer to the "tween" age as being anything close to perfect. Yet, in looking back at my life, my tween years in Central Oregon and Crooked River Grade School, were magical. Years later, in another small town (we called it Mayberry), my boys lived those years to the full, on the court, by the creek, and in the classroom of Whitworth Elementary. Those were the best years of *my* life!

These "best years" are what come to mind whenever I hear childlike. So if this is what Jesus wants, I'm in! Not that it was all a walk in the Ochoco Creek or Dallas City Parks. No age is perfect, of course, and every season has its challenges. I also understand not everybody had the charmed childhoods me and my boys did. However, I believe God has "wonder years" ahead for all of us, regardless of our proximity to the tweens.

Picturing the Kingdom

A kingdom for children. Before Walt Disney. And the little children came.

(JOHN ORTBERG)[4]

So what will heaven be like? It is definitely worth considering (and we will). But if we get our theology from The Far Side (another childlike favorite!) heaven seems to be a boring place of harps, puffy clouds, and hymns. At least it is better than accordions, smoke clouds, and rock-n-roll in the other place. But I just happen to believe there will be jungle gyms, sandboxes, finger painting, tag, and most importantly, Legos!

3. Saltzman, *Growing Up Good*.
4. Ortberg, *Who Is This Man*, 146.

3 Childlike

Confession time. I was a Lego-maniac. And I'm still a card-carrying member of the Lego Club. It's true. You can, too. But my next confession is a bit more painful. I used to play with my sister's Barbie Townhouse. Don't judge, I was five. I bet you did, too. That's enough confessing for now, though more will come later.

That's why I was riveted when I saw the commercial for the Rocket Mortgage Barbie Dreamhouse. It was one of the Super Bowl commercials we all look forward to as much as the game. But here's the kicker: Rocket Mortgage's Barbie Dreamhouse was the #1 rated Super Bowl commercial of 2022. USA Today's Lorenzo Reyes described the commercial as "A childlike approach to a very adult problem . . . It resonated very well." I couldn't have said it better.

We will never outgrow Barbie & Ken. Scooby & Shaggy. Woody & Buzz. Sylvester & Tweety. Calvin & Hobbes. Jesus & John. Jesus said:

> *But to all who believed him and accepted him, he gave the right to become Children of God. (John 1:12)*

Forever.

Life in the Kingdom

Stay playful.

(OREO COMMERCIAL)

So what are we supposed to do? How are we supposed to live? If we were to ask Scooby, all he'd say is we need is another Scooby-Snack and a nap. Yes, we should never outgrow those, either. Enter now, the greatest child ever born of a woman (according to Jesus).

John the Baptist was a radical. To say the least. His message of repentance reached to the highest levels of government and caused swarms of wayward souls to sojourn to the desert to be baptized. But did the people find a raving madman amidst the scorpions and cacti? Did they find an unhinged prophet wearing a sign reading "The End is Near" on one side and "Get Right or Get Left" on the other? It's easy to think that when considering his dress and diet. However, there was something that caused Jesus to call John the greatest. So what was it? Clever kids.

John the Baptist was another supreme example of being childlike. I believe this is what captured the attention of Jesus. That, and the fact he was his cousin. I'm thinking they might have known each other pretty well growing up; birthday parties, holidays, graduations, and all. Maybe. When John baptized Jesus, I don't think this was the first time they'd met. But perhaps it was the moment of divine revelation, when he realized the promised Messiah, for which John was called to prepare the way, was part of his family and standing beside him in the water. Divine revelation is required to see Jesus as he really is, after all. Just ask Peter.

So why would I believe this grasshopper eating guru covered in camel hair to be a great example for us and a forerunner of childlike living? I'm so glad you asked. Because John preached and lived an "upside-down and backwards" kingdom life.

Here's what I mean. The world we live in expects us to leave childhood behind. And, in fact, as we're growing up, we can't wait to do just that. How tragically misguided we humans can be. For instance, we sacrifice our health to get rich, only to later spend our riches trying to get our health back. John the Baptist shows us, and tells us, precisely the same thing. You've completely missed it, people. Repent (change your thinking)!

3 Childlike

Here is the short list we typically teach our kids so they can make something of their life:

- Be (and get) More!
- Be (and get) Big!
- Be First!
- Be Best!

John and Jesus urge us to do *exactly the opposite*:

- Be Less—*He must become greater; I must become less. (John 3:30, NIV)*
- Be Little—*I'm not even worthy to be his slave and untie the straps of his sandal. (John 1:27)*
- Be Last—*So those who are now last will be first then, and those who are first will be last. (Matthew 20:16)*
- Be Least—*Truly I tell you, among those born of women there has not risen anyone greater than John the Baptist . . . yet whoever is least in the kingdom of heaven is greater than he. (Matthew 11:11, NIV)*

The completely backwards and upside-down Childlike Kingdom. John the Baptist ultimately died an untimely, unfair, and terrible death. Yet Jesus called him the greatest. Here's another hint why:

> Instead, whoever wants to become great among you must be your servant. (Matthew 20:26, NIV)

Be Less. Be Little. Be Last. Be Least.

Just like John.
Just like Jesus.
Before I conclude, let me be clear about what I am *not* saying:

- I'm not advocating a life of irresponsibility.
- I'm not making a case for perpetual childish immaturity.

- I'm not saying we shouldn't learn, grow, and mature in our faith.
- I'm not contradicting the Bible when it says:

> *When I was a child, I talked like a child, I thought like a child, I reasoned like a child. When I became a man, I set aside childish ways. (1 Corinthians 13:11, BSB)*

What I *am* saying is we must put away *child-ish* thinking and living. Yes, we must (temporarily) leave our childhood behind us. But we should *always* have childlike in the windshield, not in the rearview. As we have seen, Jesus is quite explicit. In fact, he even made this jaw-dropping statement:

> *I tell you the truth, the Son can do nothing by himself. He does only what he sees the Father doing. Whatever the Father does, the Son also does. (John 5:19)*

Throughout his life on earth, Jesus remained dependent on his Father for, wait for it, *everything*. In the Childlike Kingdom this never changes. And we, too, will be dependent on our God for everything, forevermore.

Just like a child.

The Alphabet Bridge

Florence, Italy's Ponte Vecchio Bridge (1339)

*Mister Rogers did not adequately prepare me
for the people in my neighborhood.*

(Unknown)

How are you doing, kingdom scholars? Feeling smart and ready to impress your friends and family? Then you'd best keep reading. Especially the words of Jesus. They have always cut through culture like a Japanese Ginsu Knife going through sushi (gross). And we all do *best* to allow his words to cut *us* to the core. Regularly. It won't hurt a bit. Well . . .

In the coming pages, we'll be working our way through the Childlike Kingdom Alphabet. And, silly kids, this alphabet is for adults too! And for all times and places. An alphabet for all *ages,* get it? Again, the first and most important task in the schoolhouse is to learn to read. It is impossible to grow or even function in our educational pursuit without it. But, before complete words and sentences can be understood, we go back to the chart in the front of our elementary school classroom, where we were introduced to our ABC's. Now remember, the Kingdom of God is far more than an educational pursuit, and there is much more to learn than our ABC's. But the ABC Song is a great place for us to start. Sing it now!

Before we cross the bridge, I want to emphasize a couple points in the format. First, you'll note in the first section of each letter (Announcing the Kingdom) there will always be a pithy statement in kingdom cursive. Honestly, I'm a pretty simple guy, and this is my attempt to boil the main idea down to its *lowest common denominator.* You know, like we learned how to do in math . . . Nooooo! You could also refer to these as the "mic-drops" for each letter. Or, if you're a hopeless romantic like me, you could refer to these as the Hallmark Card statements of the kingdom. They might even get a bit mushy at times.

Also note, as the focus of the numbers was primarily ortho*doxy* (believing/*head),* the focus of the letters is ortho*praxy* (living and loving/ *hands*), though neither exclusively. Hopefully our *heart* will be engaged and filled up as we pursue both. A pastor friend of mine constantly reminds his congregation: "The depth of a message is not in the hearing but in the living." (Kevin Geer) Yes . . . *that.* We are called by Jesus to not just be hearers of his words, filling (puffing) up with knowledge alone, but doers of his words, following our king and filling up our world with all kinds of good he prepared in advance for us to do.

We've crossed another cool bridge, and now it's time for the letters. As former NFL quarterback Tom Brady (another GOAT) would say, "Let's Gooooo!"

Kingdom A, B, C's

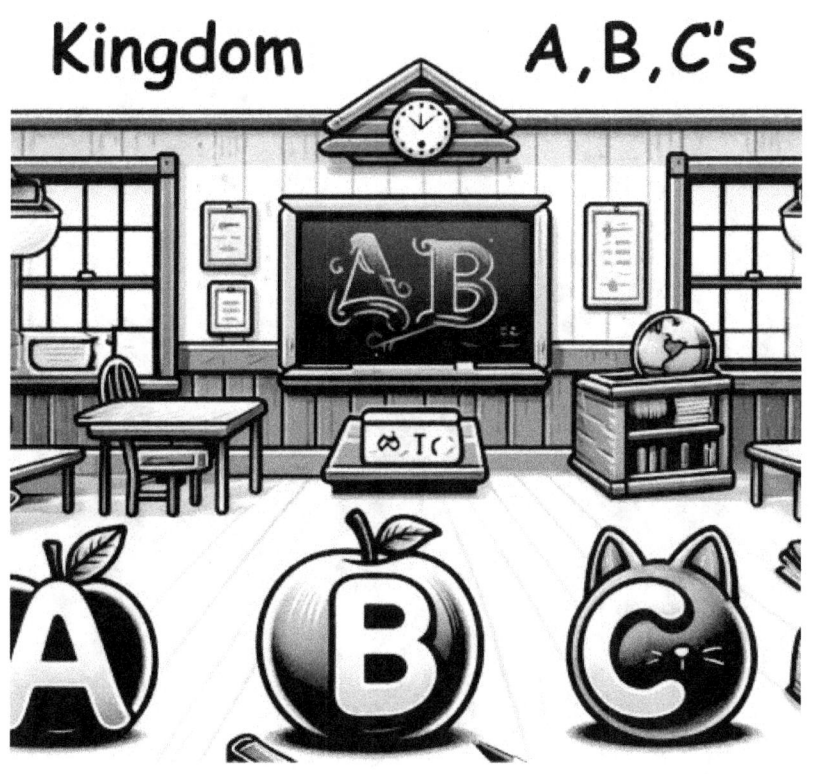

Access

I have come to make a way to access this kingdom.

(Jesus in The Chosen)

Keep on asking, and you will receive what you ask for. Keep on seeking, and you will find. Keep on knocking, and the door will be opened to you. For everyone who asks, receives. Everyone who seeks, finds. And to everyone who knocks, the door will be opened. (Matthew 7:7)

Nobody wants to pound on a door when no one is home. Nobody wants to waste their time asking if the answer is always no. Nobody wants to go on a hunt when someone has already found the treasure. Therefore, the words of Jesus here provide great encouragement, confidence, and motivation. There are no wild goose chases in God's kingdom. At least not the futile kind. For now, simply remember there is a life and death difference when we ask, seek, and knock at the door of the CLK Castle!

Speaking of difference, here is a totally unexpected kingdom announcement:

Let's break down this impossible reality:

The King is Always Available

Scripture records the story of Esther, a no name Jewish girl in foreign exile, who becomes queen. It is a royal drama so gripping Shakespeare himself surely tipped his cap. If you need to read it for the first time, or the first time in a long time, drop everything and take a trip to Persia. It's simply too good to summarize.

Are you back? I told you so! Here's the point I want to emphasize. Esther literally puts her life on the line on behalf of her people when she enters the presence of King Xerxes without an invitation. Subjects didn't just barge into the throne room, regardless of their title, if they valued their head staying on their shoulders. *"If I perish, I perish,"* this courageous young girl declares to the audience on the edge of their seats. And, as the ominous movie music reaches a crescendo, she is saved when the king extends the gold scepter to her. Her people are saved, too! It's a good thing the king wasn't having a bad day.

The unapproachable and terrifying presence of the king isn't unique to this story. Kings regularly had bad days, so it was best to wait for a summons. It was also best not to count on the gold scepter being extended. Yet, King Jesus has done this for us. He is *always* available for drop-ins. And he *never* has a bad day. Consider yourselves summoned.

The King is Fully Accessible

The Old Testament also details the construction and function of the Tabernacle of God. While the nation of Israel wandered in the desert, the manifest presence of the Almighty resided in the innermost chamber of the tabernacle, the Holy of Holies. The high priest was the only one who could enter through the heavy curtain, once he had completed all the required cleansing rituals, and only once a year, to make the atoning sacrifice for the people. In fact, they tied a rope around one of his feet so his corpse could be pulled out if necessary. Whoa . . .

The good news is that *all* the cleansing rituals have been completed, *all* the blood that needed to be shed has been shed, and atonement (At-*One*-ment) has been secured. The king himself, the final high priest, has made the final sacrifice. God and man have been brought back together, never to be separated again. Oh, and what happened immediately after atonement had been secured by Jesus on the cross? That heavy curtain of separation was torn from top to bottom, never to be sewn back together (by the way, some historical descriptions of the curtain said it was so strong two horses pulling in opposite directions couldn't tear it!). We now have *full access* to our king! And not just once a year.

The King is Actively Seeking Us . . . First

The teachers of the law didn't get everything wrong. They just regularly missed the point. They followed the law to the letter, and even added letters, just to be sure. But they missed who the law was pointing to >>> The King! They got all the religious rituals down to a science. And they missed the kingdom. They were zealous, devout, and sacrificial, but ultimately were religious guides who were seriously misguided.

Here is the kicker as it relates to *accessing* the Kingdom of God. Not only are we seeking. We are being sought! The king isn't playing Hide & Seek . He *wants* to be found. The king isn't running away from us. He's running *to* us! In Luke 15, Jesus tells three similar "lost and found" parables that once again shocked his hearers. He tells of a woman's furious pursuit of a lost coin, and the ensuing celebration when it is found. He tells of a lost son, who takes his father's money and runs, and a father who never gives up looking and waiting for his return. He also tells of a lost lamb, and the shepherd's refusal to lose even one. The message is clear: God will wait. God will run. God will seek. God will find. God will forgive. Can you see why they were shocked? Someone put it this way: "The Rabbis would have all agreed people should seek God, but it was a new idea to them that God was seeking people."

Jesus puts it this way:

> *For the Son of Man came to seek and save those who are lost.*
> *(Luke 19:10)*

Picturing the Kingdom

I've been accused of having an "old soul." I simply love old things. Old books. Old coins. Old pictures. Old churches and cathedrals. Old cemeteries. Yeah, I'm that guy. I call it being *historically sensitive*. Most people call it, "Nerd alert!"

It's why I love museums, libraries, and galleries. It's why I love literature and history. It's also why I married Stacie. Ha! I've also found myself, recently, being drawn to old doors. *Distressed* doors. With old keys. *Skeleton* keys. My doctoral cohort spent a week in Cambridge, UK, and talk about geeking out! I could fill this chapter with pictures of the doors I photographed in merry old England, including those to the red phone boxes. I can't believe I came home. Speaking of home, my oldest son and I got the chance to visit that of our first American president, George Washington. In the living room of Mount Vernon resides a skeleton key to the Bastille, the prison stormed by rebels, igniting the French Revolution. Okay, I'll move on.

One of the most famous paintings of Jesus shows him knocking on yet another distressed door. It is called Light of the World and resides on a wall in St. Paul's Cathedral, London. The door symbolizes each human heart. He doesn't use a skeleton key for entry. In fact, upon closer inspection, there is not even a doorknob for him to turn. It must be opened from the *inside*. He is simply the king who knocks. The king who waits for each to open their distressed door. To give the king full access.

> *Look! I stand at the door and knock. If you hear my voice and open the door, I will come in, and we will share a meal together as friends. (Revelation 3:20)*

Access

Life in the Kingdom

Jesus said that we must 'receive the kingdom of God' as little children (Mark 10:15). What is received? The Church? Heaven? What is received is God's rule. In order to enter the future realm of the kingdom, one must submit himself in perfect trust to God's rule here and now.[1]

(GE LADD)

There are three initial childlike *responses* to God's offer of the kingdom. It is the same response required of those who are surrendering on the battlefield. Hoist the white flag!

Ask. This again? Yes, and yes again. Don't ever stop asking. It is the *key* that unlocks life. Or you can just open the door.

> *For everyone who asks, receives. (Matthew 7:8)*

Accept. It bears repeating from earlier: When a commander is ready to surrender, he sends for the "terms of peace" from the enemy. It is the conquering king who has the right to set the requirements. So what are the terms of the king of all kings? *All.* Nothing less is acceptable. Are *you* ready to accept?

> *I tell you the truth, those who listen to my message and believe in God who sent me have eternal life . . . they have already passed from death to life. (John 5:24)*

Submit. "God's government demands complete submission. His subjects must put Him first. The Kingdom is entered only when a decision has been made and the price paid."[2] Once I accept the terms, I lay down my sword. I lay down my rights. I lay down my life. In doing so I receive (real) peace, (true) blessings, and (eternal) life. We lay it all down and receive the Kingdom of God. But there is one thing we must pick up:

> *If any of you wants to be my follower, you must give up your own way, take up your cross, and follow me. (Mark 8:34)*

---

1. Ladd, *The Gospel of the Kingdom*, 21.
2. Smith in Ladd's *The Gospel of the Kingdom*, 12.

There are also three *keys* for us to experience life in the kingdom. With these on our ring, access to all the blessings God intends for us is unlimited. We don't just have a hall pass in the castle. We have an *all-access* pass to the kingdom! Yes, even the throne room. I bet you can guess what they are. Scripture says they're kind of important:

> *Three things will last forever—faith, hope, and love—and the greatest of these is love. (1 Corinthians 13:13)*

- **Faith.** *And it is impossible to please God without faith. Anyone who wants to come to him must believe that God exists and that he rewards those who sincerely seek him. (Hebrews 11:6)*
- **Hope.** *Even youths grow tired and weary, and young men stumble and fall; but those who hope in the LORD will renew their strength. They will soar on wings like eagles; they will run and not grow weary, they will walk and not be faint. (Isaiah 40:31, NIV)*
- **Love.** *We know what real love is because Jesus gave up his life for us. So we also ought to give up our lives for our brothers and sisters . . . And this is his commandment: We must believe in the name of his Son, Jesus Christ, and love one another . . . (1 John 3:16, 23)*

Talk about life in the kingdom! These three things will last *forever*. Wait, even faith? You read it here *second*. Oh, and one more thing: We really only need one key. A *Master key!*

Finally, there are three things you don't have to *be* to gain access to the kingdom. It seems impossible, especially with how we've been taught in our culture (often including the church). But have no fear, we need not:

- **Be Rich.** "Entrance into eternal life in the Kingdom of God is no more possible for men to attain by all human resources than it is possible for a camel to go through a needle's eye."[3]
- **Be Religious.** *I tell you the truth, corrupt tax collectors and prostitutes will get into the Kingdom of God before you do. (Matthew 21:31)*
- **Be Right.** Wait, what? It's true. If we have to be right on everything to get into the kingdom, then we're *all* in trouble. If an air-tight theology is required for entrance, we're doomed! We must only be right about *one* thing . . . *who*. Don't believe me? Then what about the first followers? How much were they right about for three years

---

3. Ladd, 33.

running? That's right, not much. Jesus would much rather have us be near than right, anyway. While we should always seek truth, we must always remember our access to God is not dependent on a perfect theological understanding.

So don't be afraid, little flock. For it gives your Father great happiness to give you the Kingdom. (Luke 12:32)

Beauty

Children inhabit a magical world rich in beauty and replete with wonder . . . through the eyes of a child, beauty is abundant and mystery is everywhere.[1]

(BRAIN ZAHND)

Announcing the Kingdom

He has made everything beautiful in its time. He has also set eternity in the hearts of men; yet they cannot fathom what God has done from beginning to end. (Ecclesiastes 3:11, NIV)

When you're ten years old, what do you consider beautiful? Well, if you were like me, it would begin with mom (I love you, mommy!). Then, suddenly, there was Lara, Leslie, and Vestalee (okay, maybe it was before I was ten). But there were also crawdads in the creek, dragons in the sky (that only *looked* like clouds), and hot fudge sundaes at Dairy Queen. And new bikes. And Christmas lights. And butterflies. And pansies. Brian is right, through the eyes of a child, beauty is *everywhere!*

I am deeply indebted to Brian (Zahnd), and Bryan (James Bryan Smith), for changing the way I see the Kingdom of God. Before recently

---

1. Zahnd, *Beauty Will Save the World*, 33–34.

reading their fantastic books, I wouldn't have chosen beauty as a primary descriptor of the kingdom. I was much too spiritual, you see, so I'd have used more fancy theological words. Even at age ten. Words like *enchanting, eternal,* and *ethereal.* These are all true of the Childlike Kingdom (and kinda spiritual). But I was missing a super cool word I just learned how to pronounce. *Transcendental.* Sorry, kids. Four syllables.

"Surpassing." "Superior." "Something greater than ordinary." I needed help from both Oxford and Cambridge (Dictionaries) on this one. And these are also great descriptors of God's kingdom. But there are three that "rise above" (Go Cambridge!) the rest. Are you ready for more syllables? Repeat them after me: *Beauty. Goodness. Truth.* The three *transcendentals.* Together, they form the very *essence* of the Kingdom of God. Which leads me to say:

Everything in the Kingdom of God is transcendental.

Now that's a sentence Mrs. Serano (my all-time favorite teacher) would be proud of. But we're going to need help to break it down into bite sized chunks. This is where the Br(i/y)ans come in.

Three in One

We talked earlier about the greatest theological mystery of them all . . . the Trinity. Three Persons. One God. Father, Son, and Holy Spirit. I know. It's impossible, but true. Let me offer this childlike explanation: *You can't have one without the other . . . and the other.* Did that help? I know. I tried. The point, for now, is when it comes to the transcendentals, you also can't have one without the other . . . and the other. Otherwise, you won't have true beauty, goodness, or True Truth (one of my seminary books. True!). Help me boys . . .

> Beauty, goodness, and truth are, like the Trinity, of one essence. When all three—beauty, goodness, and truth—are aligned, you are dealing with reality at its deepest level.[2] (Bryan)

2. Smith, *The Magnificent Story*, 11.

> Truth and goodness need beauty. Truth claims divorced from beauty can become condescending. Goodness minus beauty can become moralistic. To embrace truth and goodness in the Christian sense, we must also embrace beauty.[3] (Brian)

If something is truly beautiful, it must also be good, and true. Put those words in any order you like, and the answer is still the same. This will help us to discern in our world now and look forward to a day when discernment is no longer necessary. Can you just imagine?

The Beautiful Way

We have lost our way. This isn't just true in our age. It is true of *any* age, and for mostly the same reasons. But there are unique reasons, too. Case in point, The Enlightenment. Most of us following the beautiful way of Jesus are quick to point out its shortcomings. What started out as throwing off absolute monarchy and the shackles of religious intolerance, quickly got lost in humanism, hedonism, and the pursuit of happiness. "Wait, I want to be happy!" Of course. But as *central* pursuits, these are not the most beautiful way. Nor is reason, intellect, philosophy, or individual liberty. "Wait, I want to be free!" Of course. But if our central pursuit is devoid of following the Way of Jesus, the beautiful way, it is simply destined for a museum. Or rubbish pile. Or prison.

But what the Enlightenment got right was the value of beauty. How thankful we should be for the artisans that made our world, including the church, a much more beautiful place to inhabit, and worship. We should celebrate their contributions in every genre. But we should also be wary of its extremes. For all we get right, we simply can't stop ourselves from crashing into the *pole,* whether north or south. We've done it again. Take it, Bryan: "The important thing to note is that we are living in what has been called a postmodern culture that has abandoned beauty, goodness, and truth as essential elements of life."[4]

That statement might appear of itself to be extreme, but I believe it with all my heart. Pursuing Jesus means pursuing truth. *Check.* Pursuing Jesus means pursuing goodness. *Check. Check.* But pursuing Jesus must also include pursuing beauty, or we're not truly pursuing Jesus. *Checkmate!* Modernism was another form of enlightenment. A course

---

3. Zahnd, 28–29.
4. Smith, 12.

correction from the extremes of the first one. But like any revolution there are unintended consequences. Have we unintentionally left beauty behind in our pursuit of righteousness? Far too often.

The Magnificent Story is Beauty (That) Will Save the World

This heading is a mash up of the titles of the books by Bryan and Brian. I hope it makes you want to read them. You see, the Kingdom of God is filled with beauty. It is everywhere you look if you're looking. Beauty that is also good, and true. And unexpected.

You see, Jesus was also an enlightened revolutionary. A *beautiful, good,* and *true* revolutionary. The *state* of things was ugly. So was the *church*. Jesus called them both out, and especially the latter:

> *The Scriptures declare, "My Temple will be called a house of prayer for all nations," but you have turned it into a den of thieves. (Mark 11:17)*

> *What sorrow awaits you teachers of religious law and you Pharisees. Hypocrites! For you are like whitewashed tombs—beautiful on the outside but filled on the inside with dead people's bones and all sorts of impurity.(Matthew 23:27)*

No one would argue the inside of a tomb is ugly, in every sensory way. But what about the inside of the temple? Often graveyards can be beautiful places to visit. If you've ever been to a national cemetery like Arlington, or Honolulu's Punchbowl, you know what I mean. I'm a big fan of cemeteries and monuments, the older and creepier the better. I know. The outsides are intentionally beautiful. But the truth cannot be denied. The truth couldn't be denied by the religious leaders, either. While the first followers were ogling the outside, and rightly so, Jesus saw the true state of things. What's that *smell?*

Here's good news for all people:

> *The LORD doesn't see things the way you see them. People judge by outward appearance, but the LORD looks at the heart. (1 Samuel 16:7)*

> *He had no stately form or majesty to attract us, no beauty that we should desire Him . . . Like one from whom men hide their faces . . . (Isaiah 53:3, BSB)*

Reading the Br(y/i)ans might also change how you see the gospel. Both lament how we could take something so breathtakingly beautiful and make it so boring, ordinary, and . . . *ugly*. In the Kingdom of God, *everything is transcendental,* including the very story itself. Why? Say it with me . . . Because it is *true, good,* and *beautiful!* As we finish this section, here is how the boys say it (so good!):

> The story of Jesus's life, death, and resurrection is not only the greatest story ever told, but it's also the most beautiful story ever told. This is how the gospel is made most compelling—by making it beautiful . . . What I am suggesting is that we look to beauty as a primary standard for our theology, witness, and action.[5] (Brian)

> When we see beauty as either irrelevant or dangerous, we miss out on one of God's greatest gifts . . . Beauty is made to lead us to God . . . Beauty is never ultimate. It is designed to be penultimate; to lead us to something beyond itself . . . Beauty is a portal to God.[6] (Bryan)

Beautiful!

Picturing the Kingdom

Brian Zahnd is my favorite writer on the Kingdom of God. Yet, he doesn't have a book with kingdom in the title (yet). It just bubbles up all the time in his writing. Exactly. He does have a book on beauty, and in it notes we often look to the wrong *form, shape,* or *combination* in our quest for it. It simply can't be said any better than this:

---

5. Zahnd, 2, 28.
6. Smith, 58, 65.

In order to recover the true form and original beauty that is integral to Christianity, we need an ideal form, a true standard, an accurate template, a faithful model to which we can look, to which me must conform. For historic Christianity this has always been Jesus Christ upon the cross, which is a holy irony, since crucifixion was designed to be ghastly and hideous. But this is the mystery of the cross. The crucifixion of Jesus Christ, which attains in retrospect an eternal glory and beauty through the resurrection, is the axis of Christianity around which everything else revolves. Thus the cruciform (the shape of the cross) is the eternal form that endows Christianity with its mysterious beauty. Simply put, the cross is the form that makes Christianity beautiful![7]

The *shape, form,* and *combination* of Jesus on the cross, seen through the lens of the resurrection, is the most beautiful picture of the kingdom. Again, this is foolishness to those who are perishing, but those who have embraced this picture, this *person,* it is life in the kingdom itself.

Life in the Kingdom

We're not so much tasked with running the world as with being a faithful expression of the kingdom of God through following Jesus and living the beautiful life that Jesus sets forth in the Sermon on the Mount.[8] (Brian)

---

7. Zahnd, 5–6.
8. Ibid., 13.

Heaven on Earth

I have lived in the Pacific Northwest my entire life. I'm not planning on that changing. The old Oregon license plates declare it to be the *Pacific Wonderland*. It is truly *beautiful*. Never been here? Plan on that changing. I'll be your tour guide. Seriously, I am one. I've welcomed and whisked people from around the world away, and the reaction is always the same. *Speechless* standing in front of Multnomah Falls. *Drool* on my Sprinter seats as we glide next to Haystack Rock. *Wide-eyed* looking out from the Roosevelt Patio of Timberline Lodge, over halfway up Mt. Hood. *Exploding hearts* taking in the Columbia River Gorge from Vista House. *Mesmerized* staring down into Crater Lake, a five-mile diameter of water which is 99% pure.

The Kingdom of God is found at the intersection of heaven and earth. Someday both will be made *new* . . . and *one*. Until then, heaven continues to break in and break forth whenever we live the beautiful way of Jesus.

Have you ever seen a total eclipse of the sun? For a moment its rays are completely blocked out and you can take off your cool metallic glasses. But be careful, because almost immediately those rays will begin to leak out in every direction. They simply can't be held back. The same thing happened and is happening in our world. The death of Jesus on the cross was the total eclipse. But ever since, the darkness of empire is slowly being pushed back, and the kingdom of light is slowly spreading across the land. Soon we'll be in total sunlight. Until then, every act of humble service, every gift expressed in sacrificial love, exposes a little more kingdom light in dark places. It can't be held back, but it can be accelerated.

Beauty

The Beautiful Way

The way of Jesus has been described in many *ways*. But perhaps none can compare to the most beautiful way. It's not easy. It's not pain free. It's not the fastest. It's not logical. It's not obvious. But it is *beautiful*. And where it leads, well, there isn't an appropriate adjective.

> *But the gateway to life is very narrow and the road is difficult, and only a few ever find it. (Matthew 7:14)*

But if we *seek* it, we will find it. If we *knock*, the gate will swing open. If we *ask*, the path will unfold before us. Before the disciples of Jesus were called Christians, they referred to themselves as followers of *the Way*. Make every effort to follow their lead.

A Beautiful Mind

If you've seen the movie, then you're seeing a room full of equations, from floor to ceiling, 360 degrees. There are many such minds in our world. We know them by their last names: Bezos. Einstein. Gates. Jobs. Musk. Of course, that's just the tip of the intellectual iceberg. But in God's eyes, a beautiful mind isn't reserved for those with S.T.E.M. superpowers. Here's the truth:

> *Do not conform any longer to the pattern of this world, but be transformed by the renewing of your mind. Then you will be able to test and approve what God's will is—his good, pleasing and perfect will. (Romans 12:2, NIV)*

A beautiful mind is ours for the asking. So is the beautiful will of God.

A Beautiful Heart

Who immediately comes to mind when you think of a beautiful heart? Mom? Grandpa? Those are my first two. Many would say St. Teresa of Calcutta or Florence Nightingale. They'd be right. But, once again, saintly superpowers are not required. Heaven will be filled with beautiful hearts, most of whom we've never heard of. But what a delight it will be to meet them and spend eternity getting to know them! Here's what they'll have in common, as promised by the doomsday prophet Ezekiel, of all people:

> *I'll give you a new heart. I'll put a new spirit in you. I'll cut out your stone heart and replace it with a red-blooded, firm-muscled heart. Then you'll obey my statutes and be careful to obey my commands. You'll be my people! I'll be your God! (Ezekiel 11, MSG)*

A beauty that is ours for the asking. By the way, I can't wait to introduce you to my grandpa. His name is Jerry . . .

Beautiful Feet

> *How beautiful are the feet of messengers who bring good news! (Romans 10:15)*

Need I say more? We are called to carry the beautiful, good news of the Kingdom of God to our world. To carry the beautiful and matchless name of Jesus to every tribe, tongue, and zip code. To tell the most beautiful story ever to be told. And as we do, God will be commenting on our feet! So will our neighbors.

Come, let's follow together on this most beautiful kingdom way.

Castles & Cathedrals

Kingdoms and castles vanish. Our love lasts forever.

(Hallmark Movie)

Announcing the Kingdom

The name of the LORD is a strong fortress; the godly run to him and are safe. (Proverbs 18:10)

Believe me, dear woman, the time is coming when it will no longer matter whether you worship the Father on this mountain or in Jerusalem. (John 4:21)

What is your default image of kingdom? Throne? Crown? Crown Jewels? Crest? For me, nothing comes close to a castle. I've had the opportunity to stand inside of, or in front of, a few of these architectural and strategic wonders. There is still a whole world of castles out there just waiting to be stormed! It might surprise you to know my favorite castle is not in England, but in Germany. Neuschwanstein. I even know how to spell it. I haven't visited in person (yet), but I have been to Disneyland. Yep, Walt loved Neuschwanstein, too.

There is also a whole world filled with cathedrals. I'm sure it will also surprise you to know my favorite cathedral is not in England, either. Happily, I've been in a few of these architectural and stained-glass wonders, too, including Westminster Abbey and St. Paul's in London. These alone are worth the trip across the pond. Do you know a bunch of kings and queens are buried in their crypts? So cool! Sorry.

Perhaps a cathedral isn't on your short list of kingdom images. Perhaps that's good. Perhaps not. Because, unfortunately, many cathedrals are known more for their political activities, including the self-crowning of Napoleon as French Emperor at Notre Dame. Hopefully, those activities were greatly outweighed by the spiritual activities therein. But it's often debatable. Phooey.

These images, or *signs* of kingdom, conjure up both positive and negative thoughts and feelings, as we've discussed. Semiotics, introduced earlier, is a fancy word for the study of signs. There are signs all around us of political, religious, and cultural significance. Some of these are still relevant in our world today, while others need to be (re)considered, (re)moved, or *(re)signed*. (Re)signing the Kingdom of God is my intent because I believe it was the childlike intention of Jesus all along.

Jesus was a *master* semiotician. His (re)signing of the temple ushered in a whole new understanding of the heart and purpose of God, and the role of Messiah. Yet, the temple (cathedral) remains as a significant sign, both cautionary and revelatory. There are scores more religious signs to be (re)introduced, but I want to zero in on the oft misused, and even more oft misconstrued sign of *kingdom*. Jesus minced no words when he said:

> *My Kingdom is not an earthly kingdom . . . my Kingdom is not of this world. (John 18:36)*

Yet, we keep trying to press the words of Jesus into the broken mold of empire. With disastrous results in every age. There is a much better way Jesus came to make. It begins with (re)signing kingdom, away from the man-made halls of power and opulence, impenetrable walls and soaring turrets of dominion, and coffers filled with treasures from near and far. It begins with my favorite image of Jesus. *Childlike*. Surprise. Surprise. Here is my contention:

The Kingdom of God is best (re)signed as a Childlike Kingdom.

That's where the castles and cathedrals come in. As we admire the architecture, appreciate the history, and marvel at their expanse, we must remind ourselves of what they represent, and what they don't. And, as always, let's be reminded of the words of Jesus when his first followers were awestruck looking at the temple in Jerusalem:

> *Do you see all these buildings? I tell you the truth, they will be completely demolished. Not one stone will be left on top of another! (Matthew 24:2)*

Jesus could be a bit of a buzzkill. Of course, he didn't stop with the outside of the temple, or anything else. He was most concerned about the *inside*. The temple of God was rotting from the inside out. Instead of a welcoming place of prayer and worship for all nations, it had become a marketplace for thieves and power mongers. Jesus turned over the tables and chased off the crooks, but it wouldn't be long before the walls and pillars would come crashing down, too. And despite the perceived glory of the castles and cathedrals of empire, they *all* will, too. Yes, even St. Peter's in Rome, Windsor in England, and my beloved German Neuschwanstein. Sorry to be a buzzkill, but we're called to be like Jesus after all . . .

As mentioned before, castles and cathedrals represent a lot of horrific realities and happenings. The Tower of London, home to the crown jewels of the British Empire, is also home to the head and body of Queen Anne Boleyn, which are not buried in the same place if you catch my drift. God save the king! Now here comes the much better way (and sign) of kingdom.

The Childlike Castle & Cathedral is *Safe*

One of the world's most oft sung hymns comes compliments of the pen of priest Martin Luther (probably from a German castle):

> A mighty fortress is our God, a bulwark never failing;
> our helper he, amid the flood of mortal ills prevailing.
> For still our ancient foe does seek to work us woe;
> his craft and power are great, and armed with cruel hate,
> on earth is not his equal.[1]

If it is true we have an enemy like this, seeking our harm, and with nothing on earth his equal, what are we to do? The simple answer is his teeth have been removed, his access has been limited (unlike ours), and his days have been numbered. Yet, Satan is the master of disguise and *"he prowls around like a roaring lion, looking for someone to devour." (1 Peter 5:8)* When it comes to the children of God, a roar is all he has left. But, like the young Lion King Simba, as the hyenas were closing in, we can roar back in the most impressive fashion. As long as our daddy, like Mufasa, is really the one roaring behind us. Can you tell how we decorated our boys' room back in the day?

The hyenas of life are often snarling and slobbering as they close in on us too, right? Perhaps it's just me. But if we can't make it back to the Prideland, we need a refuge to run to and a king who will fight for us. This doesn't mean living childishly reckless. It means we live with childlike *trust*. Look again at Proverbs 18 above, lest we forget. Let's not forget this either:

> The LORD himself will fight for you. Just stay calm. (Exodus 14:14)

The good news is we can run to him, our mighty fortress, in times of trouble. The best news is that, like Mufasa, the king's eye is always on

---

1. Luther, *A Mighty Fortress*, first stanza.

us, and I'll say it again, he will run to us! Even in the elephant graveyard. *Especially* in the elephant graveyard.

The Childlike Castle & Cathedral is *Occupied*

We don't have to hope and pray the king is present as we approach the castle. We don't have to pound on the door of the cathedral and hope someone hears us. We don't have to pay off the captain of the guard to let us in and look the other way. And we don't have to fear for our life, like Esther, when we walk in unannounced. The king is in the castle and on his throne. Not only are his eyes always on us but his ears are always attuned to our cry. He's already paid off the captain of the guard, the jail keeper, and the executioner. They're in his employ now. And, like the Maytag repairman, they don't have much to do anymore. This doesn't mean living with childish disrespect. It simply means living with the childlike *expectation* of being welcomed home.

> Did we in our own strength confide, our striving would be losing,
> were not the right Man on our side, the Man of God's own choosing.
> You ask who that may be?
> Christ Jesus, it is he;
> LORD Sabaoth his name,
> from age to age the same;
> and he must win the battle.[2]

The Childlike Castle & Cathedral is *Set-Apart*

The king has given us many great gifts. Too many to count or quantify. One of my favorites is the gift of *place*. Some are happy wanderers who never let the walls box them in or the grass grow underfoot. For others of us, our home is our castle, and we've even dug a moat. But everyone has a place, whether under the stars or under a ceiling fan. We have a place that has been set-apart. A cathedral in the wilderness or a castle in the suburbs. It is *holy*. Set apart. Separate. Different. Kind of like God's people.

Cathedrals can be holy places, too. But be careful, because what truly makes them special, set-apart, different, is not the stained glass, marble floors, or gilded rails. It is the presence of the king. The *set apart*

---

2. Luther, *A Mighty Fortress*, second stanza.

One. The *separate and highest* One. The *different and divine* One. The *only One*. But we must remind ourselves we don't *need* a cathedral. Any old church will do. Or castle in the burbs. Or slum shanty. Eugene Peterson talks of his family compound, on the shore of Flathead Lake (Montana), as a *thin place*. The place where it feels like God is close enough to touch through the invisible membrane keeping us from his manifest presence. Have you ever experienced that? Yeah, me too. For me, it's usually in an old growth forest of the Pacific Northwest. But it sometimes happens in my favorite cathedral. This doesn't mean we childishly run away from our world and those who need us. It simply means we *remember* who we are, *whose* we are, and *who* we can run to.

Picturing the Kingdom

My favorite cathedral is found in a most unexpected place. You'd never guess. It's just down the road from the Last Chance Stampede & Fairgrounds in . . . Helena, Montana!

Can anything good come out of Helena? Why yes, my wife Stacie! But Montana, and the Cathedral of St. Helena, is full of more than cattle and cowboys, sheep and herders, mountains and climbers, wheat and ranchers. The very presence of God is all around you in the Treasure State. Just like he is in the Beaver and Evergreen States. And even California. Maybe.

There is a reason the Cathedral of St. Helena is my favorite. Looking at it from the outside it is certainly an impressive gothic edifice. However, it pales in comparison to the exteriors of Westminster Abbey and St. Paul's. But to be honest, I was a touch underwhelmed by the interior of Westminster. But the nave of St. Paul's? Breathtaking.

I won't say the nave of St. Helena's rivals St. Paul's, though it gets me every time when I come through the entrance. The stained glass is amazing, and I've not seen its equivalent anywhere. Each large panel, two high on both sides of the nave from front to back, tells the story of Jesus and the story of the church. Beautiful.

The Cathedral of St. Helena is my favorite, however, for much more than the marble, gold, and stained glass. It is a thin place for me. Jesus and I have had a lot of heart to hearts here. Many of these conversations have been filled with grief and tears. You've been there, too. And even though my prayers at times seemed to be stopped by the flying buttresses above, they did somehow get through. On our last visit together, on the old carved wooden pew, I said these words, "God, I've done everything I can do to pursue work and your calling, and I have nothing but sand in my hands to show for my efforts. You are going to have to pursue me because I don't know what else to do." Less than two hours later, I got a call out of the clear blue Big Sky. I can't wait to go back. But I don't have to wait that long to have a visit with my priest and king.

Life in the Kingdom

Gothic architecture with its soaring arches, flying buttresses, ribbed vaults, and enormous stained-glass windows was designed to evoke an awareness of the transcendent and an overwhelming sense of awe in the worshiper. It was an architectural attempt to connect heaven and earth. The construction of these great cathedrals was itself an act of worship.[3]

---

3. Zahnd, *Beauty Will Save the World*, 164.

Thankfully, a cathedral (or castle) isn't required to experience the presence of the king. King Jesus himself declared this clearly to an unsuspecting Samaritan woman at a well outside of Sychar. You probably know the story, which is one of my favorites. Jesus (a Jew!) asked a woman (a Samaritan!) for a drink from the well, and then proceeded to read her mail. She quickly deduced he was a prophet. She had no idea. Yet.

So what is a young woman, a hated Samaritan, a reject of a backwater village and multiple spouses, to say to a Jewish prophet? She defaults to the same question we're still asking centuries later:

> *"Sir," the woman said, "you must be a prophet. So tell me, why is it that you Jews insist that Jerusalem is the only place of worship, while we Samaritans claim it is here at Mount Gerizim, where our ancestors worshiped?" (John 4:19–20)*

Jesus then proceeds to answer the most important questions of proper worship and put our castles and cathedrals in their proper place.

Where Must We Worship?

I've mentioned my Bucket List several times. It's an impressive list. I don't think, however, God is all that concerned with my list, even though the top spot requires a pilgrimage. Rome. The Sistine Chapel. St. Peter's Cathedral. I'm thinking it might even bump the Cathedral of St. Helena off the top spot. I'd love to find out. *Sigh.*

But amazingly, Sychar made it on the Bucket List of the Messiah. It was news to the woman at the well, however, because, as she points out:

> *"But sir, you don't have a rope . . . or a bucket . . ." (John 4:11)*

Sorry. But I insist he had a list! He shared it with the first followers just a few verses later, as the woman was running back to town to get her neighbors. Here it is:

> *My nourishment comes from doing the will of God, who sent me, and from finishing his work. (John 4:34)*

His list sounds so much simpler. And more spiritual. We know this unlikely woman made the list. The Bucket List of Jesus is highlighted by *people* not places, you see. This was no chance encounter. This wasn't just a shortcut. This wasn't an unscheduled stop. This was the will of the Father, confirmed by John, who reported:

Castles & Cathedrals

He had to go through Samaria on the way. (John 4:4)

Said no Jew, ever. Sure, it was the most direct line from Galilee to Jerusalem. But most Jews factored in a lengthy detour when making the same journey north or south. That way they wouldn't have to see or smell those dirty Samaritan dogs. The first followers had a surprising day, to say the least. But just wait. Here's the response Jesus gave to the woman's question, and the point of this section:

> *Believe me, dear woman, the time is coming when it will no longer matter whether you worship the Father on this mountain or in Jerusalem. (John 4:21)*

Surprise! After millennia of the primary focus being on the place of worship, the tabernacle, the synagogue, the temple, Jesus moves the focus to where it should have been all along. *Him.* Yes, God gave specific instructions for constructing places of worship. But the incarnation changed *everything*, including the place of worship. It has now become the infinite *places* of worship. Ultimately, God wants a *people* of worship anyway, not just a place. It's the top of his Bucket List.

How Do We Worship?

While Jesus was settling the *where* debate, he also settled the *how*:

> *But the time is coming—indeed it's here now—when true worshippers will worship the Father in spirit and in truth. (John 4:23)*

An annual trek to the temple is no longer required. Expensive and smelly animal sacrifices aren't either. Soon, there wouldn't be a Holy of Holies in the temple. Soon, there wouldn't be an Ark of the Covenant (are you listening, Mr. Jones?). Soon, there wouldn't even be a temple.

Here's the spoiler alert. There won't be one in heaven, either. Or a permanent one on earth. How do I know this? The same Jesus, several years (and verses) later, gave John of Patmos a tour of the New Jerusalem. Here is his eyewitness account:

> *I saw no temple in the city, for the LORD God Almighty and the Lamb are its temple. And the city has no need of sun or moon, for the glory of God illuminates the city, and the Lamb is its light. (Revelation 21:22-23)*

So how do we worship God, then? Do we need a pilgrimage? No, but we *can*. The fabulous book, Pilgrimage to Eternity, charts the journey and experience of New York Times columnist Timothy Egan, from Canterbury to Rome, on the Via Francigena. At my age, this is probably the closest I'll get to this Bucket List entry. Do we need a temple? No, but they're still worth visiting. Do we still need to offer smelly sacrifices? No. God thought they were smelly, too *(See Jeremiah 6, Hosea 6,* and *Isaiah 11)*. But sacrifice is still required. And is still worship. So is this:

Work. The woman surely didn't have worship on her mind as she went about her difficult task. But in God's nose, it smelled just as sweet. Do you see your work as worship? You should. In fact, it's our *primary* mode of worship on earth. And it is *sacred*. John Mark Comer, in his most encouraging book on vocation, says it this way: "His way is about living a seamless, integrated life, where the polarization between the sacred and secular is gone, and all of our life is full immersion in what Jesus called the kingdom of God."[4]

Rest. John Mark has also made me a believer in the practice of Sabbath. Sabbath is a *gift* the enslaved nation of Israel would've died for in Egypt. Most of them did. But Sabbath is about more than rest. Sabbath is about *holiness*. Is Sabbath the first thing that comes to mind when you think of being holy? It should. One day a week is *set aside*. It is *different*. It is a declaration that the LORD God Almighty is worth stopping for. Worth waiting for. Worthy of our songs, cheers, and even dancing! And, shockingly, the universe and the work of God will continue, unabated, without me for twenty-four hours. Again, John Mark: "At one point, Moses calls the Sabbath a gift. That's exactly what it is. The point is there is a way the Creator set the creation up to thrive. A way that God set you up to thrive. And when we Sabbath, we tap into God's rhythm for human flourishing."[5]

Play. My professor, Leonard Sweet, made this shocking statement in our very first class: "God created us for play, not for work." He then proceeded to *work* us! Comer adds, "We are made to mirror and mimic what God is like to the world. God works, so we work. God rests, so we rest."[6] Doctor Sweet, I believe would agree. But I also believe John Mark would agree, "God plays, so we play." In the Kingdom of God, now and

---

4. Comer, *Garden City*, 24–25.
5. Comer, 196.
6. Comer, 186.

then, our work is our play and our play is *worship!* Talk about a Childlike Kingdom! I call dibs on sweeping the highest turret.

Who Do We Worship?

As I've said, and will keep on continual repeat, the most important question in the Kingdom of God is who. We've consistently mucked up our worship of the king by focusing primarily on the *where* and the *how.* True worship is ultimately about *who.* These are the kind of worshippers the Father seeks.

Instead, we go about fighting over "holy" land and the Temple Mount, and our God just weeps. We take long walks, and now fly long miles, to take in a holy sight while all too often missing *The Holy.* We sacrifice like Martha (good!) but tend to forget that Jesus, more than anything, wants us to be near him, like Mary (best!). Worse, we fashion for ourselves idols, made in our own image, using *"gold, silver and costly stones,"* but God sees it as *"wood, hay and stubble." (See 1 Corinthians 3)* These idols aren't just statues, but can be institutions (even religious), power, money, possessions and . . . *people.* No wonder we can't stop fighting. Jesus said:

> *I am the way, the truth, and the life. (John 14:6, NIV)*

The who. Now let's worship as we sing the last stanza:

> That Word above all earthly powers no thanks to them abideth;
> The Spirit and the gifts are ours through him who with us sideth.
> Let goods and kindred go, this mortal life also;
> The body they may kill: God's truth abideth still;
> His kingdom is forever![7]

---

7. Luther, *A Mighty Fortress*, final stanza.

Dungeons & Dragons

It is a messy business to engage with the dark powers. Which is why Jesus taught us to pray, "Deliver us from evil."

(NT Wright)

The light shines in the darkness, and the darkness can never extinguish it.

(John 1:5)

Announcing the Kingdom

I'm not a gamer. I was, back in the day. Sorta. It all began with my cousin's Nintendo 64 game system where I was introduced to Pong and Frogger. Then, I had a life-changing experience, as I ate my first Pac-Man dots and ghosts. I would never be the same. Until *Ms.* Pac-Man arrived. Then it became my mission, at Wisner Bowl & Arcade, to eat my first pear, a bonus of 2,000 points! The day I did, I announced my retirement at the ripe old age of ten. The sad thing is the banana was next and was worth 5,000 points. I didn't care. I guess I just love pears. Some gamer.

The landscape of gaming, of course, is nothing like my childhood days at Wisner Bowl. Now they give out college scholarships to gamers, and one

Dungeons & Dragons

of my son's classmates currently hauls in $10,000 a month teaching other gamers, as they watch *him* play! What a country. I bet he ate the banana.

But more disturbing is the reality of graphic violence in many of these games. It started with Halo and degraded to Mortal Kombat. Speaking of macabre. Now, those initial bloodbaths appear tame. The power of evolution. Unfortunately, we're still evolving. But in the midst of these digital horrors, there was also the explosion of card games, including Magic the Gathering, and the still ultra-popular Pokémon. But it all began with Dungeons and Dragons. Not that I'd know.

D&D was the first of the fantasy role playing games. They say it's all about telling the story together. It is still one of the most played games in the world, as players set out on made up adventures, including characters of their choosing, chasing treasure and slaying dragons, all while trying to outwit the dungeon master. I think.

Let me be quick to point out there are plenty of adventures, treasure hunts, and dragons in real life. Just ask Scooby-Doo, who later in life experienced monsters who were *real*. And just like Mortal Kombat, that's where I tapped out. Enter player two.

So, what is it with us and the seriously disturbed, macabre, and violent? Why is it that Michael Jackson's mega-hit Thriller spent a record shattering thirty-seven weeks at #1? Why is it today Halloween is the #2 commercial holiday in the United States and horror is the #1 movie genre? Why is it that I've seen half of the horror movies considered the best of all time by Rotten Tomatoes? Now *that's* disturbing! Of course, Alfred Hitchcock's 1960 thriller Psycho is still #1 on the list, and no, I wasn't present in the theater for the release. But I did read all the Alfred Hitchcock and the Three Investigators books growing up, including Terror Castle at midnight (not recommended).

I do hope you aren't reading this letter at midnight. No, the children of God don't need to lose sleep, jump at everything that bumps in the night, or live in constant and growing fear. That's because we've crossed over the proverbial kingdom bridge. Like the scene from Lord of the Rings, where Gandolph said to the giant, glowing demon, "You

Shall Not Cross!" And it didn't. This trilogy is based in Scripture in case you didn't know. I don't think Hollywood does.

It has taken forever for us to get to the point of this letter, but admit it, like a good gamer you've loved the ride. Here at last is my main point:

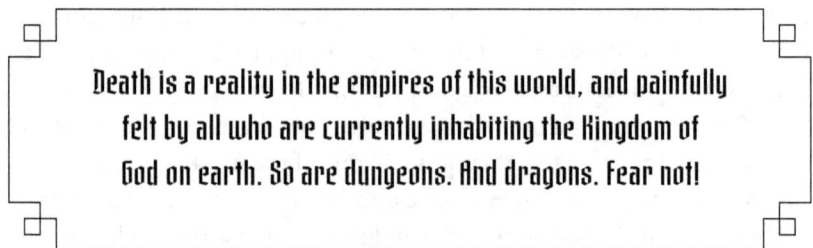

> Death is a reality in the empires of this world, and painfully felt by all who are currently inhabiting the Kingdom of God on earth. So are dungeons. And dragons. Fear not!

Just ask Anne Boleyn. And Nelson Mandela. And the Apostle Paul. And John the Baptist, who was beheaded for his efforts (in a dungeon). But eternal life has already trumped death *now*. And just wait for the *not yet* the Scriptures promise! The dragon, and his puppet emperors, are simply making their last stand. The dungeon awaits. The dragon knows it. Most of the emperors do not. But as certain as death and taxes are today, eternal life and divine inheritance are certain for those who follow King Jesus. And, as Jesus promised, his children won't have to pay taxes. Our debts, and our deaths, have been *paid in full*.

Here's the good news, and my *real* main point. It's stanza three of the hymn from the last chapter. You know, the verse that often gets skipped when we sing from the hymnal. Not this one:

> And though this world, with devils filled, should threaten to undo us,
> we will not fear, for God has willed his truth to triumph through us.
> The prince of darkness grim, we tremble not for him;
> His rage we can endure, for lo! His doom is sure;
> One little word shall fell him.[1]

Sorry, Michael, but I like this one much better.

---

1. Luther, *A Mighty Fortress*, third stanza.

Picturing the Kingdom

My love of old, creepy graveyards is eclipsed only by my love of castles and cathedrals. The best-case scenario is when you combine all three in one place. Like Windsor Castle. Or the north Oregon Coast. Huh?

One of my favorite viewpoints anywhere on earth is Ecola State Park, on a bluff overlooking Cannon Beach. On a clear day the view to the south, framing the iconic Haystack Rock is, well, priceless. If you turn to the right and gaze out a mile into the Pacific blue, you'll see Terrible Tilly. The north coast of Oregon, in addition to its matchless beauty, is also known for its nasty storms, fog, and shipwrecks. Before GPS changed the landscape, working lighthouses dotted the Pacific coastline. Lit in 1881, Terrible Tilly (officially Tillamook Rock Light), earned this nickname from the unfortunate souls who constructed it on a basalt rock island over a period of five-hundred days in mostly horrific conditions.

If you were to describe a lighthouse, *idyllic* is the best word. You can just take in the view as the cool, salty air and crashing waves fill up your senses. But Terrible Tilly has a bit more history than your average white with red trim castle. Because when it was decommissioned as a lighthouse in 1957, it was sold to a private party who turned it into, well, a cemetery! A columbarium, actually. No, they can't dig six-foot holes in that rock, but they can, and did, accept the ashes of the cremated to store inside. The owner said there was room for 300,000 urns, but alas only thirty-one took advantage of the opportunity to spend eternity at sea in quite a unique cathedral.

At last check, Terrible Tilly was for sale again for a reported $6.5 million. I imagine it includes the thirty-one urns. The current owner, Mimi Morissette, said she's proud to have had a hand in keeping standing an important part of American history. "I've been able to take something that we all have to face and sort of take the macabre out of it."

Take the macabre out of death. Hmm. Seems like someone has done that already.

Life in the Kingdom

Fear destroys curiosity and playfulness.

Now to do what millions of gamers believe to be impossible (and unnecessary). (Re)signing Dungeons & Dragons. Or, for the non-gamers, (re)signing our lives from a horror movie to a *happily ever after* kingdom story (no, not a fairy tale). Impossible, you say? You'll see.

From Pretending to the Imago Dei

I know a little more about *D&D* after doing some intense research. I Googled it, then I watched the latest movie, Honor Among Thieves. I learned how to do research in my doctoral program. Here are my findings: It appears we play the game as made-up characters of our own creation. We not only get to decide how our players look, but what they are capable of and what they're seeking. Meanwhile, there is a Dungeon Master who decides the elements of our quest, pulls the strings, puts obstacles in our path, and makes victory all the *sweeter*. Especially when your Dungeon Master is Dr. Sweet!

Tragically, our young people are being told they can do the same, even after the game is over. They're told they can decide their own identity, including their gender and their "truth," and that they control their own destiny. "You can do any*thing* you want, go any*where* the wind takes you, and be any*one* you want to be." It's the game of (modern) *Life*, with new rules or no rules. But here's what the Scriptures warn, repeatedly:

> *There is a path before each person that seems right, but it ends in death. (Proverbs 14:12)*

We have been formed by a *very* creative God. We've each been given a divine design and identity. We've each been given unique personalities, gifts, and DNA. And no dragon roar or rumor of war can keep us from releasing all of this upon our fellow gamers! Life is no game, but oh the adventures awaiting us as we submit to and follow the king and *his* plan! Jesus said:

> *The thief comes only to steal and kill and destroy; I have come that they may have life, and have it to the full. (John 10:10, NIV)*

From Addiction to Freedom

There is no shortage of avenues to addiction, whether we're selfish or scared. We can make a long list. Unfortunately, many suffering from addiction are simply thrown into dungeons or left to the dragons. I see it in downtown Portland every time I drive through. The same is true in big cities all up and down the west coast. It is tragic. It is heartbreaking. It is *real*.

Fortunately, there are *many* (though never enough), who see past the mask of pain, fear, and addiction and rescue these captives. Our best friends Marshall and Lesley did so for twenty years on the streets of Portland. Marshall was homeless himself in high school, due in large part to parents who were addicts. But he was rescued by a loving family (of a classmate), and what a difference *one* rescue has made in my city! In the midst of the darkness the work continues. It's sometimes hard to see, but the Kingdom of God is breaking through on Burnside Avenue!

This is how we know the king, and the kingdom, have come on earth:

> *The Spirit of the LORD is upon me, for he has anointed me to bring Good News to the poor. He has sent me to proclaim that captives will be released, that the blind will see, that the oppressed will be set free, and that the time of the LORD's favor has come. (Luke 4:18)*

The same Spirit of the LORD is upon us today. The time of the LORD's favor has come. It will continue to break through every addiction, in my city and yours, downtown and in the suburbs.

From a Celebration of Death to the End of Death

There were *two* who went before us in death and returned to tell the tale. Consider again the story of the raising of Lazarus. It has a lot of creepy moments, peculiar twists and perhaps the most frightening scene in all of Scripture. Has to be. Jesus waited until Lazarus had been dead four days and was wrapped up for eternity like a mummy. Then he kneels (perhaps) in front of the tomb and calls the mummy out! I don't know if Lazarus had both arms straight out making monster sounds (I bet he did), but I'm thinking a lot of tunics needed to be changed later. OMG!!! Yep, it was him. Happy Halloween everybody!

Speaking of Halloween, years ago I found the best yard decoration quite by accident. I was preparing a scavenger hunt, of sorts, for a summer youth camp I was leading and I needed to create a creepy old cemetery. Of course I did. I went to a party store looking for gravestones, and a salesman introduced me to a "bag of bones." It's as sinister (and fantastic) as it sounds, with "the thigh bone (dis)connected from the ... hip bone, and the hip bone disconnected from the ... backbone, and the backbone disconnected from the ... neck bone." C'mon kids and do The Skeleton Dance! And a creepy graveyard it was, with bones coming out of the volleyball court sand. Now you see it all the time in people's front yards. And, yes, I also found styrofoam gravestones, complete with epitaphs. Perfect.

But, unfortunately, creepy old graveyards are still a reality of life on earth. I know, because I've visited many of them. The best is in Jacksonville, Oregon, where they first found gold in my beloved state. It sits at the top of a hill, complete with a winding dirt road and scores of the creepiest trees ever. Many of the crumbling stones are from the 1800's, and, sadly, there is a separate section for coloreds and paupers who couldn't afford a marker. This place is frightening, even in the daylight. Daylight is also where I draw the line. One of my favorite commercials of all time is a Geico parody of people making bad decisions in a horror movie. "It's what you do." After hiding behind the (Texas) chainsaws, one of the girls yells, "Head for the cemetery!" when one is fired up. Bad idea, kids. The music should have given it away.

Please listen to me, my fellow dumb kids. Death is no longer to be feared. Nor dragons. There is a reason Scripture tells us, *"Do not be afraid"* 365 times! Yes, we need to be reminded *every day* not to fear. The main characters in Scripture did, too. It's not that there aren't any reasons for us to be afraid. There are still spiders in the world. And high places. And scary movies. But after Jesus conquered death, there just aren't any *good* reasons to fear.

From a Creepy Old Cemetery to a Celestial Kingdom

There is still a very real battle raging, with earthly prisoners and casualties. There are still wars. Those alive in the Twentieth Century were on hand for the bloodiest century in the history of the world. And despite its prevalence in the most popular games, there are still no good ways to die. There is a roaring, raging, raving (mad), and roaming dragon looking for opportunities to kill, to steal, to destroy, to discourage, and to distract us from living our best lives in the reality of God's kingdom.

And just like the sun breaking through the eclipse, or the wall of clouds at the end of a storm, the Kingdom of God continues to break through, to shed light on the earth, as in heaven. And someday, perhaps tomorrow, we'll catch our first sight of the king, the Son, in all his glory. And the heavenly city, the New Jerusalem, will be our new home in a celestial kingdom without end. It sounds like a fairy tale. It's not.

And we all live happily ever . . . forever.

Eternal Life

*Thrones, dominations, principalities know now with a
terrible certainty that mere force of arms has no power which
compares with that living word of the crucified Nazarene, that
bears with it Eternal Life, and directs the duty of a world of
men whom he can lead, but who bend no knee to power.*

(EDWARD EVERETT HALE)

*No government ever voluntarily reduces itself in size.
Government programs, once launched, never disappear.
Actually, a government bureau is the nearest thing
to eternal life we'll ever see on this earth![1]*

(RONALD REAGAN)

Announcing the Kingdom

If we're a teacher or a parent we're not supposed to have a favorite kid (but we do, right?). In the same way, as a Bible teacher and pastor, I'm not supposed to have a favorite book of Scripture. I just can't help it. But it might surprise you which one. Actually, I'm quite certain it will.

1. Both eternal life quotes are from Brainyquote.com. Gotta love President Reagan!

Eternal Life

I'll give you a hint. It's one of the Accounts (Gospels) of Jesus. Of course it is. You'd think, however, I would choose the one that talks about the Kingdom of God the most. Thus, it should be Matthew, where the word kingdom is used fifty-five times. Good guess. Or Luke, where it is found forty-six times. Nope. Kingdom is also found twenty times in the book of Mark. Strike three. That leaves John, my favorite, even though the word kingdom is only used five times. But please allow me to explain myself.

I learned about synonyms in Mrs. Wagonblast's (cool name for an Oregonian) eighth-grade English class. And similes and metaphors. I also learned how to outline a sentence. But I still can't explain that one. Mrs. Wagonblast, Miss Read, and Mr. Jamison were largely responsible for my love of letters. Ultimately, I blame Jesus, with a smile on my face. Even the teachers who tried to kick the lettered stuffing out of me weren't able to (you know who you are).

For those of you who have tried to forget anything learned (and done) in the eighth-grade, a synonym is "a word having the same or nearly the same meaning as another word in the same language."[2]. But it is the second meaning in my digital dictionary that tells the story, "A word or expression accepted as another name for something." So if you were to take all of the synonyms of kingdom found in the book of John, you would have . . . eighty! I rest my case.

Some of the most prominent synonyms for Kingdom of God used in Scripture are "kingdom of heaven," "the age to come" and even "salvation." The favorite choice of John the beloved? You've already guessed. Eternal life (I really should be more clever with my titles). In fact, you could even say John (re)signed the Kingdom of God as *"eternal life."* Beth Moore, one of the great Bible teachers of our day, has said it this way:

> In the totality of John's writings and in a comparison of his Gospel with the three synoptics, John has more to say about the concepts of life, light, love, truth, glory, signs, and belief than anyone else in the entire New Testament . . . Jesus offered a lot of life; John took Him up on it. Jesus shed a lot of light; John chose to walk in it. Jesus revealed a lot of glory; John chose to behold it. Jesus delivered a lot of truth; John believed it . . . Jesus lavished a lot of love; John received it.[3]

I love this! Thank you, Beth. And *thank you,* John.

---

2. Dictionary.com.
3. Moore, *John*, 179.

We can ultimately thank Jesus, of course, not only for offering eternal life, but for taking all of the mystery out of it. Well, not yet. But he did make the meaning abundantly clear:

> *Now this is eternal life: that they know you, the only true God, and Jesus Christ, whom you have sent. (John 17:3)*

That's it? That's it. The best things in life now, and *everything* in the Kingdom of God, are *relational*. Here's the eternal truth we'll be experiencing forever:

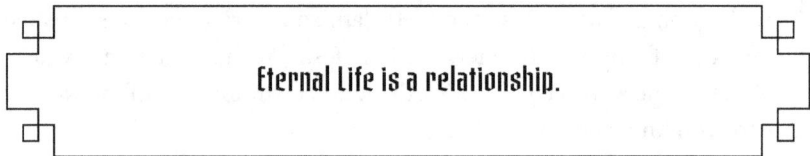

Eternal Life is a relationship.

Picturing the Kingdom

Marble Monuments

You know if you know someone, right? Not just about someone, but really know them. If someone asks you, there is an immediate recognition and response. There is first-hand and intimate knowledge. There is relationship.

If you're fortunate enough to visit Washington, DC, you'll delight in taking a tour of the monuments. The impressive marble structures are dedicated to the best and brightest former U.S. presidents, courageous citizens (like Martin Luther King, Jr.), and war heroes. There is nothing like stepping out of the Jefferson Memorial and looking across the Tidal Basin to the White House. There is nothing like standing on the steps of the Parthenon inspired Lincoln Memorial and looking across the reflecting pool to the Washington Monument in the foreground and the U.S. Capitol in the background. *Nothing.*

But even though we've been to their memorials, we can't say we know the people and presidents they help us to remember. We know certain facts about each person, such as the day they were born or the day they died (July 4, 1826, for *both* John Adams and Thomas Jefferson!), where they lived and where they died. We know what they said, how they led, and the debt they are owed for their service to their country. But none of us know them. We simply know *about* them.

The same can be true of Jesus. Many people know a lot about him. They know his teachings. They know he was a good man. Many believe he was a prophet. Many others rightly believe he was the Son of God. Many have been to where he lived, where he died, and the tomb he abandoned (there is a memorial there, too, the Church of the Holy Sepulchre). Many have even memorized a line or two of his words spoken here on earth. But do they *know* him, or do they simply know about him? Do we?

You know if you know someone. And unlike America's Founding Fathers, *this* Father (the Only true God) and Jesus (the One he has sent) *can be known*.

 ### Life in the Kingdom

> *God spoke the world into existence,*
> *but he breathed life into humanity.*
>
> (Heath Adamson)

I Am

I'm *eternally* grateful to Dr. Kowalski, my Johannine Literature professor, who introduced me to the most meaningful words spoken by Jesus. Much of what we're taught in class is buried deep within our memories never to see the light of day again. But these two words spoken by Jesus have illuminated both my heart and mind ever since.

For those who desire Jesus to *speak plainly* about himself, it doesn't get clearer than when he says, *"I Am."* In fact, one of the most hilarious scenes in all of Scripture is when Judas leads a gang of thugs to arrest Jesus. His answer to their quest for Jesus of Nazareth lands all of them on their backsides!

What is important to realize here is Jesus wasn't just describing himself. He wasn't just giving the followers some helpful metaphors. He was telling them, "This is who I am." This is his identity. This is his essence. This is what he embodies. He didn't just do resurrection, he *is* resurrection. He doesn't just declare truth or show the way to life. He *is* all the above. And more:

- *I Am the bread of life. (John 6)*
- *Before Abraham was born . . . I Am! (John 8)*
- *I Am the light of the world. (John 8 & 9)*
- *I Am the gate. (John 10)*
- *I Am the Good Shepherd. (John 10)*
- *I Am the resurrection and the life. (John 11)*
- *I Am the way, the truth, and the life. (John 14)*
- *I Am the true vine. (John 15)*
- *I Am a king. (John 18)*
- *I Am He. (John 18)*

Are *you* still standing?

The Eternal Way

Here's just some of what Jesus said regarding eternal life, as recorded by John:

Eternal Life

- *For this is how God loved the world: He gave his one and only Son, so that everyone who believes in him will not perish but have eternal life. (John 3)*
- *Anyone who drinks this water will soon become thirsty again. But those who drink the water I give will never be thirsty again. It becomes a fresh bubbling spring within them, giving them eternal life. (John 4)*
- *I tell you the truth, those who listen to my message and believe in God who sent me have eternal life. They will never be condemned for their sins, but they have already passed from death into life. (John 5)*
- *But don't be so concerned about perishable things like food. Spend your energy seeking the eternal life that the Son of Man can give you. For God the Father has given me the seal of his approval. (John 6)*

Eternal life is permanent and worth actively pursuing. But it can only be given by Jesus. And it is the difference between life and death. It is also the cure for the common, empty way of living. Beth Moore puts it this way: "Christ became *everything,* and all former things were empty without him."[4] Simon Peter captures it perfectly:

> *For you know that God paid a ransom to save you from the empty life you inherited from your ancestors. And it was not paid with mere gold or silver . . . It was the precious blood of Christ . . . For you have been born again, but not to a life that will quickly end. Your new life will last forever because it comes from the eternal, living Word of God. (1 Peter 1:18–19, 23)*

And speaking of that . . .

The Living Word

I also have a favorite chapter in John. Here's how it begins:

> *In the beginning was the Word, and the Word was with God, and the Word was God. (John 1:1, NIV)*

As a follower of Jesus, I have a deep love and reverence for the *written* Word of God. He certainly did. We should hang on every word of every page. *Especially* the words of Jesus. But the Word of God is more than the ink on the page (thank you Mr. Gutenberg), in any language. The Word

---

4. Moore, 69.

of God is *alive*. The Word of God is *active*. And in the greatest mystery in the history of the world, came to ours. Eugene Peterson put it this way:

> *The Word became flesh and blood, and moved into the neighborhood. (John 1:14, MSG)*

We have been called to embrace and follow *more* than the written Word of God. It's rather difficult to have a relationship with a book, anyway. We have been called to embrace and follow the *living* Word of God . . . *Jesus*. The person of Jesus, the God who became the flesh and blood Word. And only the living Word can give us life. Jesus also made that rather clear, and guess who recorded it:

> *You search the Scriptures because you think they give you eternal life. But the Scriptures point to me! Yet you refuse to come to me to receive this life. (John 5:39–40)*

The written Word speaks of, and points to, the living Word. From start to finish. Eugene again:

> *These Scriptures are all about me! And here I am, standing right before you, and you aren't willing to receive from me the life you say you want. (John 5:39–40, MSG)*

Simon Peter again (via John):

> *LORD, to whom would we go? You have the words that give eternal life. We believe, and we know you are the Holy One of God. (John 6:68–69)*

Will you join Peter and follow? Will you join *Jesus* and follow? Only he, the living Word of God, can give us life. Abundant. Eternal. *Now.* Always remember eternal life is not just unending existence; it's a never-ending relationship with the living God through Jesus Christ.

Eternal life (The Kingdom of God) is a relationship.

Follow

The big difference in kids and adults is that kids are always looking ahead, not back.

(JOHN CANZANO)

Announcing the Kingdom

Before becoming an Oregon Tour Guide, I was a Park Service Ranger at Olympic National Park (WA). I still have my brown hat, my grey shirt, and my US Department of the Interior patch. But I can't seem to find my badge. I know it's around here somewhere...

I'm a hopeless sentimental fool. And after a recent move, I've been digging in the treasure trove that is my memory crate. I made a big discovery, too. I found *My Life Story*. It was written at about age seven and is complete with a picture of me in my dad's size fourteen hiking boots. Regarding my former ranger role, on page one I found the evidence: "Every summer we went to Graves Creek Ranger Station in Olympic National Park where my dad and I were rangers." Boom! Any questions, hikers? Seriously, I can answer them.

Like most every kid, I wanted to be like my dad. But, as you can probably tell already, I turned out much more like my mom. Hey, she's a tough mother from the Quinault First Peoples' Reservation of Washington State (true), so there! She also has a skull tattoo on her right shoulder (not true). But my dad's scared of her, anyway. Most people are. Until they try her apple pie.

Imitation is talked about several times in Scripture:

So I urge you to imitate me. (1 Corinthians 4:16)

And you should imitate me, just as I imitate Christ. (1 Corinthians 11:1)

Can you just hear the Apostle Paul's encouragement shouting from the page? I can. "Hey kids! Follow me!" Now, Paul isn't on an ego trip in this letter. He is commanding the church at Corinth (and around the world) to participate in one of the greatest spiritual practices of them all. *Imitation.* But I will be quick to qualify. Paul did, too. Only because I'm following *him*. Another prophet of note said the same thing (without the qualification):

Follow me.

(JESUS)

But I don't think Jesus needed to shout it. I think the direct gaze and those deep brown eyes said it all. He might have even whispered it. Or simply nodded as he said, "Hey kids . . . Andrew, Bartholomew, James, John, Judas, Judas Iscariot, Matthew, Philip, Simon Peter, Simon the Zealot, Thaddaeus, Thomas . . . follow me." By the way, despite how they're shown on the screen, they *were* just kids (teenagers). They simply followed. For three years. And they grew up fast.

So what does it really mean to follow Jesus? Few questions are more important. Does it mean coming to service on Sunday? Completing a special class or catechism? Serving in the church? In the community? Reading your Bible and praying? Yes. But it's *more* . . .

The idea of discipleship originally came from the Greeks: Plato was a disciple of Socrates, and then Aristotle became a disciple of Plato. And on and on it went. According to Portland pastor John Mark Comer (a disciple of Dallas Willard), the best word in the English language for disciple is *apprentice*. We can better relate to this word in our day. Doing an internship. Having a master teacher or coach. Having a patient artisan who shows you the magic. Having a patient boss who shows you the tricks of

Follow

the trade. In earlier days, it was simply doing the family business, from cobber, to smithy, to weaver.

In the three-tiered Hebrew education system, the highest level is being an apprentice of a Rabbi (it was the Ivy League of the day). Jesus was a Rabbi, too, and, just like the others, called people to follow him. But those he called must have had shocked reactions:

"Wait . . . *me!*"

"I'm no Harvard Man."

"I'm just a simple fisherman."

"Me too!"

"Me too!"

"I'm a murdering revolutionary."

"I'm a hated *tax collector.*"

"I'm a nobody."

There was no grueling application and acceptance process with Jesus. No grueling interview. No name or family recognition. No sweetheart deals. And there were many more than twelve that followed. And since you asked, here's what was required of you for following a Rabbi: 1) Be with your Rabbi *everyday* (24/7/365); 2) Become like your Rabbi in *everything*; 3) Do what your Rabbi did and *even more*. Simple, right? Here's Rabbi Jesus's first call:

> He appointed twelve that they might be with him and that he might send them out to preach and to have authority to drive out demons. (Mark 3:14–15, NIV)

Did you see it? *Be with him. Be like him. Do what he did.*

When you follow someone on the trail, whether on horseback or in a wagon, you're going to get dust on you. *Lots* of dust. That's where this ancient Jewish apprentice blessing comes from: "May the dust of your Rabbi be all over you."[1]

Here's my invitation:

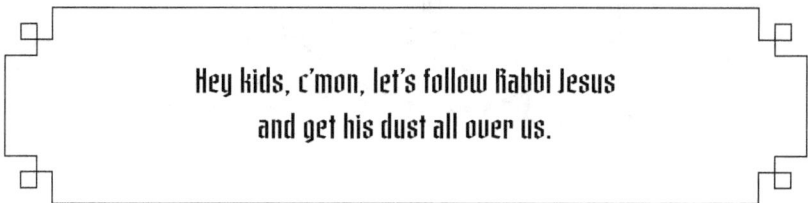

Hey kids, c'mon, let's follow Rabbi Jesus and get his dust all over us.

---

1. The above discussion was inspired and informed by John Mark Comer's *Practicing the Way*.

C'mon!

Picturing the Kingdom

It's cute, isn't it, when kids imitate their parents? Until it's not. Country artist Rodney Atkins captures one of these moments in his hit *Watching You*. He recounts the way home from a Happy Meal run with his young son in a booster seat when he had to slam on the brakes as a stop light suddenly turned red. You can imagine the mess that followed. But what Rodney couldn't imagine is what happened next. You gotta listen! I'll wait . . .

Ever been there? Yeah, me too. But aren't you thankful for second chances? Thank God for the barn to take off our hat and ask the LORD for a bit of help. Or a lot. And unlike so many country songs, this one had a happy ending. I hope my little buckaroos learned some *good* four-letter words from me along the way, too. Like pray. And that they forgot the rest of them.

I'm still trying to fit in my dad's hiking boots. Because he's been following Rabbi Jesus for over seven decades. My sweet, tough mom, too.

It's hard to imagine a greater inheritance. But there *is* one coming. It's worth the follow my friends. Every day.

life in the Kingdom

Let's talk some more about the dust of Rabbi Jesus, and how we might get a little more on *our* boots. Along the way, we'll learn a bit more of what it means to be an apprentice (disciple) of our master.

Image Bearers (Original Dust)

It's important we start here. Because apprenticeship, like everything else good in our lives, *starts* with God. The Scriptures say we're able to love because he first loved us and poured his love into our hearts through the Holy Spirit. We are only able forgive others because we ourselves have first been forgiven. We're only able to truly love our enemies, and the one's we love, because we have ourselves been loved by our Creator. And we're no longer enemies:

> *For if, while we were God's enemies, we were reconciled to him through the death of his Son, how much more, having been reconciled, shall we be saved through his life! (Romans 5:10, NIV)*

Our Creator has given us life, and continues to, every day. And because of that life, *his* life, we are able to bring life to others. Here is how we were created:

> *Then the LORD God formed a man from the dust of the ground and breathed into his nostrils the breath of life, and the man became a living being. (Genesis 2:7, NIV)*

> *So God created mankind in his own image, in the image of God he created them; male and female he created them. (Genesis 1:27, NIV)*

Of all we were created to be, we are first *image bearers*. We are the *imago Dei*, the very image of God. Of all we are called to be as apprentices of Jesus, we are foremost the walking and breathing images of God. Let that sink in for a moment. And this is true not just for us as apprentices, but for everyone you see, which includes *everyone,* you see?

The question is, do we really believe this when we drive the streets of our cities? I've spent a lot of time in downtown Portland, which in recent days has seen an explosion of houseless people. They all have significant problems, including addictions, broken relationships, catastrophic losses, or mental illness. Many people I know are now too scared to go downtown. But when we do, do we just see the problems and brokenness, or do we see the unique and precious image of God walking (and camping) on our streets? Is that what you see? Because *that is* what you see!

The very image of God is stamped on every human heart. Which makes us all masterpieces. Or Master-pieces. In fact, the name "Christian," only appearing three times in Scripture, was first a pejorative term given by an uncomprehending world. It was as if scores of "little Christs" were running around the neighborhood! Exactly.

We were all made with original dust, and each of us is an original masterpiece. And just like a piece of art painted or shaped by the likes of Michelangelo or DaVinci, there are tell-tale marks of the master, signed or not. You can always tell if it's a Van Gogh, Monet, or a Charlie Russell (my favorite). You can also tell a child of God. But we're getting ahead of ourselves.

Imitators (Trail Dust)

Once again, when we follow someone on the trail, we're going to get their dust all over us. That's the idea. When we do, everything begins to change. Which is where we return to the idea of imitation. Imitation has been called the surest form of flattery. But it is also one of the surest signs of maturity. Imitation discipleship. *Imitation apprenticeship.* This is an odd departure from *original masterpiece.* But stick with me here.

In our day, imitation most often has a negative connotation. "Be an original," a Dockers commercial urges. Of course, they still want you to wear the same pants as everyone else. *Theirs.* We celebrate the differences in our culture. The one-off's who sing, dance, and live like no one else. Enter America's Got Talent. In my hometown of Portland, our motto is "Keep Portland Weird." We take this motto *very* seriously around here.

We also take our food very seriously, too. We are all about the immediate *farm to table.* We'll take our food *organic, clean,* and *real* or not at all. Nothing artificial, frozen, or imitation for crying out loud! The Oregon Coast is just seventy-five minutes from downtown Portland with seafood right off the boat. Imitation crab on my oyster crackers? You *must* be kidding. Take it back and bring me a *real* hors d'oeuvres while I wait for my *fresh* Chinook Salmon. Shrimp Louis with *organic* cocktail sauce from Whole Foods? That's better.

But we Oregonians need not be wary when *imitation discipleship* is on the menu. The imitation I'm talking about, and our master is calling us to, is simply following an example, emulating a pattern, or copying a model. And speaking of copying, Xerox machines require a "master" if you want to make numerous copies. See where I'm going? And if office imitation doesn't ring your bell, kids, just remember some of our favorite games growing up were Follow the Leader, Simon Says, and the Hokey Pokey. Some things should never change.

Let me emphasize the imitation Paul is encouraging is *not*:

- Putting on a mask and *pretending*, like the hypocrites (ancient Greek actors).
- A *cheap* imitation, like a *Nike* (an Oregon original!) shirt bought at a flea market with a swoosh that soon falls off.
- Gritting your teeth and *trying hard*. *Real imitation* of Jesus is impossible without help. Read that again. It's true.

We've each been created as originals. Masterpieces. Yet, we're called to ~~real~~ *imitation* discipleship, to ~~frozen~~ *fresh* apprenticeship, and to be authentic *(organic)* followers. To get covered with the dust of our trail guide.

> Jesus didn't hand his disciples a textbook or give them a course syllabus. He asked each one of them to follow him—literally to "walk after" him ... Out of this unusual teaching method arose a well-known saying: you should learn from a rabbi by "covering yourself in his dust."[2]

---

2. Tverberg, *Walking in the Dust of Rabbi Jesus*, 28.

Incarnators (Pixie Dust)

I'll say it again, real imitation of Jesus is impossible without help. Thankfully, it begins with divine action *(imago Dei)* and ends with divine intervention *(incarnation)*. Our part in the middle is the easy part. Well . . .

The greatest *wonder* of the Christian faith, says Brian Zahnd, is the incarnation. God became flesh and blood and moved next door. Jesus was fully God and became fully man. You'd think the two would be mutually exclusive. This is why Jesus is our *Master copy*. We know how to be human because of his earthly life. And we know our way to God because of, and only through, *him*.

But God inhabiting man is *not* a one-time miracle. No, we'll never be fully God, but yes, we *are* the imago Dei. No, we'll never be fully as mankind was intended to be on this side of the veil, but yes, we have the perfect *example*, a model human to *emulate*. And the Spirit of Jesus is *still* in the neighborhood. And is *still* incarnating.

We are not called to powerless imitation. To a game of Simon (My favorite electronic game growing up. Google it, kids.), where it gets harder and faster until . . . *you lose*. We're not called to a fool's errand. Because imitating Jesus isn't possible without the *Spirit of Jesus*. Which is why God breathed his life into us at creation (original dust), in order for us to become living, human beings. Which is why Jesus breathed on his first followers and said, receive the Holy Spirit. Which is why he breathed the church to life on the day of Pentecost. Without his breath in our lungs, we're just like any other animal.

Instead, we are uniquely created and filled to exhibit the greatest miracle of all; a life transformed by submitting to King Jesus and incarnating the Spirit of God. We are walking images of God who are *animated* (divinely enabled) by the Spirit of God. Mickey Mouse was created by the imagination and magical pen of Walt Disney. Then animation brought he and his friends to life. Some call it magic pixie dust. Peter Pan did: "All it takes (to fly) is faith and trust. Oh! And something I forgot. Dust. Just a little bit of pixie dust."

I'm probably the first to equate the divine enablement of the Holy Spirit to pixie dust. Ha! One minute you see Tinker Bell whisk in with her magic wand and in a flash everything changes. Peter can suddenly fly! And the Apostle Peter, after being filled with the Holy Spirit, could suddenly preach! He and the rest of the 120 in the upper room were suddenly transformed, divinely animated by the Spirit of God, *incarnators* of

Follow

Jesus. Jerusalem, Judea, Samaria, and the ends of the earth would never be the same.

But let me be quick to issue a challenge as we close out another kingdom letter. We have been divinely created (original dust), and divinely enabled (pixie dust), but our divine apprenticeship (trail dust) continues. As incarnators of Jesus, we have been called to be with him, to be like him, and to do what he did. But in doing our part as imitators, we must do more than try. Two of my favorite authors make this perfectly clear:

> Trying hard can accomplish only so much. If you are serious . . . you will have to enter into a life of training. You must arrange your life around certain practices that will enable you to do what you cannot do now by willpower alone. When it comes to running a marathon, you must train, not merely try.[3] (John Ortberg)

> Following Jesus doesn't work as a hobby. The way of Jesus is a way of life. If you want to experience the life of Jesus you must adopt the lifestyle of Jesus. To live in this way takes practice. God is not looking for converts to Christianity. He is looking for apprentices to the Kingdom of God.[4] (John Mark Comer)

Jesus is still calling all of us kids to follow him . . . *like a child*. To get his dust all over us. To be his apprentices. So let's lace up our hiking boots, fix our eyes on Jesus, and follow hard after him, no matter where the trail leads. His dust is the only covering we need.

C'mon!

---

3. Ortberg, *The Life You've Always Wanted*.
4. Comer, *Practicing the Way*.

Gardencity

Our story is in between the gardens. Much more than a tidy little dash on a stone.

(BO STERN BRADY)

Announcing the Kingdom

No, I didn't forget a space in the title. It's a new word I coined. Well, sorta. It was once again John Mark Comer who inspired me with the title of one of his first books.[1] I simply did a smash up. It's a childlike thing...

The Kingdom of God is a garden. Figuratively (another biblical metaphor) and, I believe, literally. I've got a bit of biblical evidence to go on. I've also employed my logic and imagination. The last bit is the flimsier part of my case but hang on. Scripture says:

> Now all glory to God, who is able, through his mighty power at work within us, to accomplish infinitely more than we might ask or think. (Ephesians 3:20)

Infinitely more. In the ancient Greek, and the modern English languages, this means a whole lot more. Immeasurably more. Uncountable more. Like trying to count the grains of sand on the seashore more. This

---

1. Comer, *Garden City*.

is hard to believe, because, like most kids, I have a healthy imagination. So if this is true, then *at the very least* we will have lush, sprawling, and sensory overloading gardens. The kind you see all over the Willamette Valley of Oregon. Follow my logic here? Let's get back to the Scriptures:

> *Then the LORD God planted a garden in Eden in the east, and there he placed the man he had made. The LORD God made all sorts of trees grow up from the ground—trees that were beautiful and that produced delicious fruit. In the middle of the garden he placed the tree of life and the tree of the knowledge of good and evil. A river flowed from the land of Eden, watering the garden . . . (Genesis 2:8–10)*

> *Then the angel showed me a river with the water of life, clear as crystal, flowing from the throne of God and of the Lamb. It flowed down the center of the main street. On each side of the river grew a tree of life, bearing twelve crops of fruit, with a fresh crop each month. The leaves were used for medicine to heal the nations. (Revelation 22:1–2)*

We see gardens both at the beginning and end of the Scriptures. They bear a lot of similarities. Like glorious earthly gardens including Butchart in Victoria, BC, or Kensington in London, UK, this will be the place to find a park bench and stay for a while. God himself loves to be there, too:

> *When the cool evening breezes were blowing, the man and his wife heard the LORD God walking about in the garden. (Genesis 3:8)*

We also see cities in the two bookend books of the Bible. The first attempt didn't end well:

> *Then they said "Come, let's build a great city for ourselves with a tower that reaches into the sky. This will make us famous and keep us from being scattered all over the world." But the LORD came down to look at the city and the tower the people were building. (Genesis 11:4–5)*

Uh oh. God not only didn't like what he saw, he especially didn't like what he *heard*. Thus, as man created Babel, God created babble! Sorry. The final city, *The New Jerusalem*, will have a much happier ending. Actually, it won't. Have an ending that is! I'll just give you the highlights of its description, and you can read the whole chapter for yourself:

And I saw the holy city, the new Jerusalem, coming down from God out of heaven like a bride beautifully dressed for her husband . . . there will be no more death or sorrow or crying or pain . . . Look, I am making everything new . . . I will be their God, and they will be my children . . . It shone with the glory of God and sparkled like a precious stone . . . The twelve gates were made of pearls—each gate from a single pearl! And the main street was pure gold, as clear as glass . . . Its gates will never be closed at the end of day because there is no night there . . . (Revelation 21)

I've always fancied myself as a country boy. I grew up loving the wide-open spaces, the rushing streams and smooth flowing rivers, the trees and flowers, and farm fresh products. Thus, I'll be wildly happy in the brand-new *Garden of God*. But now I live in the city (albeit suburbs) with a postage stamp yard, traffic noise, and a bit more bustle. But me and my fellow city dwellers relish the convenience of Starbucks, Crumbl, Walmart, Target, and Menchie's, all within easy walking distance. I'm not a paid consultant for any of these (yet). I'm simply describing my current neighborhood. There is also an ice rink and an indoor play center about a half mile on either side of me. What a country. What a *city!* So even city dwellers will rejoice as they walk through the gates of the *City of God*.

Here's the simple truth. Here's the current (and coming) reality:

> **The Kingdom of God is a perfect smash-up . . . a Gardencity.**

Even God is (eternally) childlike.

Picturing the Kingdom

I've already mentioned I have spent several happy seasons as a tour guide. This simply means I get to go to all the places I planned on going to "someday," and get paid while doing it. And meet people from across the country and around the world. And, yes, it happily includes both gardens and cities. The beauty and majesty surrounding Portland within two hours on every side is spectacular. The Columbia River Gorge (east). The Oregon Coast (west). For garden lovers, the Willamette Valley (south). And for city lovers, Seattle (north).

But you don't even have to leave Portland for both beauty and majesty. You can see Mt. Hood from the International Rose Garden, framed perfectly over the city towers, in the 200-acre Washington Park, set aside before a single commercial building was constructed. You can lose yourself in the woods of adjacent Forest Park, the biggest city park in the country (over 5,000 acres). You can enjoy the smooth blue (sometimes) water of the Willamette River from Waterfront Park, stretching the entire length of downtown. You can even enjoy the smallest city park in the world (with a total area of 452 square inches or 0.00007205784 acres). Hey, we wanted the biggest and the smallest, okay?

But my favorite living metaphor of the Kingdom of God in Portland is our Lan Su Chinese Garden, located in Old Town. Let's just say Old Town otherwise isn't the most charming part of the city. I'll let them describe the garden for you:

> Lan Su is a tranquil botanical garden featuring rare plants native to China, decorative stonework and a tea shop . . . a result of a collaboration between the cities of Portland and Suzhou, our sister city in China's Jiangsu province that's famous for its

beautiful Ming dynasty gardens. Lan Su was built by Chinese artisans from Suzhou and is one of the most authentic Chinese gardens outside of China.

The name means "Garden of Awakening Orchids," and its plants, water features, and Pagoda is within the walls of an entire downtown city block. You can lose yourself in Portland's city gardens, and especially Lan Su. You'll never want to come back.

But someday we'll lose ourselves in God's Gardencity. It will be both, and more, and it will be *beyond our imaginations . . . beyond our wildest dreams!* And we'll *never* have to come back.

Life in the Kingdom

And even when he reached the land God promised him, he lived there by faith—for he was like a foreigner, living in tents . . . Abraham was confidently looking forward to a city with eternal foundations, a city designed and built by God. (Hebrews 11:9–10)

Garden Gate

It's *inconceivable* (Princess Bride lovers) I haven't yet been to the Oregon Garden. It's not on our normal tour routes, which is *also* Incon—(yes, *I do* know the meaning of that word). It has only been around for nearly twenty-five years now. "Someday." But my wife has, and she has testified of its beauty (she fit right in). I've also seen pictures. It even has a children's garden. So, it's high time I experienced it, don't you think? The garden gates are open (I recently drove by).

Garden gates have a romantic and mystical quality about them. Sometimes they're covered by trailing vines and foliage, like the Oregon Garden's. Sometimes they have grand and majestic entries. Other times they're modest and inconspicuous (or secret). Many times, they're wrought iron or white picket. My favorite gardens to date are Kensington (grand), George Washington's at Mt. Vernon (modest), Shore Acres on the Oregon Coast (inconspicuous), and my own (secret) backyard oasis.

Gardencity

Garden gates are entries into another world. An escape from the pressures and responsibilities of *this* world. A feast for the senses. A portal to paradise. A happy place. *My* happy place! A *sign* of the kingdom. Especially that. "Someday," more than our five senses will be overwhelmed by what we experience as we walk through the thin veil, through the garden gate into, well, *paradise*! It will be *mystical*. It will be *romantic*. It will be *forever*.

By the way, no longer will God be walking in the garden in the cool of the evening *alone*. No longer will we have to hide from God's presence because of brokenness, guilt, and shame. No longer will we *ever* have to wander in an arid desert where there is no shade or water, like the nation of Israel, David, and even Jesus did. Unless we want to. I'm kinda fond of Scottsdale, Arizona (*hot* desert), and Bend, Oregon (*high* desert), too. I'm thinking there will be Giant Sagauro Cacti in God's Gardencity, as well. And Ponderosa Pines.

City Gates

We can't underestimate the value of city gates, and city walls, throughout most of history. These days, if a city even has gates, they are simply a decorative welcome. But the safety of a city used to be reliant on the gates remaining intact in the time of attack, and the walls remaining impenetrable. They were also where grand entrances were conducted, including foreign and local dignitaries (royals), and shows of force by occupying forces.

Recently, while studying for a Palm Sunday message, I came across some fascinating history regarding Jerusalem's gates. There were eight outer gates of ancient Jerusalem with additional interior gates to the temple.

> The Eastern Gate was also known as the Beautiful Gate, the Golden Gate, and most significantly the Gate of Mercy. It was sealed up by the (occupying) Muslims for hundreds of years to prevent the Messiah from returning (Ezekiel 44:1–3). It is reserved for the Messiah's entrance in the future and thousands of graves on the slopes face it with the hope that they will be the first resurrected upon the Messiah's arrival. To prevent His arrival, the Muslims in 1541 established a cemetery to stop His path to the gate and sealed it to be certain. This is the gate that Jesus entered on Palm Sunday from the east.[2]

Yes, this *was* the gate Messiah entered. The sealing of the gate and the establishing of a cemetery came a few days too late. And why the cemetery? Because Messiah certainly wouldn't make himself ceremonially unclean by traipsing through it on the way into the city. Now for the grand (and inauspicious) entrances:

---

2. LandoftheBible.com.

Traditionally, Pilate paraded into Jerusalem on the first day of Passover Week (Palm Sunday!). He lived on the coast in Caesarea, thus entering the west gate—the front gate as impressive rulers should—with legions of chariots, horses, and foot soldiers, dressed for battle and armed with swords and spears. Rome's authority would not be questioned. The majesty with which Pilate enters the front door of the city was meant to inspire awe and fear, respect and obedience.

Meanwhile, at the east gate—the back gate—another parade is underway. This parade was just as carefully staged as Pilate's entry into Jerusalem. It was a counter-procession, a different vision of what a kingdom should be, a subversive action against the powers that ruled Jerusalem. Jesus's humble, yet triumphal, entry into Jerusalem stood in contrast to the magnificence and brutality on display at the opposite end of the city. Jesus brings peace, while Pilate brings a sword.[3]

The Kingdom of God and the empires of man were on full display in all their glory, honor, and *horror*. Here's another account:

> Pilate comes in the West Gate riding a white stallion caravanning with his entourage of Roman officers, jesters, cooks, cup bearers, and lackeys. People line the streets when Rome comes to town. Pilate is the extension of Caesar. He's the face of Rome in Israel, so when he rolls up, people notice. People cheer. People extend him the curtesy of respecting his authority, and we have evidence that proves that people threw down cloaks and palms as Pilate entered.
>
> Now imagine at the same time, over at the North Gate, Jesus enters. Rather than a war horse, he's riding an untested donkey. He's not caravanning; he's carpooling. He doesn't travel with an entourage but with fishermen and women. Nobody is supposed to notice Jesus entering. He is a nobody from nowhere.[4]

Did these two gate entries occur simultaneously? There is no historical evidence of this. But it is certainly possible, and most certainly was on the same day. What a *perfect* picture, nonetheless. A *perfect* fulfillment of prophecy. The coming of the Kingdom of God to the holy city, and most missed it!

There's a final brushstroke to this kingdom picture, compliments of John of Patmos. The city gates of Jerusalem were always closed at sunset

---

3. In Through the Back Door, sermon by Terry Gau, 2016.
4. Marcus Borg and John Dominic Crossan, The Last Week.

and reopened at sunrise. If you didn't arrive until after the gates were closed, it was going to be a long night outside. What about the gates to the *New* Jerusalem? Take it John:

> *I saw no temple in the city, for the LORD God Almighty and the Lamb are its temple. And the city has no need of sun or moon, for the glory of God illuminates the city and the Lamb is its light . . . It's gates will never be closed at the end of day because there is no night there.* (Revelation 21:22–23, 25)

The garden gates and the city gates are *always* open in the Kingdom of God. No more wars, remember? No more danger. No more death. No more night. The Messiah has come through the Gate of Mercy, and invites us to follow, where he is waiting. Someday we'll leave behind the fading gardens and failing cities of this world and step into the eternal Gardencity, where beauty, healing, and life overflow.

Forevermore.

Home

Like a blind man tapping with his cane on the sidewalk, so modern man is tapping from event to event by an everyday experimentalism trying to find his way Home. Somebody has said, "There is only one sickness, and that is homesickness."

(E. STANLEY JONES)

Announcing the Kingdom

Our favorite destination, especially during the holidays, is also our favorite four-letter word. *Home.* The desire for home, *especially for kids,* is universal and its gravitational pull is one of the strongest in the universe. We love to read about it, sing about it, and dream about it. But best of all is when we pull in the driveway. And we *never* grow out of it.

But however much the sights, smells, and feels of our hometown, neighborhood, and house are, home is not just a place. Home is a *person*. We default to a place when we think about home, and that's okay. Especially when dinner is ready. But there is an even greater reality than a white picket fence in the front and a tree with a tire swing out back. It is *who* is waiting for us on the porch. And in the kitchen. Because home isn't an empty house, just like a church isn't an empty sanctuary. The people of God *are* the church, just like our family *is* home! What would home be without mom and dad? What would grandma's house be without grandma?

I hope you are nodding your head right now because you have found this to be true. However, I know statistically many have never experienced a Home Sweet Home. I'm so sorry. But I have good news for you. Jesus, after dropping the bombshell on his first followers that he would soon be betrayed, denied, and killed, immediately dropped this seed of faith in their hearts:

> *Don't let your hearts be troubled. Trust in God, and trust also in me. There is more than enough room in my Father's home. If this were not so, would I have told you that I am going to prepare a place for you? When everything is ready, I will come and get you, so that you will always be with me where I am. (John 14:1–3)*

We'll get back to this *not yet* kingdom reality in a moment. But first let me ask you a question: Where is *your* happy place? You probably have more than one, just like I have more than one secret garden. But in relation to our happy place, this is not the greatest question I can ask. I was reminded of this when I was in my favorite shop at Sunriver (Central Oregon resort). Yes, Sunriver is my happy place. But as I was looking for something special for my girl, I was reminded of my *real* happy place on this earth. *Stacie.* It's not where, it's *who*. My home in Sherwood, where I'm currently writing, isn't home without her. "Honey, I'm home!" just doesn't work without a honey. And all my happy places frankly aren't that happy without her, either. So I bought a small wooden sign, written in black and white, with the mic-drop saying on it. You've seen all kinds of them in your favorite store. But this one is the best: *You Are My Happy Place*. Right? Right.

God has invited us to embark on a great journey. A pilgrimage from lost to found, from life to death, and from our home to his. Well, that's not quite it. This is better: *From our home to him!* The prodigal son learned this when returning from his rebellious and bankrupting misadventures. He finally came back to his senses and returned home. Upon arrival, he was just hoping to be treated like any other hired *hand* in his father's house. Instead, he was a child returning home to his father's *arms*. It was the greatest journey of his life. It is ours, too, because we have a Father waiting for us with the same breathless anticipation. And he never wants you to forget:

Home

> The greatest journey home is from a place to a person.

Picturing the Kingdom

There's no place like home.

(Dorothy, in the Wizard of Oz)

Follow the Yellow Brick Road

You've been humming it ever since you read the quote above. You might as well go ahead and sing it with Dorothy and her pals. I'll join you . . .

Wouldn't it be nice if we didn't have to just sing about it? If there was an *actual* yellow brick road that led to the actual streets of gold? (See what I did there? I'm a trained professional; don't try this at *home*.)

But all kidding, singing, and humming aside, it really is the will of the Father, for *all* of his children, to find their way home. And if they have trouble or find themselves lost, he'll even drop everything to go and find them. The parable of the shepherd who leaves the ninety-nine to locate, secure, and carry home his one lost lamb, is the story of our salvation (rescue). Each one of us is valuable enough for him to "leave everyone else to go and find *me*." *That* is the good news!

That is also the incarnation I've made such a fuss about. But Jesus didn't just leave home to seek and save the lost. He, well, I'll let Paul and Eugene say it:

> *When the time came, he set aside the privileges of deity and took on the status of a slave, became human! Having become human, he stayed human. It was an incredibly humbling process. He didn't claim special privileges. Instead, he lived a selfless, obedient life and then did a selfless, obedient death—and the worst kind of death at that: a crucifixion. (Philippians 2, MSG)*

Can you see why Brian and I make such a fuss about it? It's more than a reason to exchange gifts and chop down an Oregon Douglas Fir to decorate. The incarnation changed *everything*. It was the beginning of . . . *the beginning*. It even changed Jesus . . . forever. What? No, that's not heresy. That's his sacrifice. *"Having become human, he stayed human."* Our friend Eugene nailed it! The human form he took, though now glorified, is permanent. And speaking of *nailed it,* have you ever heard there will only be one thing in heaven that is man-made? The *nail scarred hands* of Jesus. He even showed these scars to Thomas on his glorified body.

Jesus did one other thing before his ascension. He left an *actual* yellow brick road for us to follow. It's not just a dream, Dorothy. We don't have to grope our way to Oz, hoping we'll somehow make it with our brains of straw, heart of tin, and courage of a paper tiger. The Scriptures are replete with passages promising safe passage if we'll just stay on *the Way*. The Scriptures themselves are a yellow brick road of sorts. The longest Psalm, celebrating the written Word of God, includes this truth we cling to when it seems so dark:

> *Your word is a lamp to guide my feet and a light for my path. (Psalm 119:105)*

But again, we're not just talking about the written Word of God here. We're talking about the *living* Word of God. Jesus. He hasn't just handed us a map and compass and wished us luck on the trail. He *is* the map and compass. And he hasn't just constructed a road for us to navigate on our own. He *is* that road. Yes, *Jesus* is the yellow brick road! He said it flat out:

> *I am the Road, also the Truth, also the Life. No one gets to the Father apart from me. (John 14, MSG)*

Let's sing it again . . .

> *Follow the Yellow Brick Road. Follow the Yellow Brick Road. Follow, follow . . .*

Life in the Kingdom

> *Home is somewhere we've been, not yet been, and most long to be.*
>
> (JJA)

> *Three things will last forever—*
> *faith, hope, and love . . .*
>
> (1 CORINTHIANS 13:13)

Our Perfect Home

Every one of us has an ideal picture of home. This is true no matter where we're from. Home is simply home, wherever it is. Right? And it's always worth singing about, on holidays or normal days. Have you heard John Denver's classic country song Take Me Home Country Roads? It's time. Ironically, when the greatest folk singer of all time sings the first line about West Virginia being on the border of heaven, he was singing about a place he'd never been! Perhaps his co-writers had.

But he obviously had some experience with being home, because he also sang (and wrote) Back Home Again. Yes, you might as well just listen to this one too. What a beautiful picture of his country farm, including a hot supper, hot fire, and hot wife! Well, he might have said it a little more poetically than that.

We can all add our favorite descriptions and longings of home. It's safe. It's warm. It's comfortable. It's a place, just like the store Toys R Us of old, "where a kid can be a kid." Where we're always accepted, always valued, and always cherished. It's a place of *faith, hope,* and *love.* The pure stuff. Nothing added. Nothing taken away. Eternal. I think I hear mom calling . . .

Our Mediterranean Home

My favorite speaker is someone you've likely never heard of. But he's one of the world's greatest story tellers. Coincidence? I think not. One of his most memorable messages (and pictures) describes what our eternal home will *really* be like. I emphasize that word because I know the picture forming in your mind when reading the words of Jesus above. It is the same picture I've always had. Until Dick Foth came along and spoiled it.

I grew up singing about *my* mansion in glory and have been decorating it ever since. And, of course, this mansion is on the best street, with the best view, with the best yard, and the best layout. Oh, and the best (and highest) fence and security system. I've just described heaven for an introvert. Did I mention the moat and crocodiles?

But the crowd of followers Jesus was talking to weren't picturing a first world estate high on a hill free of the riffraff. His audience was Mediterranean, so guess what their mansions were like? *Mediterranean.* Now I've never been to the Mediterranean, so I'll have to take Dr. Foth's word for it. In this tight-knit family culture, new houses weren't typically constructed when the kids got married. New *rooms* were constructed. What started out as a rambler turned into a mansion as rooms were added on, so the family could continue to *all be together in one place. That* is the picture of our eternal home. All together in one place with the people who make home . . . *home.* All together in one place with the *person* who will make home . . . *Home!*

> Jesus says, "Here's the deal! I'll leave My place. I'll come to your place. I'll take your place. And then we'll go to My place. (Dick Foth)

Our Forever Home

> *God, it seems you've been our home forever; long before the mountains were born, Long before you brought earth itself to birth, from*

Home

"once upon a time" to *"kingdom come"*—*you are God. (Psalm 90, MSG)*

Perhaps you didn't realize how strong a theological concept home is. So strong, in fact, that two theological heavyweights from Yale made the following statement: "The purpose of theology is then to help human beings identify God's home as their home and to help us journey toward it."[1] Read it again. What a profound truth! And like all the best aspects of the Kingdom of God, it's so simple even a child can understand it. And live it.

The Flourishing Triangle

Speaking of, for those who still struggle with the loaded metaphor of kingdom, they helpfully add, "the 'kingdom of God' and the 'home of God' are metaphors for two sides of the same reality."[2] Now *that's* loaded! We'd best unpack this suitcase, in our old room, before heading downstairs to dinner. These two New Haven smarties make it easy for us (can you say that about *your* professors?). We have only to back up a bit from the above ellipse to find the two words which capture their theology of theology . . . "The Flourishing Life." Most of their book, happily, gives their vision for a flourishing life, summed up simply as "Life led well, life going well and life feeling as it should." Sign me up! Of course, we could

---

1. Volf and Croasmun, *For The Life of the World*, 71.
2. Volf and Croasmun, 181.

substitute *abundant life, eternal life,* or *Kingdom of God* for flourishing life if we'd like. It's all the same, and only made possible by the completed work of our king.

Part of the reason I love these Bulldogs (Yale), is because they continually focus on the Kingdom of God. They say, "In the New Testament, there is no metaphor more important than the kingdom of God."[3] A-men, boys! They conclude this thought saying: "The kingdom is where and when God rules in such a way as to make the world fit in its entirety to be God's home and therefore humanities true home as well."[4]

In a world of temporary shelters and passing pleasures, Jesus offers us a home that will last forever. May we fix our hearts on him, our sure foundation, and our eternal dwelling place. Hey, look at us (smarties) doing theology. Piece of cake, right?

Homemade cake, of course.

---

3. Volf and Croasmun, 17.
4. Volf and Croasmun, 17.

Identity

Find your identity in Jesus and nothing else.

(Leonard Sweet)

I identify as a kite.

(Bumper Sticker)

Announcing the Kingdom

We live in confusing times. We've *always* lived in confusing times. This is true no matter *who* you are, *where* you come from, *how* you were raised, *what* you believe, or *why* you should care. We can be confused by any number of things, which is why two of the biggest sections in a bookstore are self-help and spirituality. Well, and the children's area, which is where most of the fun is. And much less confusion. Well . . .

Perhaps the biggest point of confusion and contention in our day is over *identity*. Unfortunately, this also includes kids. Most especially so. Remember junior high? I know, I'm trying to forget, too. So instead, let's go all the way back to the playground at Crooked River Elementary School (Go Cougars!). Yes, some of our best, and worst, lessons came on the playground. Like learning to share the swings (get out of my bathtub!), who was king of the mountain (or log), who was "in" and who was "out." Of course, that last part could change between morning and afternoon recess.

But perhaps no "lessons" are more controversial right now in the classroom than grappling with issues of identity. It is a curriculum unit where even angels fear to tread. We've gone from reading, writing, and arithmetic being the primary concerns for parents (and safety on the playground), to what is being taught to students about their values, morals, and identity. And these discussions and distinctions are starting at a younger and younger age.

Our identity used to be a lot more straightforward. Like picking out toys in the store for boys or girls used to be. Now it's not so simple (and stereotypical). Now don't panic, I'm not going to go down a political or social rabbit trail. But I will simply say we are often asking the wrong questions and focusing on the wrong "stuff" (Ban Mr. Potato Head? Seriously?). This is not to downplay the significance of these relevant discussions and conclusions, but simply to point out one of the reasons for the rampant confusion in our day. Sadly, the classroom has now become a hotbed for the red & blue, black & white divides. Years ago, Pink Floyd famously told teachers to leave their poor, unsuspecting students alone. Sounds like they still haven't learned *their* lesson. Fire up the band. God help us.

Fortunately, he has. No, you won't find the answers in Scripture to whether boys should wear pink, girls should play football, or bathrooms should be unisex. I wonder if they still have the annual Powder Puff football game in school these days? I imagine I'm rather dating myself and am woefully un-PC. But c'mon now, those Central girls looked great in football jerseys! I'm just sayin'. Sorry. They often make good quarterbacks, too. Like the girl they made a movie about from a school in our league, a half hour away from Central High. True.

But what we *will* find in the Scriptures is helpful counsel for our perpetual cultural propensity for identity crises. And while my intent is not to oversimplify these issues, I believe it is critical we review the basics of life that, in Geometric terms, used to be considered *givens* by most people in the world. So let's get down to brass tacks. Or whatever color of tacks you prefer:

Identity

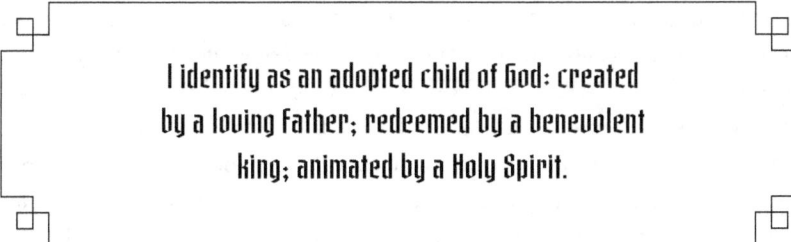

I identify as an adopted child of God: created by a loving Father; redeemed by a benevolent king; animated by a Holy Spirit.

That's a serious mouthful, so let's quickly break it down into smaller bites.

Adopted

> *Long before he laid down earth's foundations, he had us in mind, had settled on us as the focus of his love, to be made whole and holy by his love. Long, long ago he decided to adopt us into his family through Jesus Christ. (Ephesians 1, MSG)*

Our identity includes our *family* and *geographical* origins but goes way beyond them. Jesus has a more expansive view of family, anyway. *Much* more. In fact, Jesus has a much more expansive view of just about everything, especially borders. Sure, we can wave our national flags during a parade, but when Jesus looks at our planet, he sees the same borders our astronauts see. *None.* So it follows Jesus doesn't really notice our family crests in our home entries, either. And when it comes to children, well, let's just say our Father has a few, favorites *all,* and always has room for more. No DNA or ancestry.com searches are necessary. If you want in, you're in! And your new identity?

Child of God!

Created

> *So God created human beings in his own image. In the image of God he created them; male and female he created them . . . Then God looked over all he had made, and he saw that it was very good! (Genesis 1:27, 31)*

Our identity includes our *physical make-up* and *personality* but goes way beyond them. We could spend a lot of time here, but I imagine you're aware of the big issues of our time, and where both sides stand. But instead of throwing gender grenades and personal pronouns at each other, how about we ask and answer the first and most relevant question. Do you believe God created? And do you believe God created . . . *you*. How you answer this question is foundational to your beliefs in *all* physical issues, sexuality or otherwise. Scripture won't try to convince you, it simply begins with this assumption, in the very first words of the very first chapter of the very first book. God stamped us, sealed us, and celebrated us! Thus, it is not we humans who determine our identity and value, despite what you hear in the classroom, see on your favorite show, or read from your favorite well-meaning self-help guru. It is our Creator alone, and he created us *good*. It's the imago Dei again. We were made in the very . . .

Image of God!

Redeemed

> *Do you not know that your body is a temple of the Holy Spirit, who is in you, whom you have received from God? You are not your own; you were bought at a price. Therefore honor God with your body. (1 Corinthians 6:19–20)*

Our identity includes our *choices* (good and bad), and *accomplishments* (winners and participants), but goes way beyond them. It's not only the Old Testament that celebrates our physical creation. And it's not only the New Testament that urges good works and good choices. Yes, how we were created physically determines a large part of our destiny, and we had very little say in the matter. At 6'7" I am not destined to fit into a compact car, and my clothing choices are often limited. And while I had *some* value on the basketball court, I had very little value on the wrestling mat or as a horse jockey.

But when it comes to a life full of good works and good choices, I have a lot of say in the matter, and my choices will absolutely impact my health in *every way*; physically, emotionally, socially, and spiritually. Yet, Scripture declares, despite my most despicable acts and lack of good deeds, I have been redeemed. I have been bought back at a heavy price, the very life blood of Jesus, in the greatest act of sacrificial love in the history of the world. I should *never* doubt my value, and *never* doubt the identity defining and confirming . . .

Generosity of God!

Identity

Animated

> ... the LORD God formed the man from the dust of the ground and breathed into his nostrils the breath of life, and the man became a living being. (Genesis 2:7, NIV)

Our identity includes our *passions* and *pursuits* but goes way beyond them. I spoke earlier of my love for Mickey & Minnie, and the creator who brought them to life. Without the animation of Walt Disney and his many generations of pals, some of *our* favorite pals, including Pluto, Goofy, and Donald, would simply not exist. And without the very breath of God being (gently) forced into our lungs of dust, neither would we. And we're only two chapters into the Holy Scriptures. But we're not a one-time act of animation. The very Spirit of God continues to breathe life not just into our temporary physical bodies, but into our eternal souls. As long as he is welcome. When we throw open the doors of our hearts, whether French, wooden, or wrought iron, we will receive fresh animation, renewed identity, and the overflowing . . .

Life of God!

Picturing the Kingdom

Today you are you! That is truer than true!

There is no one alive who is you-er than you!

(Dr. Seuss)

I will continue to shout from the mountaintops of Oregon that *every* person on the planet has been uniquely wired and is inherently valuable! We are not only *masterpieces* but are master *prints*. Each one of us is an original, even the Elvis impersonators. You are a perfect model, and God has thrown away the proverbial mold. True. And *good*, despite what you think you see in the mirror.

I imagine all of us have gotten hooked on one of the myriad options of crime genre, whether it be network dramas or real-life documentary series. Some of these I call *creepy rodeos*, but my wife loves them anyway. Our time investment undoubtedly makes us perfect jurors because we know our forensics. Of course, lesson one of being a successful criminal is to leave behind no fingerprints. We practically yell it into our 140"

TV's when the hot, young thief we're pulling for doesn't wear gloves. Our fingerprints are indisputably unique, enough so that the investigator we *should* be rooting for only needs a partial print to nab the criminal.

If this is true of our physical fingerprints, then how much more so our *soul prints*. Mark Batterson says it this way: "Your fingerprint uniquely identifies you and differentiates you from everyone else who has ever lived, but your fingerprint is only skin-deep. You possess a uniqueness that is soul deep."[1]

This is why doppelgangers and celebrity imitators always fall so far short of the originals. They might fool us for a while with their physical characteristics, but they can only hide their fingerprints and disguise their soul prints for so long. Elvis *really is* dead, despite what the drive-thru worker at Taco Bell saw in Memphis last year.

Scripture sometimes compares us to *vessels*, full or empty, clay or bejeweled, noble or ordinary. These metaphors aren't designed to denigrate, degrade, or discourage, but rather to *distinguish*. Each have been fashioned for a purpose and derive their value from their Creator's desires. And *fingerprints*. Every vessel has their Creator's fingerprints all over them, which gives them significant value. I imagine you can see where this is headed, so I'll just say it:

The fingerprints of the Master are all over you. Soul deep. And you are signed.

---

1. Mark Batterson, *Soul Print*, 6.

Identity

Life in the Kingdom

Don't let daylight in on the magic.

(THE CROWN)

It occurred to me then that identity is a hierarchy. We are primarily one thing, and then we're primarily another, and then another, and so on, until death—in succession. Each new identity assumes the throne of Self, but takes us further from our original self, perhaps our core self—the child. Yes, evolution, maturation, the path towards wisdom, it's all natural and healthy, but there's a purity to childhood, which is diluted with each iteration. As with the hunk of gold, it gets whittled away.[2]

(PRINCE HARRY)

Royals

Now for the fun part! Not only are we part of God's family, with all the requisite blessings, but we're also *citizens* of his kingdom, with all the rights and privileges included. But not just any citizen. We are *heirs*. But not just any heirs. We are *royal* heirs. We're a member of the royal family. And someday, like the prodigal son returning home, not only will we be welcomed with open arms, but we'll be *robed and ringed as royals!* We'll have full run of the castle, and full access to the throne. And in this kingdom, the magic will be real and exposed to broad daylight. Eat your hearts out Tudors, Yorkies, and Windsors! Am I gonna get in trouble for saying that?

Royal Value

So what does this mean? It means as sons and daughters of the king, full heirs, and members of the royal family, that our *value* is undeniable, and of far greater worth than all the royal jewels in all the empires of our world. In fact, Scripture not only repeatedly calls us heirs, but says that

---

2. Prince Harry, *Spare*, 304.

we will *be* the royal jewels of the kingdom, shining like stars in the sky. It means we're more than servants, ladies in waiting, or even court jesters. It means we eat upstairs, not down, and that we'll use the family China, crystal, and silver as we eat at the "big boys and girls" table. The big table, in the Kingdom of God, *is* the kid's table! I told you this was fun.

This also means we kids have been *invited, noticed,* and *announced.* We're not just the family appendages they hope will behave themselves at the palace ball. We have a name card on the table. We're announced by the doorman in a loud voice. We're noticed by the important people. We *are* the important people. How different from the way kids have been treated by most cultures, even ours, if we're not careful and intentional. Do *we* notice and engage the kids around us on the street, in the sanctuary, or at the family reunion? Jesus certainly does.

A Royal Voice

This also means we're *heard* and *responded to.* We don't have to beg the servants for a refill. We don't have to beg the grown-ups to listen to our story. We don't have to worry whether we have the king's ear. It will be like an old commercial from when I was a kid. EF Hutton was an investment firm, and when EF Hutton spoke, everyone stopped what they were doing and listened. Yeah, like that.

But the voices being heard will go both ways. Jesus said of a shepherd:

> He calls his own sheep by name and leads them out. When he gets them all out, he leads them and they follow because they are familiar with his voice. (John 10, MSG)

Jesus called himself the Good Shepherd and promised we'd know his voice as we go out, too. But even better, when we're led in (to the Royal Ballroom), we'll know the voice of the king, too! Yep, same person. Talk about the end of confusion.

Royal Vestments

Scripture says in the Kingdom of God we'll be robed in white. Not coincidentally it also calls us the *Bride of Christ.* This means we'll exchange our filthy rags of sin for our beautiful gowns of purity. Scripture also says nothing impure will ever enter so fancy duds are on the way.

But Jesus wants to help us change our duds for dinner *now*. In Downton Abbey, you didn't show up for dinner dressed casual or even business casual. It was a formal affair requiring the women's best gowns, and the men's tuxes with tails. In fact, in one of the stories of Jesus one of the guests gets thrown out for not having proper garments on. Fortunately, Jesus has taken care of our needed duds for our new digs. We will be clothed in *his* righteousness. But we can put on these *righteous* clothes right now. In fact, the king insists. See *Colossians 3* for a look at the wardrobe, which notably includes humility. And by the way, in the Kingdom of God the emperor *will* have clothes on!

Royal Priesthood

One final and important note: We're not *independent* royals, like Harry & Megan. Our identity as royals is determined by the king but is embodied as a family. We are *together* the royal family, and what is true for us as *children* of God is especially true for us as the *family* of God:

> We identify as the adopted family of God, the very bride and body of Christ: created by a loving Father to be a chosen generation; redeemed by a benevolent king to be a royal priesthood; animated by the Spirit to be a holy nation.[3]

In a world of confusion and counterfeit identities, Jesus offers us a rock-solid foundation for knowing who we are and whose we are. We have been adopted, created, redeemed, and animated by the God who not only makes us royalty but treats us as royals as well.

And he's turned light on the magic.

---

3. See Ephesians 5; 1 Corinthians 12; 1 Peter 2.

Jubilee!

> *Sing Ho! For the life of a Bear! I don't much mind if it rains or snows, 'Cos I've got a lot of honey on my nice new nose, I don't much care if it snows or thaws, 'Cos I've got a lot of honey on my nice clean paws!*[1]
>
> (WINNIE-THE-POOH)

Announcing the Kingdom

Most people are transported back, *waaay* back, to the hillbilly holler when they hear the word *jubilee!* Am I right? Did you hear the backwoods banjo as you read the title? The haunting harmonica joining the faraway fiddle transporting you to a lonely land? One of my favorite songs from one of my favorite country groups is Ozark Mountain Jubilee by The Oak Ridge Boys. It's as old as the hills, and so are the Boys, but it's a goodie. If you have a Bluetooth speaker, it will be the perfect background for this letter.

Imagine my surprise when my doctoral professor said *jubilee!* is the best word to use in describing the Kingdom of God. In fact, he had the audacity to suggest we use jubilee *instead of* kingdom! *Now that's just about enough out of him,* I thought to myself as I was taking notes in our snobby Cambridge classroom. Then, come to find out, he used to own a

---

1. Milne, *The Complete Tales of Winnie-the-Pooh*, 109.

country store in the mountains of West Virginia. Now it makes sense. Ha! By the way, I used to look down on those mountaineers of West Virginny, until I found out my roots trace back there. *Hee Haw!*

Scripture, however, directly supports adding harmonicas, fiddles, and banjos to our kingdom band. They add great texture to the large harp section. Scripture even declares *jubilee!* in both Hebrew and Greek. When Jesus returned to his hometown of Nazareth, he made a beeline for the synagogue on the Sabbath, as was his custom. When it was his turn to read from the Scriptures, he was handed the perfect scroll to make his introductory kingdom announcement. I'm sure it was a coincidence. Jesus *rolled* almost all the way to the end of the scroll and read the best declaration of the Kingdom of God in all of Scripture. No wonder it's repeated no less than three times, in the Law, the Prophets, and the Gospels:

> *The Spirit of the LORD is on me, because he has anointed me to preach good news to the poor. He has sent me to proclaim freedom for the prisoners and recovery of sight for the blind, to release the oppressed, to proclaim the year of the LORD's favor. (Luke 4:18–19, NIV)*
>
> *I must preach the good news of the kingdom of God to the other towns also, because that is why I was sent. (Luke 4:43, NIV)*

Jesus began his public ministry *announcing the kingdom*. He announced it with more than words but with a demonstration of kingdom power and authority. It was not lost on his Jewish audience, and it got him into immediate hot water, even among his childhood peeps. His direct connection of the *Year of Jubilee* to the Kingdom of God (and to him) wasn't lost on them, either.

Leviticus 25 introduces this expression of Sabbath which was both for the people and the land. Every fiftieth year, after seven sabbaths of years, was to be set aside as holy. On this year everyone returns home to their clan and their land to rest and celebrate. All debts are cancelled, all slaves are set free, and all mortgaged lands are returned (redeemed). And then the party commences, with no planting, no tilling, and no harvesting for an entire year. It is a full year to celebrate the LORD's presence among them, his mercy in them, and his kingship over them. Oh, and their kinship with one another. *Jubilee!*

As John the Baptist was rotting in Herod's prison, he undoubtedly had a few bad moments. After being the first to announce Jesus as the long-awaited Messiah, getting to baptize him, seeing the divine dove and hearing the heavenly voice, he was now dealing with a bit of human doubt and disillusionment. So he dispatched some of his minions to bring back a bit of confirmation. Jesus essentially told them the *ultimate jubilee!* had come and was now currently in progress:

> *"Are you the one who was to come, or should we expect someone else?" "Go back and report to John what you have seen and heard: The blind receive sight, the lame walk, those who have leprosy are cured, the deaf hear, the dead are raised, and the good news is preached to the poor." (Luke 7:20,22)*

Do you recognize the list? The kingdom had arrived, in power and authority, and you can see and hear:

- Freedom!
- Healing!
- Good news!
- Life!
- Favor!

Rosen up the bow. *Jubilee!* has come.

Picturing the Kingdom

Mardis Gras

Of course, the jubilee band can involve instruments other than the Ozark kind. Have you ever been to Bourbon Street in New Orleans? You'll see a few bands around. And you'll hear a few instruments. On each corner, I'm told. Which, shockingly, includes world famous Clarinet player Doreen Ketchens, right there on the street! In a recent interview with Ted Koppel, she talks about the funeral parades of New Orleans. A funeral procession is probably not your go to picture of *jubilee!*, but just listen:

Jubilee!

It starts slow and somber. Expresses grief. Honors the person. But once the last family car passes the trumpet player gives a 'call' and the crowd says "Hey!" And it symbolizes that the time of bereavement is over, and the time of rejoicing has begun, because that person has gone on to a better place.[2]

Have you ever been to a funeral like this? True, the reception often has a bit more of a celebratory air, especially if there is good potato salad. Dancing in the streets is one thing but shouting "Hey!" and then dancing in the sanctuary, right in front of the casket? Not on your *life!* Sorry. What's next, breaking into raucous laughter during the Eulogy?

Parties in the Kingdom of God are, and will be, a whole different *animal*. Perhaps you've been to Bourbon Street during the annual Mardi Gras? It will pale in comparison to the upcoming *Jubilee!,* I assure you. The great feasts of the Old Testament give us a *taste* of what's to come. Weddings and the receptions following are even closer since Jesus uses this metaphor in his invitation to the upcoming *Marriage Supper of the Lamb*. But we can also see and hear the Kingdom of God in the funerals of the righteous:

- Freedom!
- Healing!

2. CBS Sunday Morning, aired February 2022.

- Good news!
- Life!
- Favor!

"Hey!"

Life in the Kingdom

I . . . I . . . I remember the Alamo!
(PEE WEE HERMAN'S BIG ADVENTURE)

Now let's return to the classroom in Cambridge. But only for a quick moment. Despite my professor's comments about kingdom, I still took good notes. And before we headed back downtown on the cobblestone streets, Dr. Sweet ended with a flourish. He told us: "Jubilee invites us to remember, rejoice, and reset."

Remember

The massacre at the small little mission in San Antonio (including Davy Crockett!), became the rallying cry for Texas independence. On most days they still shout it, deep in the heart of the Lone Star state. You can also hear the inspiring voice of Mufasa (James Earl Jones) telling his son *Simba,* the next Lion King . . . "Remember who you are!"

Remembering is critical to our faith because, like the nation of Israel, we have short memories (and attention spans). We need *frequent* reminders. That's why Jesus gave us the *feast* of the Eucharist. My pastor, in a recent sermon, said, "Whenever God wants us to remember something he gives us a meal."[3] (Tyler Staton) Eucharist literally means thanksgiv-

---

3. Tyler Staton, sermon October, 2024, delivered in Portland, OR.

Jubilee!

ing, which for most of us is our favorite feast of the year. It is always good to pause and remember the blessings of the past year, before diving into the stuffing. God knows it is good for us to pause and remember what he has done, and what is now finished. He also knows we need to eat.

The Year of Jubilee, like the annual feasts of Israel, was also a critical time for the nation of Israel to remember. To remember: *"You belong to me, I am the LORD your God!"* To remember: *"All this land belongs to me, because it was I who brought you out of the land of Egypt."* To remember: *"It is I that brings the harvest and feeds you and your children! I am Jehovah-Jireh, your provider. You have only to wait."*[4]

But the nation of Israel, and now the church of Jesus, needs another critical reminder. It should be our constant rallying cry, not merely a seasonal sentiment: *Remember the poor.* God truly, and deeply, cares about the poor. That's why care for the poor among you, including the aliens (immigrants), was *baked* into the law. The Year of Jubilee was but one of numerous provisions for the needy. It wasn't optional then, and it shouldn't be seen as optional now, because it is also baked into the teaching of the New Testament. Paul, in recounting a discussion with James, Peter, and John, said:

> *All they asked was that we should continue to remember the poor, the very thing I had been eager to do all along. (Galations 2:10, NIV)*

Then there's Jesus, who was always talking about, and talking with, the poor. The same was true of sinners. Jesus even had the audacity to suggest they should be invited to banquets. The hosts were appalled. Jesus said to one of them:

> *But when you give a banquet, invite the poor, the crippled, the lame, the blind, and you will be blessed. Although they cannot repay you, you will be repaid at the resurrection of the righteous. (Luke 14:13–14)*

We all love a good banquet, especially if there are important people there. But Jesus said kingdom banquets should be altogether different (like everything else). This is the kind of *ball* Jesus has called us to *throw!* Let the self-important host their own affairs.

---

4. See *Leviticus* 25 and *Isaiah* 61.

Reset

But *jubilee!* (and Eucharist) demands we do more than remember. It demands we *act*. Therefore, release your brothers and sisters and their children from all their debts, and from slavery. Therefore, give back the land to its rightful clan, and give the land a year of Sabbath from its production, because it is I who provides the harvest and makes sure you and your children are fed. It is the divine reset, a button God called Israel to press every fifty years. It recalibrated the community for the next fifty. It was a gift to *all*, not just some, but *especially* the poor. Now God wants *us* to press the reset button of forgiveness *every day*, times without number (70 x 7). And as we do, we're reminded we were once *poor sinners*, and then God hit the divine reset that is the cross. *Jubilee!*

Rejoice

With news this good, there is nothing left for us to do but rejoice:

- We have been set *free*, from our debts, despair, demons and death!
- We have been *healed*, of our diseases, disabilities, and debts (sin)!
- We have received *good news*, embodied in Jesus!
- We have been given *life* in the land of death; light in the land of darkness!
- We have been given *forgiveness* (mercy) and *favor* (grace)!

Dr. Sweet ended his most recent book talking about our calling to keep *ringing the bell* of hope in our world, no matter the circumstances. It's only appropriate that he, and Doreen, get the last word on *Jubilee!*: "My hands were clasping that clapper while writing this book, ringing the bell, the bell of Jubilee, God's dream for this world."[5]

"*Hey!*"

---

5. Sweet, *Jesus Human*, 448.

Kings & Kingdoms

*Kings and kingdoms will all pass away, but
there's something about that name.*[1]

(BILL & GLORIA GAITHER)

Announcing the Kingdom

We've already talked about what the Kingdom of God is. Now it's time to highlight what it is *not*, by looking at the empires of this world. This is a bad news/good news kind of thing for me. The bad news is Highclear Castle (home of Downton Abbey), is a relic of the past. Like so many other English manors, it is no longer the hub around which the rest of the community revolves. Where they once generated revenue and employed many, now they are a financial black hole the government must prop up.

This is eventually true of every manor house, castle, and fortress around the world and throughout history. The walls once impenetrable are now crumbling. The powers once invincible, already have. The current powers are headed for the same fate, despite how things appear today. We have only to look to the Romans, Greeks, Turks, Persians,

---

1. There's Something About That Name. Words by Gloria Gaither; Words and Music by William J Gaither. 1970 Hanna Street Music (BMI). All rights reserved. Used by permission.

Spaniards, Germans, Mongols, French, and English. It is hard to imagine, when looking at the US Capitol building and the amazing monuments and museums of marble throughout Washington, DC. But history *will* eventually repeat itself. The empires of this world, without exception, are *not* made for the long haul. So if you haven't been inside the Jefferson and Lincoln Memorials, you'd best get moving.

There was also a sole superpower as Jesus walked Galilee in sandals. It was imperial glory, might, and borders like the world has never seen, before or since. Rome was still at the zenith of power when Jesus began to subversively establish his kingdom on earth. The political and religious powers noticed and were not amused. It eventually got him killed. Enter Pilate.

For three years Jesus prepared his first followers to announce his kingdom, but it turns out none of them were the first to do so. That honor went to the ruthless Roman governor of Judea himself. Talk about a most unlikely source. As we *constantly* say in the Kingdom of God, "You can't make this stuff up!" Not only did he clearly announce it, but he did so in three languages on three placards. "Let there be no doubt," Pilate proclaimed (unintentionally):

> JESUS OF NAZARETH THE KING OF THE JEWS. (John 19:19)

Incredibly, it is only appropriate. Because in Pilate, the representative of political power, and in Caiphas, the representative of religious power, we see the difference between the empires of man and the Kingdom of God in the starkest relief. They joined forces in the greatest abuse of power and travesty of justice in the history of the world. Can you fathom the religious leaders of the day uttering these words . . . ?

> *The high priests answered, "We have no king except Caesar." (John 19, MSG)*

Exactly. While the local political leader of Rome was announcing King Jesus, the religious leaders of God's chosen people were pledging allegiance *to Caesar!* Unfortunately, this too is but one example of the unholy alliance between *Rome* and *Israel*. Fill in the blanks with your favorite *religious* and *political* characters in history who were in cahoots. Can we ever learn from history? There appears to be no evidence.

After all of that, are you ready for the good news? The truth is beautifully simple:

> When we compare the Kingdom of God with the empires of this world, we quickly realize there is nothing but contrast, and the kingdom Jesus offers is beyond compare.

We indeed could make a list of contrasting elements from A to Z, and from One to Infinity (and beyond!). Here are just a few to get us started:

Kingdom Elements	Empires of This World	Kingdom of God
Rule	Power Through Violence	Love Through Forgiveness
Freedom	Continually Fought For	Once Died For
Reign	Temporary	Eternal
Realm	Has Established Boundaries	Can Be Anywhere
Reality	Injustice/Chaos/Happiness	Righteousness/Peace/Joy
Resources	Limited (Natural)	Unlimited (Supernatural)
Values	Power/Wealth/Status/Pleasure	The Beatitudes
Starting Place	Carnal/From Without	Divine/From Within
Permanent Place	Destruction/Death/Footnote	Love/Life/Glory

Picturing the Kingdom

Sandcastles

Some of my happiest memories in life are on the beach. I've been blessed to have experienced beaches of both white and black sand. But the beaches I'm most familiar with are Pacific Northwest grey. On most days this describes the color of both the sand and sky. As a tour guide, I tell my guests as we approach the Pacific shore, those coming to the Oregon Coast in their bikinis and toting their coolers find themselves quickly running to the store for a hoodie and extra-hot latte. We're famous for our coffee and outdoor stores (Eddie Bauer, Columbia, REI) for good reason.

I've already told you the best coastal town of Oregon is Cannon Beach. There are many reasons for this, including the fresh seafood, the

Chocolate Café (!), fresh saltwater taffy, Sleepy Monk coffee, and the art boutiques. And when you get to the beach, the most iconic image of Oregon awaits, the 235-foot rock monolith of Haystack Rock that looms over the coastline. It's perfect.

Like any tourist town, Cannon Beach hosts scores of special days and festivals to bring in the crowds. There is the annual Stormy Weather Arts Festival, Get Lit at the Beach (for readers, get it?), and the Corgi Festival. I heard a rumor Queen Elizabeth II herself even brought her lads one time! Okay, I might have started that one. But the biggest event of the year is the annual Sandcastle Contest.

If you've never been to a sandcastle contest, it is truly a wonder to behold. The creativity and intricate skill of the artisans is remarkable. And at Cannon Beach, these temporary works of art are created right in front of Haystack Rock, which also features a natural rock outcropping resembling a castle. Perfect. But, of course, there is one big problem . . .

As amazing as a sandcastle is, its value and life span is only good until the next high tide. But we've been called to persevere through *many* high and low tides, God-willing. Ultimately, sandcastles are built in the *wrong place* at the *wrong time* with the *wrong materials*. Does that remind you of anything? Most castles aren't made of sand and were built in perfect places to provide safety and fortification for the empire and its people. But they might as well have been made of sand because high tides eventually reached even them.

Jesus and Paul both addressed this reality as they urged us to build our lives on a solid foundation. However, this applies to kings and kingdoms, as well. It also applied to the nation of Israel he was looking in the eye. And just a few decades later the high tide indeed came, and washed the temple away, just as Jesus said it would. With this in mind, let's listen afresh to their admonitions:

> *But anyone who hears my teaching and doesn't obey it is foolish, like a person who builds a house on sand. When the rains and floods come and the winds beat against that house, it will collapse with a mighty crash. (Matthew 7:26–27)*

> *But each one must be careful how he builds. For no one can lay any foundation other than the one already laid, which is Jesus Christ. If anyone builds on this foundation using gold, silver, precious stones, wood, hay or straw, his workmanship will be evident, because the Day will bring it to light. (1 Corinthians 3:10–13, BSB)*

Kings and kingdoms will *all* pass away . . . except the only one not made of sand.

Life in the Kingdom

Now it's time to do a little (re)signing. To review, when we (re)sign we take familiar symbols and images and the meanings they convey and infuse them with new meaning. In the process, we'll learn a lot about life in the kingdom, and death in the empire.

The Crown = *Eternal* Glory

> *My dentist told me I needed a crown. I'm like, I know, right?*
>
> (STITCHED ON A PURSE)

> *She didn't rule by fear. She ruled by humanity and humility.*[2]

---

2. Alisa Anderson, ABC News Royal Contributer. Funeral of Queen Elizabeth II. Sept. 19, 2022.

As kings and queens go, Elizabeth II of England was close to perfect. But in the end, she too was buried, as the world watched in rapt attention, *without* her crown. For a record seventy years she had regally worn the purple crown of the United Kingdom, replete and resplendent with jewels, large and small, and of every color. I saw it with my own eyes, along with the other gaudy crown jewels, when I visited the Tower of London. Yet, though the crown stayed on the top of her casket until just before it was lowered into the crypt of Windsor Castle, it ultimately returned to the state she served, and now the son she bore. And in another grand ceremony full of pomp and circumstance, the crown was laid on the head of Charles III, as the Archbishop of Canterbury led the chant, "Long live the king!"

Jesus was crowned too, but his coronation lacked pomp and circumstance, and his crown lacked gold and jewels. It was fashioned by the sticks of a *Crown of Thorns* bush, and the large spikes were driven into his skull, turning the crown of Jesus blood red. It was no less a coronation, and it turns out his world-wide audience is like the sand on the seashore. It was only appropriate he be crowned this way, since he told his followers:

> *For even the Son of Man did not come to be served, but to serve, and to give his life as a ransom for many. (Mark 10:45, NIV)*

The Netflix series The Crown, tells the story of Queen Elizabeth II's reign. It lets "light in on the magic." It turns out she and her family were, and are, *far* from perfect (just like our families). Yet, from the moment she turned twenty-one, she declared to her future subjects: "My whole life shall be devoted to your service." Five years later she would be queen and would make good on that promise for the next seventy.

The crown of Jesus is the crown of righteousness. He came not only to serve, but to make things *right*. Elizabeth II did her best to do the same, but in the end, only King Jesus could. And can. And in the end, the glory of the twisted red crown far outweighs that of the purple, or any other color.

Long live the King!

The Throne = *Righteous* Power

> *Righteousness and justice are the foundation of your throne; love and faithfulness go before you. (Psalm 89:14, NIV)*

- *Righteousness* is less about purity. In the Hebrew it is *making things right through generosity and kindness.*
- *Justice* is less about right and wrong. It has everything to do with honor (over shame).
- *Love* is clearly shown to us by the cross of Jesus.
- *Power* is clearly established by the resurrection of Jesus.

All other thrones pale by comparison, wouldn't you say? Even Solomon's, whose steps were flanked by twelve majestic marble lions. All who saw his splendor were left speechless. Jesus, however, *is* the Lion on the throne.

The Scepter = *Eternal* Life

The scepter of the king, or queen, is also a dazzling display of jewels and ornamentation. It is the symbol of power. But we just saw what true power is like in the Kingdom of God. Jewels weren't on the scepter given to Jesus, either. It was more like a broken reed, which *Isaiah* also prophesied would be the sign of the true king. But that broken reed, for us, means life.

The most memorable scene of a king and scepter is found in the story (and book) of *Esther*. Twice she went into the presence of the Persian King Xerxes without an invitation, an act punishable by death. Unless the king had mercy and extended the scepter, which Xerxes did for Esther, twice. The power of life and death was literally in the hands of the king. Elizabeth II had an ornate scepter, too. It is also not found in her sarcophagus. Now Charles III carries this symbol of power.

There is only one king, however, who carries the *eternal* power of life and death. And he has chosen to extend it to *all* his royal subjects. It is the scepter of mercy, and our king always chooses to *lead* with it, not judgment. Not too many heads of state have ever followed suit. No, *not one*. And our king calls on us to exercise mercy in the same way. The scepter of life and death has exclusively become the scepter of life! He has it extended to you and me this day. No wonder we sing . . . !

Kings and kingdoms will all pass away, but there's something about that name.

Love / Everything

> *Beware you be not swallowed up in books: an ounce of love is worth a pound of knowledge.*
>
> (JOHN WESLEY)

Announcing the Kingdom

The love of my life is a girl from Montana. I might have mentioned it already. The big question people have for their parents or friends when it comes to love of their life is, "How do you know he/she is the one?" Well, if you must ask, it's probably not who you're with. That certainly was my experience. It didn't take long to determine Stacie was my happily ever after.

The best thing about Stacie is, well . . . *everything!* Happily, where she is from is on the list. After experiencing western Montana for the first time, she never had to beg me to go back to visit my mother-in-law. But one holiday visit, a sign caught my eye and immediately weighed on my heart. It was the Ten Commandments, written not on stone but on giant billboards. It turns out they were all over the state because the churches all got together to do a joint campaign. What's wrong with that, you might ask? Well . . . *everything.*

To be clear, there is *nothing* wrong with the Ten Commandments. If all the children of the world, red & yellow, black & white, would simply live these out, our world would be an entirely different place. *Absolutely.* But if we're sharing God with our world, should we be *leading* with the law? Absolutely . . . *not!* Paul makes it clear, in no uncertain terms, the law is *not* the ultimate revelation of God. So does Jesus. *Jesus* is the ultimate revelation of God the law simply points to. So let's lead with *him,* and let the law chip in later.

When Jesus was asked what the greatest commandment is, he didn't hesitate or even choose one of the Ten. Instead, he said:

> *Love the LORD your God with all your heart and with all your soul and with all your mind. This is the first and greatest commandment. And the second is like it: Love your neighbor as yourself. All the Law and the Prophets hang on these two commandments.* (Matthew 22:37-40, NIV)

Now *that* would make a great billboard! Surely this was not the answer the teachers of the law were expecting (or teaching). Love is greater than the law. Aren't you thankful? If you hesitated, perhaps you need to read the Books of the Law again. And best of luck trying to live them all out. That's the point, anyway, because the law, and all of Scripture point to the same *person* . . . Jesus. And Jesus told us, and showed us, love is not only *over* the law but:

Love is over everything!

To be sure, we're talking about a certain kind of love. My friend Bob (not Goff, yet), purveyor of deep thoughts, said it this way recently: "In fallen man, eros and phileo are present and readily available. But we don't have agape without the presence of God." (Bob Tinnin) Eros (romantic) and phileo (friendship) are wonderful expressions of love. But the kind of love Scripture is most concerned with is the unconditional kind, *agape.* And this kind of love only comes from God himself, poured into our hearts by the Holy Spirit *(see Romans 5).* And this kind of love is over everything.

This kind of love is a law unto itself. We're no longer under the Old Testament rule of law. We're now under the law of love. It is important to realize the commands don't go out the window with love, but that love is the ultimate command. Josh McDowell calls it "the one moral absolute." And when we follow this absolute *absolutely,* here is what happens:

> *A new command I give you: Love one another. As I have loved you, so you must love one another. By this all men will know that you are my disciples if you love one another. (John 13:34–35, NIV)*

I have a ruler on my desk. It's not just any ruler, it's a *kingdom ruler.* At least that's what I call it. Yes, it's wood and has numbers and lines on it. And the *Golden Rule* printed on it. But it also reminds me of the one moral absolute, the greatest command, the highest calling. It should also be on a billboard. We are ultimately *measured* by our love. So don't forget the golden rule (I have a golden ruler, too, but that's another story), and don't forget the kingdom ruler. Because our Ruler *is* love.

And Jesus is over everything.

Picturing the Kingdom

The Standard of the Kingdom

According to the Cambridge Dictionary, a standard refers to "a level of quality" (measurement) and a "moral rule that should be obeyed" (ruler). But here's the fun word play giving us an even clearer picture of the Kingdom of God. A standard is also "a flag used as the symbol of a person, group, or organization."

If you visit Buckingham Palace when the monarch is in residence, you'll see The Standard of the United Kingdom flying high above. That's because The Standard follows the sovereign wherever they go. The flag represents the kingdom, yes, but it first and foremost represents *the person* who is sovereign. So the kingdom is wherever the king is. You smart kids see right where this is going. My professor says it this way: "The Kingdom of God is wherever Jesus is" (Leonard Sweet).

Talk about a mic-drop! And what is *The Standard* of the Kingdom? *Agape*. So perhaps we can even say the Kingdom of God is wherever agape is. Talk about an expansive kingdom! We have no idea. So the next time you see someone living out loud *Matthew 22*, or *1 Corinthians 13*, or *John 13*, you see the Kingdom of God. And where the Kingdom of God is, Jesus is. When you've seen Jesus, you've seen the kingdom. When Jesus preached, *"The Kingdom of God is near,"* he wasn't kidding! Here is how one of the greatest musicals of all time pictures it: "To love another person is to see the face of God." (Les Misérables)

Life in the Kingdom

The biggest challenge is not to do acts of love on certain days, but to become love every day.

(Tyler Staton)

Love goes above and beyond, and beyond some more.[1]

(Steve Hartman)

The Axis

If there was one book introducing love as the *axis* of the kingdom, I'd have you read, well, the Bible! But the second is Beauty Will Save the World. This is one of my favorite books on the kingdom. Here's how the author (Brian again) presents it:

> The truth of power enforced by violence is the axis around which the world ruled by the principalities and powers

---

1. Steve Hartmann, CBS Sunday Morning, aired April 30, 2023.

revolves . . . Ultimate truth is not power enforced through violence, but love expressed through forgiveness.[2]

If Pastor Zahnd never wrote another book, or preached another sermon, this truth he expounds, alone, would be enough. Especially when it comes to the Kingdom of God being upside-down and backwards from the empires of this world. The difference between kingdom and empire isn't just the window dressings. It's the very foundation. It is the very axis upon which the entire reality revolves. Zahnd illustrates this with a history lesson and painful commentary:

> . . . the historic problem the Roman Catholic Church struggled with in the West was the temptation to be too conformed to the Roman Empire. And I dare to suggest (or even insist!) that the problem that is distorting American evangelicalism is that it has become far too accommodating to Americanism and the culture of a superpower . . . It becomes American culture with a Jesus fish bumper sticker.[3]

Ouch! But I believe he's spot on. The Kingdom of God doesn't wield power as the world does, enforcing it with superpower violence. Rather, it wages peace through sacrificial agape and undeserved forgiveness! *Ahhh!* There is so much more I'd love to quote from this book (I have ten pages of notes!), but this puts the finest point on our *doxy* and our *praxis*:

> Yes, believe the orthodox doctrines of his virgin birth, his divine identity, and his bodily resurrection. But also believe the gospel he proclaimed—a gospel of the kingdom of God where the ordering principle and central axis is co-suffering love and radical forgiveness.[4]

The Praxis

If there were two books on love being the ultimate praxis of the kingdom, it would be Bob Goff's *Love Does*, and *Everybody Always*. If you haven't yet met Bob, you are in for a treat when you read these books. Bob is the most outrageous, outlandish, and out and out crazy purveyors of love this world has seen! *Crazy* being the key word. I was first introduced to

---

2. Zahnd, *Beauty Will Save the World*, 67, 69.
3. Zahnd, 4.
4. Zahnd, 80.

Bob by my work receptionist Sherri, who asked me if I'd read his first book. No. After a scolding look, I got the book. Then, upon reaching the end of the book, I came across his cell phone number. I called it. And he answered! Like I said, crazy.

While I don't wish to spoil every delightful surprise within Bob's pages, allow me to share just a couple. One thing you'll find out is he's a lawyer and his office in on Tom Sawyer Island, in Disneyland! If you have a legal appointment with Bob, you must first pay admission to the park. He invites everyone who comes to sign underneath *his* table. You can also sign it without an appointment, which I did. But the best stories are the incredible lengths he will go to in love. Like he and his family putting on a New Year's Day parade for their neighbors. Or arranging fireworks for a special night for two love birds on the bay in San Diego. It goes on and on and on. That's the idea. I love it! I love *him*.

He takes seriously, and hilariously, God's ultimate calling on our lives. He also has a boatload full of mic-drops on love. Here are two of my favorites:

- It will be our love, not our opinions which will be our greatest contribution to the world.
- When I think someone ought to be more loving, it's usually me.

The Bottom Line

Finally, another word from my hero, Josh McDowell. Josh is known as one of the great apologists of the faith, certainly in our day. His book *More Than a Carpenter* is one of the best-selling books worldwide in the history of books (seriously). But of the scores of his books that fill multiple shelves, he has another masterpiece called *Love Is Always Right: A Defense of the One Moral Absolute*.

In my more legalistic days, I grappled with matters of conscience and the complexities of situational ethics. For example, is it *always* wrong to lie? What if I'm doing so to protect a loved one from harm? What about going even a mile over the speed limit? Does that make me a lawbreaker and violator of God ordained authority? What if I'm rushing my wife to the hospital as she's in labor, like my dad did on the day I was born? I used to agonize over some of these things in my zeal for righteousness. After all, I had devoured Josh's apologetics, including his Right From Wrong campaign where he stressed absolute truth means it is true for "all people in all places at all times." Period. And then I picked up *Love Is Always Right*. Here is how he and co-author Norm Geisler help to clarify our moral dilemmas:

> There are no exceptions to absolute commands, but there are some exemptions in view of higher priorities of love. There is always a greater good ... Therefore, whenever we are faced with a conflict between good alternatives or between good and evil, the morally right course of action is always the greatest good or the most loving response.[5]

Corrie Ten Boom's account in *The Hiding Place* is the perfect story to bring this discussion home. She and her Jewish family were protected behind a wall in an upstairs attic, in the home of a loving non-Jewish family. When Nazi officials knocked on their door, rounding up all Jews to send to concentration camps, this family lied to protect them. Tragically, her family was eventually discovered and sent to these death camps, where most of her family perished. But, unbelievably, years later she was able to forgive her captors, who had tortured and killed her family. She even offered a hand of forgiveness to one of the guards, who had become a believer. She writes it was the hardest thing she'd ever done, *but she did it!*

All the empires of the world, rotating around the axis of power enforced by violence, will eventually go the way of the Nazi's. The Kingdom of God, revolving around the axis of sacrificial love enforced by forgiveness, will ultimately triumph and *never perish*. This is why agape love is our highest calling and why forgiving others is non-negotiable. Such love is the very essence, power, beauty, foundation, and lifeblood of God's kingdom. It radiates from Christ our king, who embodies the standard, bedrock, and absolute truth of this kingdom.

And this king, and the agape he embodies, *is over everything.*

---

5. McDowell and Geisler, *Love Is Always Right*, 60, 62.

Manifesto

It is said that this manifesto is more than a theory, that it was an incitement.[1]

(OLIVER WENDELL HOLMES, JR.)

You and I are meant to be living epistles—that is, "Jesus Manifestos"—in our world.[2]

(LEONARD SWEET AND FRANK VIOLA)

Announcing the Kingdom

Jesus had several coming out parties as he began his public ministry. The first was *literally* a party, a wedding in Cana, where he seemed somewhat reluctant to perform his first miracle. He told his mother Mary it wasn't his time, but in the end, I guess it's hard for anybody to say no to mom. However, it wasn't exactly a public declaration since most of the guests were either drunk or in the dark as to what had happened. The only people who were in on this first miracle were mom, the twelve, and the *servants* who filled the jars with water. This is such a perfect picture

---

1. Bartlett, *Familiar Quotations*, 645:5.
2. Sweet and Viola, *Jesus Manifesto*, iBooks, 59.

of the ministry of Jesus, and of the priority group Jesus came to reveal himself to. And as persuasive as Mary could be, I don't believe this was unplanned. It's just too perfect.

The second was indeed a public affair, at the Feast of Tabernacles. Like a Jewish wedding, the prescribed religious feasts were multiple day events. Of course, every faithful Jew was sure to participate. But Jesus waited, which caused his brothers to sarcastically call him out. Jesus wouldn't be baited. However, on the final day of the feast his time came, and he made himself known. In a loud voice he said:

> *If anyone is thirsty, let him come to me and drink. Whoever believes in me, as the Scripture has said, streams of living water will flow from within Him. (John 7:37-38, NIV)*

However, his greatest teaching was still to come. On a Galilean hillside, home to sheep and lowly shepherds, the Good Shepherd uttered the greatest sermon in the history of the world. The thousands in attendance that day were *thunderstruck*. The Sermon on the Mount, as it is traditionally known, left no doubt as to the values, expectations, uniqueness, and authority of the Kingdom of God. Jesus laid it out and laid it on the line in the most memorable of terms. But it was more than a sermon, invitation, or simple announcement. It was his *Kingdom Manifesto*. The proverbial gauntlet had been thrown down, the dye cast, and there was no going back to his anonymous life of construction in Nazareth because it was now:

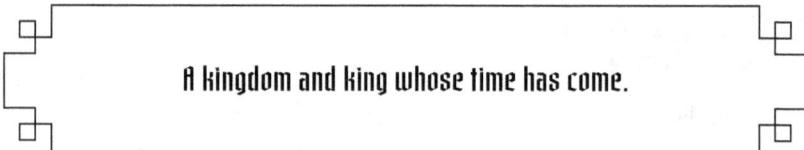

A kingdom and king whose time has come.

Picturing the Kingdom

Jesus went home to Nazareth as he began his public ministry. I've already mentioned the first recorded sermon of Jesus had him announcing, "The Kingdom of Heaven is near." However, his first Scripture reading at his home synagogue couldn't have been more dramatic, both his words and the response of his hometown. It appears to be happenstance when he was handed the scroll of Isaiah to read. Funny how many perfect coincidences there were around Jesus. He immediately unrolled it near the end:

The Spirit of the LORD is on me, because he has anointed me to preach good news to the poor. He has sent me to proclaim freedom for the prisoners and recovery of sight for the blind, to release the oppressed, to proclaim the year of the LORD's favor. (Luke 4:18,19/ Isaiah 61, NIV)

A kingdom mission statement if there ever was one. And one he would repeat when John the Baptist was rotting in prison and seemed to be second guessing Jesus as Messiah. Jesus wasn't what he had expected, either. Therefore, he sent some of his followers to Jesus, just to be sure. But Jesus didn't read from the scroll again. He simply told them to go back and tell John *what they had seen.* They had seen the prophecy of Isaiah being fulfilled right before their eyes! And they believed. But tragically, Jesus's fellow Nazarenes couldn't see it, and didn't believe it, even though Jesus told them right after rolling up the scroll:

Today this Scripture is fulfilled in your hearing.

Then they tried to kill him. But, again, that time had not come, either. Yet.

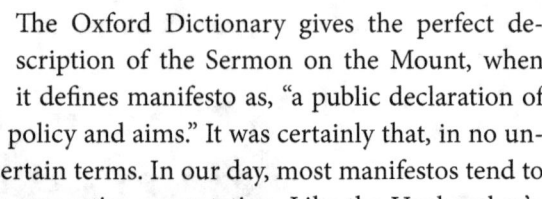

Life in the Kingdom

The Oxford Dictionary gives the perfect description of the Sermon on the Mount, when it defines manifesto as, "a public declaration of policy and aims." It was certainly that, in no uncertain terms. In our day, most manifestos tend to have a negative connotation. Like the Unabomber's, penned in his small cabin in Lincoln, Montana (an hour from my wife's hometown). Or the more recent Safeway shooter, in Bend, Oregon (a half hour from *my* hometown). And I was a mile away when it happened, and a dear friend was inside the store! Later, authorities found his disturbing manifesto online.

Undoubtedly, many find Jesus's written manifesto *(Matthew 5–7)* unsettling. His words challenge us to a higher standard of living, demanding our hearts and lives. The biggest difference in this manifesto is that its aim and policies lead to *life,* not death. Yet, the tension in the air must have been palpable as the crowd listened in awed silence. Jesus wasn't undoing the law; he was doubling down on it:

> *Do not think that I have come to abolish the Law or the Prophets; I have not come to abolish them but to fulfill them. (Matthew 5:17, NIV)*

This did not appease the religious elites and scholars of the law. Quite the opposite, because he was calling them out, and all who thought the law was enough. His appeal was to purity, yes, but it was an inward reality not an outward display. He appealed to righteousness, yes, but not just for personal gain but rather to *set things right* in our world. He called all to holiness, certainly, but not just to be set apart from our fellow man, but to be set apart for the glory and pleasure of God and benefit of our fellows. It was a call for Israel to return to its original call:

> *But you are a chosen people, a royal priesthood, a holy nation, a people for God's own possession, to proclaim the virtues of Him who called you out of darkness into His marvelous light. (1 Peter 2:9, BSB)*

The call of Jesus is to *embody* his Kingdom Manifesto. Paul says it this way:

Manifesto

> *You show that you are a letter from Christ . . . written not with ink but with the Spirit of the living God, not on tablets of stone but on tablets of human hearts. (2 Corinthians 3:2–3, NIV)*

But it all starts with hearing Jesus's words, whether on a hillside or by the water's edge, and consciously choosing to submit and obey. The very thing Israel struggled with most throughout its history. The very thing the people of God still struggle with most today. Jesus paints the memorable picture of the result of this intentional decision:

> *Therefore everyone who hears these words of mine and puts them into practice is like a wise man who built his house on the rock. The rain came down, the streams rose, and the winds blew and beat against that house; yet it did not fall, because it had its foundation on the rock. (Matthew 7:24–25, NIV)*

As we've already seen, it beats a sandcastle at low tide and especially at high. We build our lives wisely, not foolishly, by hearing the words of Jesus and putting them into practice. As we do, we fulfill our calling, for the glory of God and the good of all mankind.

We've skimmed the body of the Sermon on the Mount, and even skipped to the end. But Jesus saved the best for . . . *first!* No single description of kingdom living is more clear, concise, and potent than the Beatitudes. The Beatitudes are simply *beautiful.* The children of God and the collective community are, too, when we make these words our story and song:

Blessed are the poor in spirit, for theirs is the kingdom of heaven.
Blessed are those who mourn, for they will be comforted.
Blessed are the meek, for they will inherit the earth.
Blessed are those who hunger and thirst for righteousness, for they will be filled.
Blessed are the merciful, for they will be shown mercy.
Blessed are the pure in heart, for they will see God.

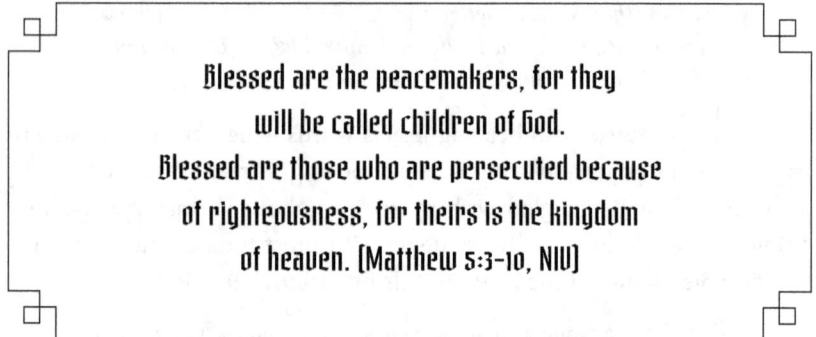

Blessed are the peacemakers, for they will be called children of God. Blessed are those who are persecuted because of righteousness, for theirs is the kingdom of heaven. (Matthew 5:3-10, NIV)

Jesus himself embodied and sang the Beatitudes for all to see and hear. He is the very picture of beauty. Breathtaking beauty:

> If we ask, 'What is Jesus like?,' we can give no better answer than to say Jesus is like the Beatitudes . . . If we attempt to understand Jesus apart from the Beatitudes, we inevitably get Jesus wrong. Getting Jesus right is absolutely essential if we are to recover the beauty of Christianity, because Jesus is the beauty of Christianity![3]

Take time today to review, memorize, and even *sing* the Beatitudes. But most importantly, pray the Spirit of God will burst forth out of your life like living water, so you will *embody* them. And all creatures great and small, and all things bright and beautiful, will sing along with you. This time Brian Zahnd gets the last word:

The Beatitudes lead us into the life of the kingdom of God.[4]

---

3. Zahnd, *Beauty Will Save the World*, 207–8.
4. Zahnd, 222.

New Creation

> *God's plan is not to abandon this world, the world which he said was "very good." Rather, he intends to remake it. And when he does he will raise all his people to new bodily life to live in it. That is the promise of the Christian gospel.*[1]
>
> (N. T. Wright)

Announcing the Kingdom

Now that we've crossed the halfway mark of the kingdom alphabet, it's time I came out of the closet. I'm not ashamed to say I have a strong feminine side I've fully embraced. It leaks out in my love of chocolate, romance movies, and interior decorating. Then it overflows in my Downton Abbey obsession, which cost me my *man card* with my two sons. It was worth it. So while I was at it I threw in the Disney Princesses (my first movie date with Stacie was The Little Mermaid) and the Princess Diaries. In fact, I even took my young boys to that movie and when the lights came up, we were the only boys in the theater! They're scarred for life. But don't let them fool you, they loved the movie, too. There is hope for them yet.

But little did my boys know, but I had already given up my man card at a very young age. I don't know how it happened, perhaps it was a gene

---

1. Wright, *Simply Christian*.

I was born with, but from nearly day one I have been a butterfly man. The scientific name for it, I discovered, is an *entomologist*. My wife and boys aren't impressed. In fact, Stacie split her gut when watching me on the chase for the first time. She's a bad person. But it was in our first year of marriage, so by then it was too late. I'm a smart person. I did hang up my net for a season, however. Now I just don't let her see me in my hunting gear. I guess I'm not fully out of the closet. But confession is good for the soul. Are you impressed? Never mind.

Now that you've heard my confession, let me be quick to *chase it* with a caveat. It turns out I was much more spiritual than my childhood pals at Crooked River Elementary. Because as I was ogling Monarchs, Swallowtails, and Fritillaries, I was also witnessing the miracle of transformation. The wonder of an ugly, fuzzy, crawling caterpillar becoming a winged wonder of spectacular color and beauty, soaring over the earth instead of grounded to it. I even captured caterpillars and put them in large mouth glass jars with their favorite food, watched as they spun their pupae, and waited until the day when their temporary home would split open, their wings would unfold and dry out, and then they were ready to fly. Well, actually they were ready to be ethered, pinned flat, and put in a display case. Okay, I can be a bad person, too.

What I have just described is the process of *metamorphosis*, and it turns out it isn't just for butterflies. Silly *Lepidoptera*, it's for kids, too! And don't forget the earth. And the heavens. Scripture says it flat out:

> *I saw Heaven and earth new-created. Gone the first Heaven, gone the first earth, gone the sea. (Revelation 21, MSG)*

What we are seeing and experiencing today is a caterpillar in comparison to the wondrous reality of tomorrow. However, the good news of the gospel of the kingdom, as I've said over and over, isn't limited to the *not yet*. It is also, *expressly,* about *now!* And like God's good creation, *now* had a starting point. Can you guess what it is? I'll give you a hint: *Easter.* I know, I'm such a pushover teacher, but I know you clever kids catch on fast, anyway. So I'll ask another question (or two): What is the one event the entire gospel of the kingdom *relies* on? What is the one foundation this gospel *rests* on? What historical (and cosmic) event changed the trajectory of the universe *forever?* You got it. *Resurrection.* Without it, faith, hope, and agape disappear into a black hole. With it? *Transformation. Metamorphosis. New Creation.* Here is the kingdom reality *now:*

New Creation

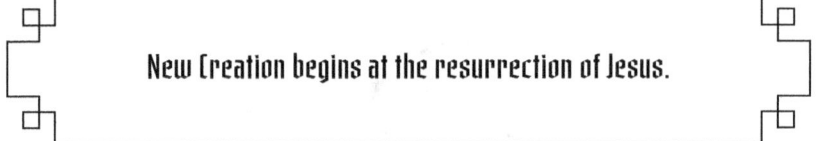

New Creation begins at the resurrection of Jesus.

New creation is breaking through the temporary confines of our earthly bodies (pupae's) and earthly home (dirt). And like the beautiful wings of a Monarch, it is slowly unfolding. New creation, like the Kingdom of God, is near. New creation, like the Kingdom of God, is *here*. And even though we *groan inwardly,* longing for our new bodies *(see 1 Corinthians 15)*, while chewing away on our Milkweed leaves, we crawl forward in faith, hope, and agape today. Because the *not yet* is on the way, so:

Fellow caterpillars, prepare to fly!

Picturing the Kingdom

The Transformation Will Continue

Like the Monarch, or whichever is your favorite, we are *currently* in the process of transformation. If we give the Holy Spirit full access. But happily, someday our transformation will kick into high gear and become fully visible to us, to the *great cloud of witnesses* Scripture talks about, and most importantly to our Creator God. He already sees our folded-up wings and knows what is coming. But he will undoubtedly still delight on that great someday. Here's why I believe this to be true:

> *Precious in the sight of the LORD is the death of his faithful servants. (Psalm 116:15, NIV)*

It is precious to our LORD for more than one reason: No more sorrow, pain, suffering, or death will ever touch his most beloved creation again. The thin veil of separation will never ever separate this relationship again. And, oh, how beautiful his child will be on that day, and every day to come! Just as he always planned.

Not only do butterflies transform, but many other creatures do, as well. Perhaps not as dramatically. But the dragonfly's metamorphosis is dramatic indeed! I came across this story in the folder of a recent funeral I attended. Pull out a tissue before you read it:

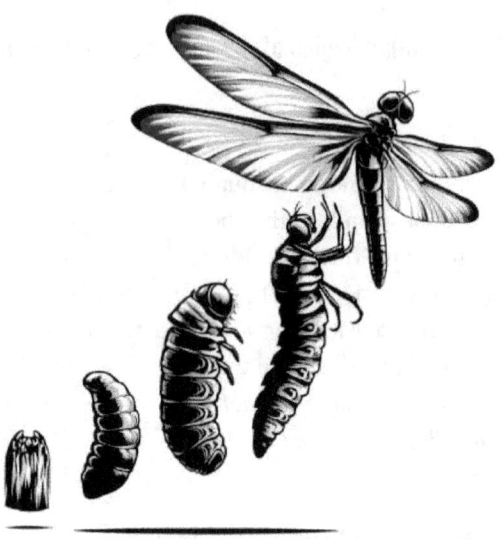

In the bottom of an old pond lived some grubs who could not understand why none of their groups ever came back after crawling up the stems of the lilies to the top of the water. They promised each other that the next one who was called to make the upward climb would return and tell what happened to him. Soon one of them felt an urgent impulse to see the surface; he rested himself on the top of a lily pad and went through a glorious transformation which made him a dragonfly with beautiful wings. In vain he tried to keep his promise. Flying back and forth over the pond he peered down at his friends below. Then he realized that even if they could see him they would not recognize such a radiant creature as one of their number. The fact that we cannot see our loved ones or communicate with them after the transformation, which we call death, is no proof that they cease to exist. (Walter Dudley Cavert)

Are you encouraged fellow travelers? There is so much we don't understand and so much we can't see. But there is a reality, just beyond the veil, just above the shimmering waters, where this corruptible shell of mine with its aches and pains, blemishes and scars, will put on the incorruptible and away I will fly, shimmering wings and dazzling colored body released! Grub no more. And as much as we'd like to go back and tell what has happened to us, our fellow grubs will just have to wait for the day when they can't help themselves but climb the eternal lily to their new divine *pad*.

Someday.

Life in the Kingdom

We will morph indeed.[2]

(JOHN ORTBERG)

I don't just love butterflies. I love creation. All of it (except spiders). I'm equally happy hugging a tree, hugging a mountain trail, or hugging a steaming cup of (organic) coffee. I live in the perfect place. We've been over this. But what we haven't been over, and what I can't get over, is this creation won't be able to shake a (walking) stick at the new one. It's impossible to imagine. There are a lot of foretastes in the Kingdom of God: the *Holy Spirit* (a *deposit* guaranteeing what is to come); the *church community* (What I call a *Taste* of the Kingdom. Which might be the title of the second CLK book. Shhh!); the *resurrection of Jesus* (*first fruits* of ours); and *creation* (God still calls it *good*). It's enough to get a person riled up! And you don't have to settle down and get back in your seats.

God has in mind for everyone, and everything, a total transformation. For us, this will include our head (thinking), heart (loving), and hands (living). Oh, and our bodies. It's fascinating to me that after his resurrection, Jesus was hard to recognize. The twelve were *pretty sure* it was him when he first appeared, but they still wanted to ask. Mary, in the garden on Easter Sunday, talked to Jesus thinking he was the gardener, until he spoke her name. The couple returning to Emmaus talked to Jesus *for miles*, only recognizing him when he broke the bread (is that when they saw the nail scars maybe?). How I wish the writers had been more descriptive of the post-resurrection Jesus, though we know he could walk through walls. Cool! The rest will have to wait.

God's creation, including all the above and more, is a *Wow!* But God's new creation, including all we can imagine and more, will be a *Whoa!!* It will be *life to the overflowing*, not just to the full. It will be agape

---

2. Ortberg, *The Life You've Always Wanted*.

far beyond *all* conditions. It will be *light for all mankind,* and the darkness will never overcome it *(see John 1)*.

Speaking of *John 1,* New Testament scholars often refer to it as the *new creation* account. That means both testaments have a creation account. But the new account introduces us to the incarnate Christ, who moved right into the neighborhood he created. And because he did, those who believe and receive he gives . . .

> . . . *the right to become Children of God—children born not of natural descent, nor of human decision or a husband's will, but born of God. (John 1:13, NIV)*

A lot of people talk about change, from politicians to self-help gurus, pastors to personal trainers. But what drives real and lasting change? Here's a hint, it's not:

- **Resolutions.** It's okay to make them, and sometimes they might even stick. But it's best to have low expectations of these resolves, because for most it takes more than will-power.
- **Information.** We're in the throes of the information age and it's all a click or two away. And as I write this, *Chat GPT* is poised to take over the world. But change requires more than information, and, unfortunately, most education today is an info dump. Now I love education more than most, but it's not the path to lasting change.
- **Remuneration.** The pursuit of money has eclipsed life, liberty, and the pursuit of happiness for most people. But real change requires more than "throwing money at it," or *"storing up more in barns."* Jesus has a word for it: *"Fool."*

So what does lasting change truly require? It demands:

- **Transformation.** Think princess kissing the frog.
- **Metamorphosis.** Think butterflies and dragonflies.
- **New Creation.** Think resurrection.

The Holy Spirit is the primary agent of transformation. Without the Holy Spirit, transformation is as likely as a fulfilled resolution. With the Spirit working in and through us, *everything* changes. Here is the change Scripture says we should pursue (and expect), with the aid of our *Helper:*

New Creation

- **Heart.** *I'll give you a new heart . . . I'll cut out your stone heart and replace it with a red-blooded, firm-muscled heart. I'll put a new spirit in you. (Ezekiel 11, MSG)*

- **Soul.** *So you have not received a spirit that makes you fearful slaves. Instead, you received God's Spirit when he adopted you as his own children. (Romans 8:15)*

- **Mind.** *Don't copy the behavior and customs of this world, but let God transform you into a new person by changing the way you think. (Romans 12:2)*

- **Strength.** *If anyone serves, they should do so with the strength God provides, so that in all things God may be praised through Jesus Christ. (1 Peter 4:11, NIV)*

The LORD hasn't just called us to love him in this way. He has made it possible, through the resurrection power of Jesus, made available to us *today* by the Holy Spirit.

This is where new creation, and life in the kingdom, begins.

One

There is no them; there is only us.[1]

(BRIAN ZAHND)

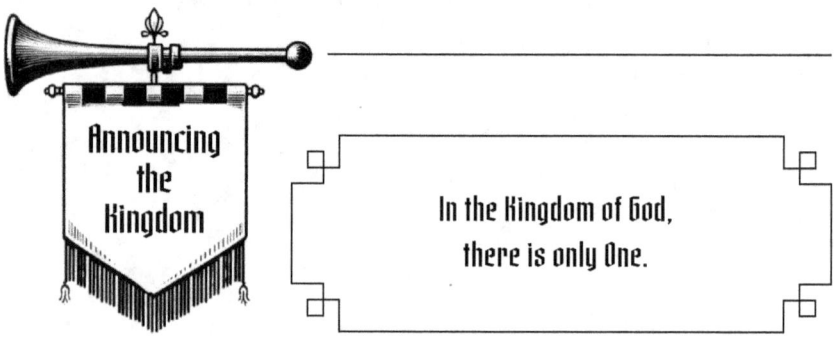

Announcing the Kingdom

In the Kingdom of God, there is only One.

One God

> *Hear, O Israel: The LORD our God, the LORD is one.* (Deuteronomy 6:4, NIV)

As the modern description goes, the LORD God "is one of one." Actually, he's *"One of One!"* To a polytheistic ancient world, the God of Israel declares himself the *only* One, and *himself* as One. To a pluralistic modern world, the LORD of all continues to stand, and reign, *alone!*

---

1. Quotefancy, Top 80 Brian Zahnd Quotes, 2024 Update.

One People

1 + 1 + 1 = One

> *You were all called to travel on the same road and in the same direction, so stay together, both outwardly and inwardly. You have one Master, one faith, one baptism, one God and Father of all, who rules over all, works through all, and is present in all. Everything you are and think and do is permeated with oneness. (Ephesians 4, MSG)*

One represents the heart and intent of our One God, for all. He doesn't have a plan two. For those who are fans of the cult movie classic *The Princess Bride* (I'm the biggest), you'll remember Miracle Max, who saved the day for our heroes. After giving Wesley a specially formulated pill to bring him back to life, he sent the boys off to storm the castle and save the girl. Any questions? As they were riding away, Max's wife asked him, "Do you think it will work?" His answer is the same answer required for unity in the body of Christ: "It will take a miracle." Yes, Max, it will. So let's heed the words of Mary, Mother of Jesus, just prior to his first recorded miracle in Cana: *"Do what he says,"* and properly align ourselves with the true heart and intention of God.

One Way

Before the first followers of Jesus were called Christians, they were referred to as followers of *the Way*. I wish we'd still call ourselves that, as our world doesn't see "Christian" in a positive light. And that's mostly our fault. The reason is simply that we don't truly and fully follow the Jesus Way. If we did, we'd appear and act altogether different from our world. We'd have different values and priorities. We'd have a different vision and purpose. We'd have a genuine faith, hope, and love bubbling out of deep wells of eternal life from within. Listen to this early description of the followers:

> *The whole congregation of believers was united as One—One heart, One mind! They didn't even claim ownership of their own possessions. No one said, "That's mine; you can't have it." They shared everything. The apostles gave powerful witness to the resurrection of the Master Jesus, and grace was on all of them. (Acts 4, MSG)*

Yes, there remains One way, One person, One name that leads to truth, life, and the Kingdom of God. But never forget, on all the roads of life; from Emmaus to Damascus, from Canterbury to Rome, from Mecca to Jerusalem, there is One you'll find on each and every path, ready and able to lead each willing child of God home.

One Prayer

> *I have given them the glory that you gave me, so they may be One as we are One. I am in them and you are in me. May they experience such perfect unity that the world will know that you sent me and that you love them as much as you love me.*
> *(John 17:22–23)*

Of all Jesus could've prayed for just before being arrested, he made unity his cry. It is no ordinary prayer and represents no ordinary pursuit. The outcome of our unity, according to Jesus, is genuinely staggering! No wonder he prayed for it. This is not just an "all for one and one for all" kind of appeal. This is more than learning the handshake, singing the fight song, or wearing the uniform. What Jesus is praying for is a loving Oneness with everyone who will believe, just as he and the Father have. Nothing ordinary about that! He also knows that our Oneness is essential to our *witness*. In the Kingdom of God there is only one witness . . . *ours*.

Picturing the Kingdom

The Wave

Being a football fan from the Pacific Northwest means I lay claim to The Wave. If you've been to a major sporting event you've probably participated in one, not realizing that Seattle is where it all began. It starts with one section of fans standing and throwing their hands in the air and yelling "Whoa!" and then it makes its way clockwise around the arena several times. It used to be one of the greatest traditions in sports, and until 2017 it was surely the greatest *wave*. Not anymore.

Stead Family Children's Hospital is a twelve-story complex overlooking Kinnick Stadium, home of University of Iowa Hawkeyes football.

One

The view from the twelfth story "press box" is the best in the stadium, reserved for the courageous kids admitted for a variety of critical procedures and illnesses. In 2017, a single Facebook post from a good-hearted Hawkeye fan led to, well, we'll let them describe it:

The Hawkeye Wave is the best tradition in college sports. When the Kinnick clock hits zero, at the end of the first quarter, 70,000+ football fans turn their attention from the field to the UI Stead Family Children's Hospital. In unison, they wave to the pediatric patients and their families watching the game. The patients and family members view this genuine act of kindness as life-changing, inspiring . . . a wave of hope.[2]

To add to this heart-felt tradition, a Kid Captain is selected for each home game, who spends the entire game with the team on the sideline. This child also gets to select the song that will play during the Hawkeye Wave. Now, when the clock hits 0:00 at the end of the first quarter, the song plays and the entire stadium stands, turns, and waves until the end of the song. This includes the players, coaches, cheerleaders, and fans of *both teams*. It's a tear-jerker every time.

---

2. University of Iowa Athletics, https://hawkeyesorts.com>wave.

But not only is it a tear-jerker, it is one of the greatest pictures of unity I can imagine. For about five minutes rivalries are set aside, and life is put in perspective as all participants join together in an act of agape those kids will never forget. No one in the stadium will, either. Because for one song, everybody in the stadium is *One*.

Life in the Kingdom

E pluribus unum

(Traditional motto of the USA).

The above motto, on the Great Seal of the United States and all its coins, is Latin for "Out of many, one." It's a great motto. If only it were true. As I write, my country has never been more *furiously* divided. While divisions have always existed, now, instead of coming together like King Arthur's knights at the round table, we dig trenches and lob grenades at one another. Sure, at times we pull together, in a crisis and immediately after, but we *live* divided. This is eventually true of all nations, time immemorial.

Of course, this is also true of God's church, both big C and little c. How tragic, for all involved and for all watching. Our witness has been compromised by our division. We often wonder why such a growing number of young people want nothing to do with our faith communities. Our lack of unity is one big reason. Perhaps we should start right there.

But how is unity made possible for more than one shining moment? Is it even possible? The answer is impossibly easy: *Yes!* But that answer is also impossibly hard to live out. But in the Kingdom of God, the impossible becomes possible. But only as we follow the way of Jesus. Here are some *one* thoughts for us to consider and put into practice.

The United Kingdom

The empires of this world believe unity is sustained by the tip of the sword or end of a double barrel. The history we continue to insist on repeating, has witnessed otherwise. These witnesses include the one-hundred-year Pax Britannica, the two-hundred-year Pax Romana, and the three-hundred-year Pax Ottomana. Fleeting imperial reigns of history that now *are* history. The communists employed their hammer and sickle, but their zenith lasted less than a century. The United States, as the latest world superpower, is 247 years and counting. Only time will tell if it endures beyond a fleeting historical moment.

The Kingdom of God, however, has been *forcibly advancing* ever since the resurrection of Jesus. By forcibly (some translations say *violently*) this is not to say by the same violent means as the armies of middle earth. It simply means good luck stopping it! Despite how it looks, the moon shadow that once blocked out the sun's rays is slowly sliding away. And not only will this kingdom be filled with inextinguishable light, but the best part will be that it is One. It will be *the* United Kingdom that will never divide. No swords, sickles, or sledgehammers will ever be required. No border gates, agents, or passports either.

What Brings Us Together

For several years I hung out with a group called The Fellowship. Based in the Washington DC area, this was an influential work with *no political agenda*. Most people don't believe that's likely, let alone possible. Sure, there's an agenda, but it has nothing to do with promoting the Donkeys' or Elephants' agenda. It is simply a peacemaking work. Doug Coe, an original Oregonian, helped to guide this work for over five decades, and in the process became a trusted advisor to presidents and leaders all over the world. The Fellowship also helps facilitate the National Prayer Breakfast, attended by US Presidents, world leaders, and purveyors of business, entertainment, and religion from A to Z.

I had the opportunity to attend two National Prayer Breakfasts, and it is the best representation of what the Kingdom of God is supposed to be I've ever experienced. So just what is it that would cause over four-thousand people of every color, creed, and persuasion to drop everything to gather for prayer and inspiration? Doug Coe, one of the greatest peace-makers of our generation most have never heard of, puts it this way:

> We join together as brothers and sisters, the family of man, and we focus on what we have in common, on what brings us together. Regardless of who comes, we all can agree on four things: 1) We care about peace; 2) We care about the poor; *3) We care about kids;* and 4) We care about Jesus.

I had to italicize #3 for obvious reasons. It is not a watered down gathering that stands for everything, and therefore for nothing. It is decidedly focused on the *person and teachings of Jesus*, believing *he* is the answer to the worlds' problems and the only true way forward. It is beautiful!

But each time I attended, I left lamenting we couldn't stay together for more than a power breakfast. We *can*. This belief has seen prayer breakfasts started in scores of cities and countries. Like the first quarter break at Kinnick Stadium, it gives us just a taste of what the Kingdom of God is and will be. Good luck stopping it! But who would want to? It is beautiful, and yes, it is possible as we follow the way of Jesus together.

Bridges Not Fences

> *Each person is given wood with which to build fences or bridges.*
>
> (DOUG BURLEIGH)

I remember clearly the evening I was crossing the two-mile long Glen Jackson Bridge of Interstate 205 near the Portland Airport. I found myself, as I often do on bridges, marveling at the engineering and amount of work (almost twenty years!) it took to make such an easy crossing over the mighty Columbia River possible. It was then that I heard the unmistakable whisper of the Spirit saying, "I've called you to build bridges." Being terrified of heights, I dismissed it as the pizza.

The reality is God has called *all of us* to be bridge builders. If you want a fancy title to put in front of your name, you are welcome to use *ambassador*. God would love it if you did. An *ambassador of reconciliation*, to be specific. When we reconcile, we bring two opposing sides together, like the Glen Jackson bridge does for Oregon and Washington. We restore friendly relations. We become *peacemakers;* a bridge building vocation Jesus specially blessed:

> *Blessed are the peacemakers, for they will be called Children of God. (Matthew 5:9, NIV)*

One

Draw a Bigger Circle

Our cultures, and our own insecurities, drive us to draw circles of inclusion and exclusion. We draw them just big enough to include ourselves, and those who are like us, and small enough to keep the "others" out. Consider all there is that divides us: Ethnicity. Nationality. Race. Religion. Class. Money. Education. Teams. Politics. Family. Friends. The ways we can divide ourselves are nearly infinite, and unfortunately, we take this work seriously. But Jesus calls us to draw bigger and bigger circles of inclusion.

Our world (including religion), however, pushes us to draw smaller and smaller circles. We are taught to live and relate categorically and not relationally. Sometimes these categories are easy to see. At other times the categories are harder to determine. Consider the example of the Hutu and Tutsi tribes in Rwanda. Originally, they could tell who-was-who, but after years of intermarriage it was difficult to distinguish. Yet in 1994, over a period of one-hundred days, over 800,0000 perished in one of the world's worst recorded genocides. How tragically sad it is to realize that official Rwandan ID cards had to sometimes be consulted to determine who was Hutu or Tutsi, who would live and who would die.

The above is an extreme example of the result of our never-ending quest to divide (and conquer). Unfortunately, it isn't an isolated example. Violent circles of separation are drawn all over our world. Jesus came to tear down the religious "veil" and would like to dissolve the lines and dashes that separate us, as well. By the way, how big is the circle of inclusion that Jesus draws?

It's as big as the globe itself!

Peace

Imagine World Peace
                    (BUMPER STICKER)

Imagine Whirled Peas
                    (ANOTHER BUMPER STICKER)

Announcing the Kingdom

My birthday is on New Year's Day, which is fantastic for many reasons. The best is never having to go to school on your birthday, and I've only had to work on it once. And there is football. And fireworks. And everybody seems inclined to celebrate with me! The only problem is people have gift fatigue and no money. And my parents missed out on a big tax break for the year 1967 by less than twelve hours. They still remind me.

I'm not a big fan of staying up late, either, but I make an annual exception. It's a fun tradition to get my first "Happy Birthday!" at midnight. And one year, 1990, my first words of the new year and new decade were, "I love you." It was the first time I said it, and eight months later I married that girl! But most of the time we simply watched Dick Clark, and now

Peace

Ryan Seacrest, count down the minutes, watched the drunken revelers in Times Square, and listened to the first song of the year. Imagine.

I'm not a big fan of the song, either, but I understand the sentiment. There is hope for a better world in the coming year. A world with less division, strife, and selfishness. A world of renewed community; a brotherhood (and sisterhood) of humanity. A world of *peace*. But that peace lasts about as long as a song, and then the other shoe drops. And more bombs. And we *resolve* to try it all again next year. But if everyone around the world sings along with John, and would trade in all their resolutions for peace, why does it remain so elusive? Why can't we, in the words of my basketball coach, "Figure it out!"? Why can't we, in the words of Nike marketers, "Just do it!"?

Because we *can't*. Not without help, that is. Because, in the words of another John, the *"lust of the flesh, the lust of the eyes, and the pride of life" (See 1 John 2)* kick in again. The drive to be first, be big, and get more, immediately shifts in to overdrive. We believe the same old pursuits, values, and solutions will surely work this year, if we just try a little harder. And we play it all again, same old story, same old line.

But there *is* a better way. It's a political *platform*, but not one that will win an election. It's a military *posture*, but not one that will win an earthly war. It's a worldly *pursuit*, whose victory requires heavenly resource. It's a *person*, whose platform, posture, and pursuit changed his creation forever. Enter Christmas. Isaiah prophesied of the coming of Messiah in words that anchor The Hallelujah Chorus:

> *For to us a child is born, to us a son is given, and the government will be on his shoulders. And he will be called Wonderful Counselor, Mighty God, Everlasting Father, Prince of Peace. Of the greatness of his government and peace there will be no end. (Isaiah 9:6–7)*

Which leads us to the proper conclusion:

> **Lasting peace is only found in the Prince of Peace.**

Picturing the Kingdom

I Heard the Bells

Enter Longfellow.

It was 1864 when Henry Wadsworth Longfellow penned these unforgettable words: "I heard the bells on Christmas day, their old, familiar carols play; and wild and sweet the words repeat of peace on earth, goodwill to men."

For Wadsworth, however, his reality was anything but. The Civil War was still raging, a conflict that would claim three-quarters of a million American lives. His son, Charles, he'd just learned, was one of the casualties, seriously wounded in battle. Three years earlier, his wife Fanny tragically burned to death in a freak accident at home, and Henry was so severely burned in trying to save her that he couldn't attend her funeral. A recent article I read described it this way:

> Grief, someone once suggested, is love that has nowhere to go. Such everlasting love would consume Longfellow, perhaps making him more susceptible to a feeling of hopelessness as he pondered the world around him, the way a lot of us feel these days when confronted by a daily barrage of chilling crime, rampant greed, virulent hatred, and toxic politics. So Longfellow continued to write: "And in despair I bowed my head: 'There is no peace on earth,' I said. 'For hate is strong and mocks the song of peace on earth, goodwill to men.'"
>
> But Longfellow was also a man of faith and knew if faith doesn't work in the worst of times, it doesn't work at all. So, believing in the story of an angel who announced the birth of a savior to shepherds watching their flocks at night, he reached the conclusion that transformed his poem into the much-loved carol it's been for the past 155 years:
>
> "Then pealed the bells more loud and deep: 'God is not dead, nor doth he sleep; the wrong shall fail, the right prevail, with peace on earth, goodwill to men.'"[1]

---

1. "Meaningful words worthy to remember: 'Peace on earth, goodwill to men.'" Joe Fitzgerald, Boston Herald, published December 24, 2019.

A-men, Henry.

Life in the Kingdom

A Peaceful Platform

Jesus is the person whose platform, posture, and pursuit changed his creation forever. Let's look closer at this peacemaker from Galilee.

I used to believe Jesus wasn't political. The only time he directly called out a king he called him a "fox," after all. Now I know better. Jesus made his political platform clear, but most of us miss it, because it's not what we're looking for, or think will work. It seems like I've said this already.

In political terms, rallies don't get bigger or more significant than the Sermon on the Mount. Jesus took full advantage of the moment, and left the crowd spellbound. But they were awed not just because of his rhetorical skills, but because of his obvious *authority*. "Who is this man?" has been asked by generations ever since. "Who does he think he is?" was the sentiment of both the religious and political elites. They certainly didn't miss his message and intention. He wasn't just a well-meaning backwater prophet with some memorable one-liners. He was a king from another world come to take over this one. It led to his political and religious execution.

Yet, the political leaders, like the religious leaders, completely misread the intentions of the Messiah. They couldn't believe a man with such a following didn't have armed insurrection in mind. All the other would-be messiahs before him, like Judah Maccabees, certainly did. Jesus even had a zealot among his first followers. But the teaching of Jesus, led by the peace dripping Beatitudes, and chased by the sacrificial love of your enemies, represented zero threat to Caesar's iron political grip. The threat was to the religious elites, though again, not as they imagined. Jesus didn't need to take over the temple because he *is* the temple. And Jesus didn't need to throw off the oppressive, deadly reign of Rome or any other occupiers. He planned to break the power of death, period, and with it the empires who relied on it to survive.

If there is a statement that crystallized the subversive political intentions of Jesus, it is the Olivet Discourse. Like the Sermon on the Mount, the Olivet Discourse is packed with kingdom descriptions and demands. This latter discourse, however, is more apocalyptic and cryptic. As usual, Jesus taught using stories to illustrate shocking realities, now and in the days to come. At the end of this epic bombshell is the parable of the sheep and goats. Most modern-day preaching focuses on our personal response to those in need. However, Brian Zahnd points out this story isn't directed to individuals but to *nations*. Brace yourself, here come the politics.

What is the Kingdom of God like, and what is to be the responsibility of nations *now*? Candidate Jesus of Nazareth, please tell us your plan. A more robust and diverse economy? A better outfitted and trained army? Less governmental interference and lower taxes? Not exactly. *Here is my six-point plan:*

- Feed the hungry.
- Give the thirsty a drink.
- Give the homeless a room.
- Give the cold and exposed something to wear.
- Visit the sick.
- Don't forget those who are in prison.

"You do-gooder *liberal!*"

"What kind of nonsense is that? We have *real* problems!"

"That will *never* work."

But have you ever heard a better platform? I assure you this coming election you won't, either.

A Peaceful Posture

My first *real* sermon came at the end of a summer youth ministry internship at my home church. It's a large church, so they certainly didn't trust the *trainee* with a Sunday morning, but the Sunday PM service was still a coveted gig. I remember the sermon well, and I still have the cassette recording! The passage I selected is still a favorite, taken from *the book of joy*, written from a jail cell. In this passage we learn a peaceful posture, from a former religious terrorist with blood on his hands:

> *Rejoice in the LORD always. I will say it again: Rejoice! Let your gentleness be evident to all. The LORD is near. Do not be anxious about anything, but in prayer and petition, with thanksgiving, present your requests to God. And the peace of God, which transcends all understanding, will guard your hearts and your minds in Christ Jesus. (Philippians 4:4–7)*

Once again remember, this letter is written to groups of people (churches), not just individuals. So let me ask you, does this sound like the posture of your church? Does gentleness, thanksgiving, and unconditional joy prevail? It certainly isn't our posture as the world's superpower. But has the same bloodlust and patriotic fervor seeped into our faith communities? What is our first reaction to being attacked, accused, or undermined? Be honest. Empires respond in kind. An eye for an eye! A tooth for a tooth! It's a default call to arms.

Jesus called us to be a different people, a holy nation, who respond differently when provoked. How is this even possible? It starts by cultivating peaceful *hearts* and peaceful *minds*. And this peaceful posture will lead to peaceful *hands*. *This* is the kingdom Jesus came to offer, and make possible, even to hell-bent zealots like Paul. Here is Paul's prescription for peace:

> *Finally, brothers and sisters, whatever is true, whatever is noble, whatever is right, whatever is pure, whatever is lovely, whatever is admirable—if anything is excellent or praiseworthy—think about such things. Whatever you have learned or received or heard from*

me, or seen in me—put it into practice. And the God of peace will be with you. (Philippians 4:8–9)

Still in?

A Peaceful Pursuit

The *Jesus Way* is the path of peace. The hippies of the 1960s and beyond certainly grasped the message and intention of Jesus. A recent movie, Jesus Revolution, depicted their lifestyle and pursuits, as well as the response of a straightlaced California preacher from the suburbs. Fortunately, he was able to get over his initial attitude, reticence, and prejudice, leading to one of the greatest moves of God our nation has ever seen. *Peace!*

The Kingdom of God is a realm of perfect, lasting peace. It is made possible and made permanent by the Prince of Peace. But it is a realm and reign that must be pursued. We must intentionally follow the Way of Jesus. We must fully embrace his platform. We must decide to employ a peaceful posture. We are called to be peacemakers, a people of peace, continuing the political agenda of Jesus to reconcile the whole world to himself. It is, and will be, the greatest miracle of all.

Peace out! (Hippie Farewell)

Questions

It's not that I'm so smart. But I stay with the questions much longer.

(ALBERT EINSTEIN)

Ask no questions and you'll be told no lies.[1]

(CHARLES DICKENS)

Question Authority

(HIPPIE MANTRA)

Announcing the Kingdom

Let's return to our tiny first-grade desks again. When it comes to "learning to read" in the kingdom, this would be the first lesson. If we truly want to understand how to think and live according to Jesus, this is the time to sit up and pay attention. Don't worry, there will still be time for lunch and recess.

What is the first question out of the mouth of every child? *Why?* Often it is out of curiosity, but just as often out of exasperation. "Why can't I?" "Why do I have to?" "Why do you have to be so mean?" Then they graduate to the *How?* stage, which is a lot

---

1. Charles Dickens, *Great Expectations*, Public Domain.

more fun. At least for people who know how to do things. Sigh . . . sorry Kyle & Calvin. The other *W's* follow in quick succession; *When? Where?* and the most important question we can ask, *Who?*

We talked earlier about exercising proper orthopraxy. This begins (and ends) with our Rabbi Jesus. Jesus is the greatest teacher who ever lived, and his methods were simple. Hmm . . . a coincidence? Jesus told stories using people and images his listeners could easily identify and relate to. He also asked great questions. When know-it-alls tried to trap him, he would most often respond with another question. As promised, then, let's return to the basic questions: What? Where? Why? How? *Who?*

Specifically, let's look at five of the best questions we can ask. They are questions that help us, in math terms, reduce things down to the lowest common denominator. Or what we often refer to as the basics of life. Are you ready, students? Here are the questions:

> What is the gospel?
> Where do I start each day?
> Why am I here?
> How do I navigate this life?
> Who do you say Jesus is?

Picturing the Kingdom

The Sludge Test

Like most students, I loved science. That is, if I had a great teacher. But unfortunately, many science teachers take our passion and curiosity and pound it to dust (or vapor). One of those teachers was my IPS (Introduction to Physical Science) teacher my freshman year. I won't say his name because he was a *really* great guy. But let's just say I didn't look forward to second period. We did do a lot of cool experiments, though, some of which I actually understood. Our final experiment was, of course, the toughest. The dreaded Sludge Test.

Questions

My eighth-grade teacher was another science *killjoy*. Okay, he was the worst of the bunch, and I'm struggling not to call him out here. But he did teach us the basics of how to measure liquids, use a beaker, and fire up a Bunsen Burner (An eighth-grader and Natural Gas? What could go wrong?). So when I arrived in ninth grade and donned my white lab coat, I was *ready!* Yeah, let's go with that. Anyway, during the freshman final, the assignment was to reduce the sludge down to its *basic elements*, and report on which ones we found in the mix. To do this, we were to employ any means of separation necessary, from simple filtering to burning the sludge with the Bunsen. It would've been fun, I guess, if my full ride to Harvard Medical School wasn't on the line. Oh well, I guess it was better I got filtered out early, too.

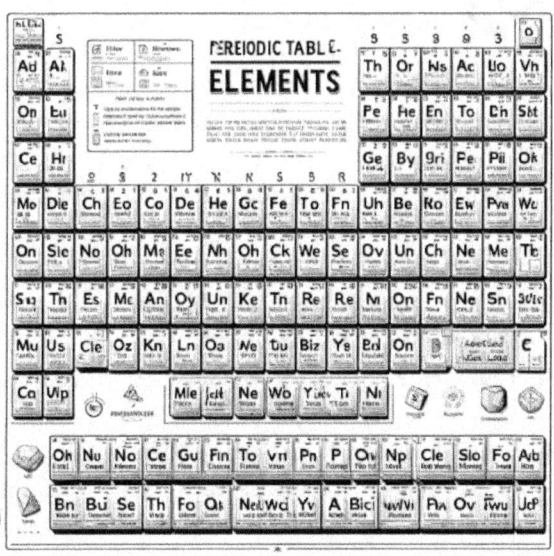

Life is also a Sludge Test of sorts. At the very least, there certainly *is* a lot of sludge. Nature, as all good science students know, can also be boiled down (or otherwise separated), into the *basic elements*. You see here a Periodic Table, which unlike the five elements I introduced earlier, there are a full 118! Are you reliving the nightmare of Chemistry? The aforementioned Mrs. Jobe was also my Chem teacher, and she was the best. But the nightmare was still real.

Most of what we see, taste, touch, smell, and hear are compounds; a combination of elements, like water (H_2O), salt ($NaCl$), and coffee

(ASAP10). Much of our life is, as well. But our existence can get sludgy, so we need frequent reminders to return to the basics. Every business, faith community, family, and individual needs to do this regularly. If we don't, the crises of life will force us to. When you reduce to the basic elements of life, *your* common denominators, what do you see? Perhaps we should make our own Periodic Table. Perhaps these five questions will help the basic elements bubble to the surface.

Life in the Kingdom

Faith and doubt make great dance partners.

(TIM JOHNSON)

If you follow Jesus long enough, you will experience seasons of doubt. My biggest came my freshman year of Bible college. Most people believe doubt is a *really* bad thing, so let me encourage all of us kids by asking, "Why?" God is not offended by our questions. You're not sinning when you *genuinely want to know*. You may not get an immediate or adequate answer but ask away! I love the childlike image my former pastor gave us of faith and doubt dancing. It was a gift to our congregation. It was a gift to me. We can question. We can wrestle. We can cry out in pain or frustration. But just remember, faith will *always* be a required element.

Let's get back to the five elemental questions I introduced above. I was challenged with these questions after I'd been in pastoral ministry for over two decades and had a master's degree in my pocket. But spending precious moments with Doug Coe challenged me to think about these basics of faith and life in a whole new *light*. Yes, these were light bulb moments! But even when we start with one of the others, the most important questions always seem to lead to *who*.

What is the Gospel?

Most believers when asked this, including me, answer by pointing to the Four Spiritual Laws, the Romans Road, or the story of Easter. Telling the story of Jesus is a great start but it is even more! Doug would put it this way: "The gospel (good news) is not a book of the Bible, the plan of salvation, or a theology of heaven and hell. The gospel is a person. That person is Jesus."

I remember when the power of that statement sunk in for me. The light bulb switched on in my understanding. This understanding changes everything:

- We are not following a religion. We are following a *person*.
- We are not presenting the message and mission of a church. We are presenting the life and teaching of a *person*.
- We are not taking a stand for the truth. We are pointing to the *person* who is the truth.
- We are not believing in a plan to gain heaven and avoid hell. We are believing in, and following, a *person*.
- Jesus not only announced the good news . . . *he is* the good news!
- The gospel is not just a message *about* Jesus. The gospel *is* Jesus.

I mentioned the history of a gospel as the good news declared when kings conquered a territory, city, and people. Of course, they didn't just announce it once, but constantly. But many, like King Nebuchadnezzar, took it a drastic step further, declaring themselves as a "son of god" worthy of worship. Daniel and his Jewish friends faced the lions and the fire to declare he had gone too far. I recently learned that the Romans did the same with their Caesars, putting on their coins Caesar is "king of kings" and "lord of lords." So what was it that got Paul, ten of the first followers, and scores of others politically executed? When they declared Jesus as King of Kings and LORD of LORDs, they were subversively saying Caesar was *not*. Remember these ramifications the next time you sing. Jesus *is now* the ruler of all, and his reign will last forever.

Where Do I Start Each Day?

> *Everyone thinks of changing the world, but*
> *no one thinks of changing himself.*
>
> (Leo Tolstoy)

Here's another doozie: "Who is the most important person for me to reach?"

According to our Sunday School teachers and pastors, it is always somebody else.

Mind you, it's usually a good idea to focus on others and not ourselves all the time. A great idea, even. However, if we're going to make a difference in anybody else's life, we need Jesus to make a difference in our life first. As the saying goes, we can't give what we don't have. Therefore, I need to lead *myself* to Jesus, daily.

According to Jesus, the most important person for me to reach *first* is always *me*. He gives us a picture most everyone will recognize because we often use it as a grenade to lob at others. We find it, again, in the Sermon on the Mount:

> *Why do you look at the speck of sawdust in your brother's eye and pay no attention to the plank in your own eye? You hypocrite, first take the plank out of your own eye, and then you will see clearly to remove the speck from your brother's eye. (Matthew 7:3,5, NIV)*

The point Jesus is making is not that we shouldn't help our brother or sister, but that *we* need to get help first. He is commanding us not to judge others first, which is a difficult assignment! However, it is made much easier when we, in another of Michael Jackson's songs, start with the man in the mirror. This is true in any room, any situation, any time, with anyone. Yes, even the one you *know* has missed the mark by a mile, or is the very epitome of arrogance, selfishness, or evil. Do we really believe Jesus is currently working in the lives of everyone on the planet, *right now?* It's true to the tune of over eight billion and counting! Therefore, instead of being holy hypocrites with a loaded moral bazooka, let's join Jesus in the work he has already started and longs to complete. Beginning with us.

Why Am I Here?

Doug Coe was always quick to clarify the purpose of life. What would be your immediate answer? Most of us would likely give different answers. Here is Doug's: "Our primary purpose is to love God with all our heart, soul, mind, and strength and our neighbors as ourselves. Love is our purpose—the God-given purpose for every person." It's not the only purpose in life, but no purpose is more significant. Remember, *love is over everything.* And who do we love? *Everyone,* even our worst enemy. Perhaps we can just say we're called to love *Two Who's* . . . God and neighbor.

Questions

How Do I Navigate This Life?

There is an old Sunday School joke those who attended at an early age can appreciate. It has been said there are three basic answers to any question a Sunday School teacher asks: "God," "Jesus," and "The Bible." A teacher once asked her class who built the ark and gathered two of all the animals. A young boy raised his hand and said, "I thought it was Noah, but I guess it must be God or Jesus." Classic. But it's not too far off as we consider our steps and decisions:

- **Jesus.** True North is a fixed point on a compass. It *never* changes and can *always* be relied on to point us in the right direction and help us home. Sound familiar?

- **Scripture.** The longest chapter in Scripture, *Psalm 119*, is also a celebration of Scripture. The most familiar verse, *105*, tells us the word of God is *"a lamp to guide my feet and a light for my path."* If you've ever turned off your flashlight or lamp in a cave and experienced *total* darkness, never cease to be thankful for this reality.

- **Family & Friends.** We are wired for community. We *must* live our lives together, especially as followers of Jesus. This is where the church (faith community) comes in. But remember the sludge? Navigating faith communities can be messy at times, too. Doug Coe often said: "We are a family of brothers and sisters following Jesus; not a religion, organization, or an institution." Read that again. Does that describe your church, or how you see church? Perhaps it's time for a Bunsen Burner?

- **The Holy Spirit.** Jesus promised us the Holy Spirit will guide us into all truth. He's a gentle, faithful, and reliable guide indeed. Here is my favorite encouragement regarding the work of the Holy Spirit: "For the Holy Spirit of Christ is 'the key that unlocks for us the treasures of the Kingdom of Heaven.'"[2] (John Calvin)

Who Do You Say Jesus Is?

This is the most important question of all! Jesus directly asked his first followers not just what people were saying, but what *they* believed about

---

2. Calvin, *Institutes of the Christian Religion*, 3.1.4.

him. Peter, shockingly, nailed it (see *Matthew 16*). Someone else who nailed it is the man born blind who Jesus gave his sight. It is not only a joyous story of miraculous healing, but a tragic story of religious leaders who, ironically, refused to see.

This story also shows the significant journey this man took in his understanding and testimony of who Jesus is. His first statement, as he was being interrogated by the religious leaders, was simply: *"The man they call Jesus made mud and spread it over my eyes." (John 9:11)* Not so significant? John later states: *"This is how you can recognize the Spirit of God: Every spirit that acknowledges that Jesus Christ has come in the flesh is from God." (1 John 4:2, NIV)* Jesus coming in the flesh is an undeniable fact of history. The evidence is overwhelming! The (hu)man Jesus is a good place to start.

As the interrogation continued, the religious leaders pressed the man: *"'What's your opinion about this man who healed you?' 'I think he must be a prophet.'" (John 9:17)* So they called in his parents to verify he had actually been born blind. Then the threats and name calling intensified. But what a significant statement the man in question made. He told them no one has ever heard of opening the eyes of a man born blind. Thus, he reasoned if this man were not from God, he could do nothing. So far so good. But our world is full of people who believe Jesus was a good man and a good teacher, even a prophet sent by God. It is a conclusion Jesus himself affirms: *"You call me 'Teacher' and 'LORD,' and rightly so, for that is what I am." (John 13:13, NIV)* But wait, there's more!

Here is where we (and the man born blind) need help. After the man gets thrown out of the presence of the religious leaders for daring to suggest they might want to become his followers too, Jesus sought him out. The question he led with was most unexpected: *"Do you believe in the Son of Man?"* But his response, unlike the religious leaders, was perfect: *"'Who is he, sir? I want to believe in him.' 'You have seen him . . . and he is speaking to you!'"* And the story had a happy ending after all: *"'Yes, LORD, I believe!' And he worshiped Jesus." (John 9:35–38)*.

The journey of faith this man unknowingly embarked on is tremendously significant to our own. Sometimes this journey happens all at once, as it did in this story. However, there are many still on this journey. All three of these confessions, according to Scripture, are critical. It begins with believing in the *fully man* Jesus. Following Jesus, making him our Rabbi, and recognizing his authority as one sent from God *(prophet)* comes next. But embracing Jesus as the divine son, *fully God* come in the flesh, declaring him LORD and worshipping him is where it all comes together! It's then we can say, along with Peter:

> *You are the Messiah, the Son of the living God. (Matthew 16:16, NIV)*

Rescue

For the Son of man came to find and rescue the lost.

(Luke 19:10, MSG)

Announcing the Kingdom

Heroes in a half-shell . . . Turtle Power!

(Teenage Mutant Ninja Turtles)

Stacie and I could open a toy store. Sentimental fools that we are, we just can't bear to part with the plastic trappings of childhood. Thus, we got the largest plastic tubs we could find and filled them with G.I. Joes, Hot Wheels, Fisher Price play sets (including 2 castles), Legos, stuffed animals, and Rescue Heroes. Each of these major categories *still* fill their very own crate. I can't wait to move again. This is in addition to my antique metal Tonka Trucks, Dapper Dan & Anne, Raggedy Anne & Andy, in the toy box my grandpa made for me. Don't judge, we're a childlike family, okay?

But here's a fun twist to our toy boxes; they can help us understand the greatest desire of our God. And what is that? Three words:

Saved

The Rescue Heroes came along late in the *game* for the Andersons, but we made up for lost time. Rescue Heroes are like Transformers in that the rescuers and the method of rescue are one in the same. Thus, the police officer has a built-in motorcycle, and the fire fighter a built-in helicopter. Can you see why we kept them? We must have fifty of them. There are a lot of people still needing rescue.

Perhaps you haven't heard your pastor use the word rescue lately. But I'll bet you our crate of Rescue Heroes you've heard the words *saved* and *salvation*. I believe the best definition of salvation is rescue. I also believe, and Scripture declares:

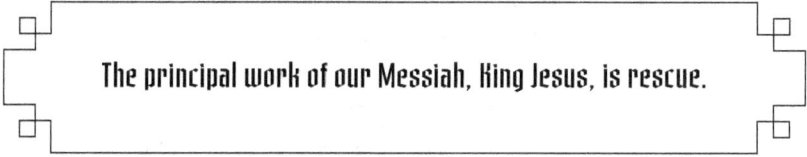

The principal work of our Messiah, King Jesus, is rescue.

Delivered

The Marvel universe was created in 1939 by Martin Goodman. I wonder if he could have imagined the blockbuster Hollywood movies his comic characters would spawn. Now we're nearly one-hundred years in and we never seem to run out of them. It's a good thing because there are Jokers, Penguins, Riddlers, and Green Goblins everywhere! And that's just the tip of the sinister iceberg. So shine the spotlight and fire up the Batmobile because Gotham City is in need of deliverance.

Despite decades of heroes with all the superpowers in the universe, it's no less true of our world today. I know it's all in good fun but there is always a glaring omission at Comic Con. *Moses.* The greatest deliverer the world had ever seen was this adopted son of Pharoah, with forty years of shepherding experience on the backside of the desert. If you haven't watched The Prince of Egypt lately, speaking of Hollywood blockbusters, you need to hear the theme song again. Deliver Us plays as the nation of Israel cries out from their crushing yoke of slavery. Enter the deliverer.

But we all know the greatest deliverer was still to come. You likely won't see him at Comic Con, either. Well, he's no fun anyway, right? But the good news is there is a deliverer who doesn't need to change in a telephone booth or get bit by a spider to be able to save the day. What did Jesus deliver us from? We could make another entire A-Z list. Why don't you try it? Yes, right now. Here's a head start: *Accuser (the satan). Death. Evil. Fear. Oppression. Slavery.* By the way, what is one of the greatest signs the Kingdom of God has come? *Deliverance* from demonic spirits. He sends them packing, pigs or no pigs! The deliverer has come, but we still need to sing:

Deliver Us!

Healed

Our default when we think of healing is physical needs (body). Thankfully, this *is* part of God's kingdom agenda. But it goes beyond this to every aspect of our lives (soul and spirit) and our communities. Healing in the Kingdom of God is *wholeness*. Yes, there are *now* and *not yet* aspects of wholeness. The reality is, there is sickness, injury, loss, and death we are currently not immune from. Even Lazarus died again. But our ultimate healing began with the resurrection and that life is available to us *now*. So is divine healing. But why doesn't God heal everybody now? I don't know. I just attended the funeral of a thirteen-year-old boy today. But he *has* made provision for our wholeness, and we may experience his healing power *today,* or it may be *tomorrow*. But we *will* be made *whole*. Here's the truth:

> *The LORD hears his people when they call to him for help. He rescues them from all their troubles. The LORD is close to the brokenhearted; he rescues those whose spirits are crushed.* (Psalm 37:17–18)

Picturing the Kingdom

Doernbecher Dolly

Have you ever been to a children's hospital? If you have then you've witnessed heroes in action. Most won't be wearing capes and tights but rather scrubs and white lab coats. If you ever want to catch a glimpse of angels on assignment, I believe this is the best place to look. If God is close to the brokenhearted (and he is!), and if he values every child as precious (and he does!), then where better to find Jesus in Portland than Doernbecher, Randall, or Shriners? I believe you'll see him there because I have. Just look for the scrubs and lab coats.

Stacie and I have been beyond fortunate to have only had one experience admitting a child at Doernbecher. It was our youngest son Calvin, at age fifteen, for an outpatient knee surgery. It was traumatic enough for us, and we got to take him home at the end of the day. For many families, and brave kids, Doernbecher *becomes* home for an extended period. And many families won't ever be able to take their child home again. It is unimaginable. Some of you, my readers, have experienced this, and all I can say is my heart breaks for you and with you. We lost our first grandchild, CJ (Caroline Joy), at seven months gestation, and it is the deepest grief I've experienced. God's continued grace to all who grieve today.

How is it these doctors, nurses, and support staff can look into the eyes of these kids, every day, who are suffering? How is it they can stare untimely death in the eye, every day, and be able to return the following? Having walked with friends through the passing of their son to cancer, at the age of two, it is *still* unimaginable. But for the grace of God, *none of us* would be able to stand.

But for the generosity of good-hearted men and women, these places of care and healing wouldn't be possible. The picture of the kingdom you see is Doernbecher Dolly, an image I see at Costco every year during an annual fundraising campaign. How wonderful to see Dolly after Dolly dotting the walls and hanging from wires, denoting another gift for our kids and their families. God-willing you won't have to walk the halls of a Doernbecher or a similar facility, but you and I can be heroes on behalf of kids, too. Our generosity can literally rescue a child. God bless *every* Dolly.

Life in the Kingdom

There is a character in Scripture I decidedly cannot relate to. Zacchaeus, the short guy in the tree. But not only is Zacchaeus a short guy, he's a bad guy. He's the most hated of all bad guys, the dreaded tax collector. Tax collectors were well-known cheats, exacting more than was owed to Rome to pad their own bank accounts. They were despised outcasts of Jewish society, which made Zacchaeus the perfect lunch date for Jesus (and Matthew a perfect choice for a first follower). It comes as no surprise this one encounter with Jesus led to his transformation. As a result, Zacchaeus makes this shocking vow:

> *I will give half my wealth to the poor, LORD, and if I have cheated people on their taxes, I will give them back four times as much!* (Luke 19:8)

Talk about metamorphosis! I imagine it took the Jerichoans awhile to believe it. Until they got their check in the mail. Even on his lunch hour Jesus was fulfilling his mission of rescue. I sure wish Scripture recorded what Jesus said to bring about this most unlikely 180. Did he talk with his mouth full? Did he have to say *anything*? I personally believe it was the latter.

Speaking of healing, here are three more theological words that clarify our calling as God's agents of healing:

Reconciliation

When I'm on vacation in my beloved Central Oregon, I love to visit Antioch Church. Recently, when looking at their statement of vision, this caught my eye:

> We inhabit this world as visitors from the future, seeking to live as a sneak peak of God's coming kingdom on earth—a kingdom

marked by peace, love, justice, and hope—as we join God in the reconciliation of all things.

The reconciliation of all things is the focus of *all* their activities. So much for beach trips and potlucks. I've already mentioned a couple times our calling as ambassadors of reconciliation. Of course, this includes reconciling people to God himself. It also includes helping people be reconciled to one other (peacemakers). But it goes beyond this to include our communities, our institutions, and our organizations. Oh, and the earth. This is a calling many followers of Jesus don't take seriously enough. Yes, God desires *spiritual* reconciliation. Yes, Jesus desires *social* reconciliation. But he also desires *soil* reconciliation. He cares about clean water, abundant crops to safely feed the hungry, and our beautiful creation remaining beautiful and functioning as designed. *All things.* Oh, and one more thing God is working on right now: The reconciliation of heaven and earth. Someday bridges will no longer be needed.

Righteousness

In the same way we default healing to the physical only, we can also default righteousness to purity only. Certainly, purity is a crucial aspect of righteousness. But righteousness in the eyes of God and through the lens of Scripture is to *set things right*. Right here. Right now. All things. The prophet Micah, led by the Holy Spirit, described a *righteous* lifestyle:

> *He has shown you, O mortal, what is good. And what does the LORD require of you? To act justly and to love mercy and to walk humbly with your God. (Micah 6:8)*

Wanna be a hero? Wanna be righteous? Start here. Make justice a priority. Lead with mercy in all your dealings. Be known, by God and others, for your humility not your personal accolades. One of my favorite Bob Goff stories is his rescue of an innocent child from a prison in Uganda. He's a lawyer and is so passionate about justice prevailing in our world, and in this Ugandan prison, that he literally took the jail door off its hinges and brought it back to the United States! *Beautiful.*

Consummation

This final word is primarily a *not yet* reality. To consummate is "to make something complete or perfect."[1] Someday, God's rescue project will come to a *perfect* conclusion. *All things* will be made subject to King Jesus, and then Jesus will turn over the entire kingdom to the eternal jurisdiction of the Father. God's children will be whole. God's children will be safe. God's children will be home. God's covenant, bearing a signature in Messiah's blood, will once and for all be signed, sealed, and delivered! Luke captures it perfectly:

> *But God was fulfilling what all the prophets had foretold about the Messiah—that he must suffer these things. Now repent of your sins and turn to God, so that your sins may be wiped away. Then times of refreshment will come from the presence of the LORD, and he will again send you Jesus, your appointed Messiah. For he must remain in heaven until the time for the final restoration of all things, as God promised long ago through his holy prophets.* (Acts 3:18–21)

My oldest son has a picture on his wall I love. It's his roommate's, so I can't swipe it. Phooey. Remember earlier when I talked about Jesus *running* after us? The picture shows a shepherd running around a tree and away from the fold of ninety-nine to rescue one confused and straying lamb. This is the image of Messiah, come to seek and save . . . *me!* This is the God of rescue. The God who saves. The Good Shepherd. The Healer.

99<1 (Jesus)

---

1. Cambridge Dictionary.

Story

It is a sin to make the Bible boring.

(Rick Enloe)

Announcing the Kingdom

Years ago, I started writing love stories for Stacie at Christmas. It began in a moment of illumination at the grocery store. I know it's not the most romantic of origins, but we *desperate househusbands* must take inspiration wherever we can get it. Stacie picked up the latest edition of a woman's magazine and immediately turned to a one-page love story. She'd deny it today, but she *swooned*. I saw it, and as I did, *I got an idea! An awful idea! I got a wonderful, awful idea!* "I could do that, and all those brownie points would be mine!" *The Grinch* would be proud. So I wrote my first love story on Christmas Eve, and wrapped it up and gave it to Stacie the next morning. It was set in a Starbucks, of course, and it's still the best of them all. I've been swimming in points (and staying up late every Christmas Eve), ever since.

Everybody loves a good story. We are *moved* (swooned) by a good story. What's more, we are *motivated* by a good story. We are *connected* by good stories (culture). We can even be *changed*. Enter Rabbi Jesus, the master teacher. Jesus not only told stories around the campfire; he told stories *everywhere*. Scripture says:

> Jesus always used stories and illustrations like these when speaking to the crowds. In fact, he never spoke to them without using such parables. (Matthew 13:34)

Jesus told the *best* stories, but they weren't designed to entertain his audience (though they did delight them). He told *parables*; "a simple story used to illustrate a moral or spiritual lesson."[1] His parables were relatable, memorable, and powerful to his first audience. They have only grown more influential over time. Who can imagine a world without a Good Samaritan? Who can hear lost and found without immediately thinking about a Lost Sheep or Coin? Who can imagine a story of redemption and reconciliation without using *prodigal* in the description? In fact, Charles Dickens believed The Prodigal Son to be the best story ever written.

Jesus, of course, didn't just tell stories, he *was* the story. I talked earlier about the dual spotlights of Scripture; the Old and New Testaments pointing to and illuminating the entire point of Scripture: Jesus. But don't miss this critical point: All of Scripture is *one* story. God's story. In fact, there is an entire camp of biblical theology built on this premise. I've pitched my tent there. We even have our own translation of Scripture. Well, not really, but The Story is a fantastic must read that will change the way you read the Bible forever. We must never forget:

> **Scripture is not an owner's manual or rule book.**
> **Scripture is God's story; the greatest story ever lived.**

The Bible isn't boring. It's the story of the ages. We simply must tell it right. I'll never forget hearing the words of Rick Enloe (above) in a youth ministry class at college. I doubt anyone in the room will either. But how guilty we all have been of not only making it boring, but *thinking* it is boring. Enter James Bryan Smith to help us *repent* (change our thinking):

---

1. Dictionary.com.

> The thesis of this book is that there is a magnificent story, which is the most important thing happening on this earth. It is our only hope as individuals, communities, countries, and a species. But for a variety of reasons the gospel message we often hear, the story often told, is shrunken and distorted. This is why we see so many frustrated, disappointed Christians. It is not that they are bad people, but they have never heard the magnificent story in its fullness.[2]

As my professor would say, "Bingo!" He also has said: "Epitaph Of Mainline Protestantism: 'We failed to let the story shine'" (Leonard Sweet).

Unfortunately, this can be said of most every church and denomination. Scripture is a story. It is what *connects* us as followers of Jesus. It should always *move* us; always *motivate* us; always *change* us. The magnificent story, God's story, will *shine* in the darkness.

There's nothing boring about that.

Picturing the Kingdom

Introducing Pat & Percy

Like any good parent, I read stories to my boys at bedtime. Educators tell us there is nothing more impactful to a child's academic success. *Nothing*.

But one night they asked *me* to tell them a story.

I looked around their room for inspiration. I found it on the wall in a picture painted by Charles Russell, the famous western painter from Montana. On my first trip to Big Sky Country, I was introduced to Louis L'Amour from Stacie's stepdad Walt's bookshelf. I was immediately hooked and have since read them all at least once. On subsequent visits I was introduced to the brush strokes of Charles Russell, and he's still my favorite by a *country* mile. So is Louis. So as my eyes locked on the painting of a young miner and his trusty horse at their campsite, I said to the boys, "Let me introduce you to Pat & Percy."

That bedtime tradition lasted for years afterwards. Drawing from both Charles and Louis I spun yarns on the spot, much to the delight of the boys and the surprise of me! When I'd climb in bed Stacie would ask, "How do you do that?" I'd always respond, "I have no idea, but that was pretty good!" At least on most nights. I even made a cassette tape for the

---

2. Smith, *The Magnificent Story*, 13.

boys on our longest trip away from them, so they could listen to part of a story each of the eighteen nights. Yes, I did say cassette tape. Hush.

I'm introducing Pat & Percy to you now because I'm hoping someday you'll find them on the shelf of your local bookstore. In fact, The Adventures of Pat & Percy became my first completed book. It was for a Royal Rangers (similar to Boy Scouts) Summer Pow Wow, where I was the speaker. The boys got a chapter at each session. The theme of the event was The Wild, Wild West. Perfect. They loved it! But they also had to help me pitch my tent.

It was just recently, however, that I stumbled on to a perfect connection between The Childlike Kingdom and The Adventures of Pat & Percy. It's too good not to share! Someday soon, God-willing, you'll not just meet Pat and his surefooted horse Percy, but also Sir Patrick and Percival. I can't wait! Here is an initial snapshot of our new friends, in their Charlie Russell getup.

Like you and me, Pat & Percy have a story that *must* be told. And it will be told. Jesus is called the *author* and perfector of our lives, after all. He's the master of the empty canvas *and* the blank page. If we'll allow it, he'll create a unique masterpiece and unbelievable non-fiction classic. It won't be brush stroked or written exactly how we'd like, but I promise, we'll love the ending!

Story

Life in the Kingdom

We can learn the lines (doctrine, instructions), but not know the story.

(Bo Stern Brady)

We can trust the story.

(Leonard Sweet)

For a short span of my career, I was a school superintendent (just like my daddy). It was the sweetest of seasons for many reasons. Ha! The *primary* (and intermediate) reason was getting to read to Mrs. Shelton's and Mrs. Smith's first grade classes every Friday. It was the highlight of my week. We were all introduced to Lady Lollipop (a royal pig!) among others. Talk about my happy place. Just a few weeks ago, I ran into one of the students after speaking at the high school. He's a *senior* now. Sigh. He came up and introduced himself to me and said, "You probably don't remember this . . ." Oh yes I do, Carter!

The Greatest Story Ever Told

The story is much bigger and better, more profound and compelling, when we see the fullness of who Jesus is.[3]

The story of Scripture is the story of Jesus. He's the hero, the moral, the climax, and the aftermath of the story. When we focus on him; his *profound* words, his *compelling* actions, and the *fullness* of his life, there's no way the story can be boring and lifeless. It's only when we're mining for doctrines, rules, and religious practices that the biggest story becomes small. There's little reason to tell *that* on the mountain, over the fields and everywhere . . .

There are scores of books, articles, and movies about Jesus. God-willing there will be "four-score-and-seven"[4] more soon. We all have our

---

3. Smith, *The Magnificent Story*, 106.

4. All you good history students will recognize the first four words of Abraham Lincoln's most famous speech, now engraved on the marble walls of the Lincoln Memorial: The Gettysburg Address. A "score" is 20.

favorites. My favorite (so far) is Who Is This Man?[5] It's also my favorite book title. Here are a few of the ways Pastor Ortberg made the story of Jesus *bigger* and *better* for me:

- A new time had come with Jesus, a time when thinking about kings and children would begin to shift . . . Jesus said it wasn't the child's job to become like Herod. It was Herod's job to become like the child.
- One of the most impressive aspects of Jesus is how he was impressed by unimpressive people.
- People invite this man into their lives, and heaven starts invading earth through them.

What a gift writers like Ortberg are in helping us to understand, embrace, and tell the greatest story ever written about the greatest person ever. Thank you all. And let's keep them coming, kids!

The Greatest Story Ever Lived

> *May the best story win.*
>
> (COLLEGE FOOTBALL PLAYOFF 2024)

Great authors bring great stories to life. So do movies. They help you see things in a whole new light. They introduce ideas and images you've never considered. And they, too, can change lives. The late Bill Bright probably shared Jesus with more people than anyone who has ever lived, including Billy Graham. He talked with thousands of students through the ministry of Campus Crusade for Christ. But his development and release of the movie *Jesus* has rewritten cinematic (and evangelistic) history:

> According to The New York Times, Jesus is likely the most-watched motion picture of all time. The Jesus Film Project states that Jesus has been viewed almost 5.6 billion times . . . Over 225 million people have indicated a decision to follow Christ after viewing the film.[6]

---

5. All quotes below are from Ortberg, *Who Is This Man?*
6. TrueChristianity.Info.

A more recent release (2004) is Mel Gibson's *The Passion of the Christ*, depicting the "final" twelve hours of the life of Jesus. As of 2023, according to Box Office Mojo, it is the highest-grossing R-rated (due to graphic violence) film ever in the United States and the highest grossing independent film of all time world-wide.

Fast-forward to 2017 and the release of *The Chosen*, the multi-season portrayal of Jesus created by Dallas Jenkins, and released by Angel Studios:

> With the intention of differing from previous portrayals of Jesus, he crafted a story arc which focused more on the people who encountered Jesus and viewed him through their eyes. He has stated in interviews that he sought to present Jesus in a way that was more "personal, intimate, [and] immediate." The show's producers have primarily used crowdfunding on the Angel Studios platform to finance production, and it continues to be the most successful crowdfunded TV series or film project . . . According to a 2022 analysis commissioned by the show's producers, 108 million had seen at least part of the show through the app and streaming platforms. Translation into as many as 600 languages is being funded by the Come and See Foundation.[7]

In 2024, Season Four of The Chosen is being released in theaters. I'm thinking it will do quite well at the box office. The story of Jesus is bigger and better than any other story out there and told right has an unprecedented audience in any medium. In fact, years ago The New York Times stopped putting The Bible on its non-fiction best-sellers list, because it crushes the competition *every year* to this day!

The story of Jesus isn't just the greatest story ever told, in print or in living color. It is the greatest story ever lived, by Jesus himself, and by those who have followed and will follow all throughout history. I have a Jesus story, and it fits perfectly within his-story. And the rest is . . . As long as I remember who the main character is (it's not me). Bo Stern Brady says our problem is "we always cast ourselves as the hero." She encourages us: "Don't lose your place in the story . . . I'd rather play a small part in a big story than a big part in a small one."[8] But we need a near constant reminder that it's not about us and the world doesn't revolve around our fannies. Or maybe it's just me.

---

7. Wikipedia.com, The Chosen (TV series).
8. Bo Stern Brady, 2022 sermon, delivered in Tualatin, OR.

The Rest of the Story

I've been taking a few walks down memory lane, but this chapter is about *story* after all. Some of you are too young to remember the greatest voice in the history of radio. I can still hear his signature sign-off from his daily reading of the news: "Paul Harvey . . . Good day!" His cadence and inflection could turn an ordinary piece of news into a headline. But Paul Harvey is perhaps best known for his segment (and books) The Rest of the Story, written by his son, Paul Jr. The stories featured notable people, places, and major events, but they weren't unveiled until you heard details you could never imagine could be true of them, or that. Like the beautiful actress Elizabeth Taylor being born hideously ugly, with hair all over her body (true). Once Paul and Paul had us on the hook with the introductories, the story would take a turn to a dramatic conclusion. And Paul Sr. would sign off every episode saying, "And now you know . . . the *rest* of the story!" Radio (and literary) magic.

The Bible book of Acts is the rest of the story to the Accounts of Jesus. He even makes a dramatic appearance on the road to Damascus, changing *everything* for the murderous Pharisee Saul who was on the war path. The renamed Paul shares his testimony several times as the story unfolds, in front of the political elite of the day, including eventually Caesar himself (though the book ends just before this). It is a powerful story of transformation, beginning with one man and spreading throughout Asia Minor and to the ends of the earth (Note: the ends of the earth used to be considered a spot on the north coast of Spain, showing their rather limited perspective of planet earth. But, of course, God has no such boundary. Muy bueno, Senor!).

Paul wasn't the only star in the unfolding drama of The Acts of the Apostles. The other apostles, the original first followers of Jesus, were also featured in the story. Philip and Peter get special billing, but they were all actively introducing Jews and Gentiles alike to *the Way*. We also see them start getting picked off (martyred) one by one. It is as compelling as stories get, as we follow these men (and women) on missionary journeys risking life and limb and eventually all succumbing, carrying the name of Jesus to all who would hear. Not only would the world, then and now, never be the same, but Scripture says of these and others who gave all, *"the world was not worthy of them"* (see *Hebrews 11*). And despite how things looked, and it looked bleak at many junctures, all of them were overcomers. How do we know this? The final book of Scripture, written by the "last man standing" (not really), John of Patmos, who from his island prison heard this divine declaration:

> Then I heard a loud voice in heaven say: "Now have come the salvation and the power and the kingdom of our God, and the authority of his Messiah. For the accuser of our brothers and sisters, who accuses them before our God day and night, has been hurled down. They triumphed over him by the blood of the Lamb and by the word of their testimony; they did not love their lives so much as to shrink from death. (Revelation 12:10–11, NIV)

What a vision John was given! And it was given, like much of Scripture, to encourage all enduring persecution and death. Things looked bad with the dreaded Romans in charge and will only get worse. But the story is still unfolding, and John is given a sneak peek of the end, a glimpse of the New Jerusalem, and the coming New Heavens and New Earth. Don't lose hope and don't waver in your faith, because now you know . . .

The Rest of the Story!

Treasure

Wherever your treasure is, there your heart will be.

(JESUS)

Put your money where your heart is.

(OVERHEARD)

Announcing the Kingdom

Most kids dream of a treasure hunt. An actual, bona fide, pirates and palm trees, swashbuckling adventure where "X" marks the spot. Tales have been written and produced, picks and shovels have been purchased, and ships have been launched. After all, it isn't just coins to find but *doubloons!* "Wait up, Indiana Jones, we are coming with you!"

Of course, Indiana always finds his treasure. He has the good sense to ignore the other items that glitter along the way to find and possess that of greatest value. It is storytelling at its finest. Robert Louis Stevenson started it all in his classic tale, Treasure Island. But treasure hunts of all kinds are still going on to this day (National Treasure anyone?), with all manner of riches, be they monetary, archeological, or spiritual. Let the expeditions commence!

However, not every desired pursuit passes the heavenly "quest test." We are faced with the choice of seeking either treasure that *"moth and rust destroy,"* or a life that accumulates *"treasures in heaven." (Matthew 6, ESV)* Jesus gives us a treasure map of sorts in the Sermon on the Mount, but we don't need to book passage on a Caribbean bound vessel to find it. It is an all-together different destination and "trove" than that of the world (big surprise), which has its own map.

So there is a choice. A life and death choice! Here are the maps, Indiana. *You must choose wisely . . .*

The Isle of Deadman's Bones

The Isle of Living Treasure

There is a path before each person that seems right, but it ends in death. (Proverbs 14:12)

Seek the Kingdom of God above all else, and live righteously, and he will give you everything you need. (Matthew 6:33)

Not much of a choice, right? Yet, most of us wake up each day, put our pants on one leg at a time, drink our coffee, read the morning paper (never mind), and *launch* out the front door into the wild blue seas of life with our compass set on that very island of dead man's bones. We don't mean to, necessarily, it's just what we've been taught to do. Taught at every turn in our culture from movies, television, the morning paper, self-help books, and even Robert Louis Stevenson. *Argh!* We shouldn't be surprised by this. Where we should be surprised, however, and deeply grieved, is we hear it just as often from followers of Jesus. It's not just the prosperity gospel peddlers who are the guilty parties. We need to be reminded, continually, where our passions and priorities should be focused. God help us. *Seriously.*

So where do we begin?

> According to Jesus, true righteousness always begins with the heart.

You can't read the Sermon on the Mount without the above being your biggest takeaway. Murder, lust, and divorce. Making oaths, taking revenge, and loving enemies. It all begins with the heart, not the law. And the Beatitudes? *All* about the heart. And Jesus shoots right through the heart, in the middle of his address:

> No one can serve two masters. Either he will hate the one and love the other, or he will be devoted to the one and despise the other. You cannot serve both God and money. (Matthew 6:24, NIV)

Many have tried. Many are trying. Many more are lined up in caps and gowns.

No one.

Picturing the Kingdom

Like most people, I collect things. But unfortunately, over the years I've had way too many collections. I've mentioned my butterflies already, but have I told you about my bottlecaps? I had *thousands,* in big boxes on the side of our shed. My parents deserve a medal. We also lived in rockhounding paradise during my wonder years, which meant agates, mica, fossils, and thundereggs. For a short time, I tried stamps. Now I've graduated to collector pins, Christmas ornaments, and books. There's more. *Sigh.*

Treasure

But one collected item has remained consistent. Coins. Everyone has a coin collection of some sort, though most today are in the form of paper, or are digital (Wha?). My oldest son has such a collection. He even got my wife and I to buy one of these new bits of currency for a small fortune. That fortune is now much smaller. *Sigh*. But I'm talking the actual copper, silver, and gold kind. And the older the better. But alas, this hobby is a rich man's game, so my collection is far from impressive. But you wanna see something cool? Of course you do. The picture you see is British Pence coins in the available denominations. But these particular coins shown, minted in 2008, when arranged just perfectly form the Crown Shield of England. *Argh!*

One reason I love to collect is I'm a sentimental fool. Another is I'm a lover of history. So I don't just love stuff, I love *old* stuff. My grandma and grandpa had really cool stuff, like Norman Rockwell plates, hand painted China, and baskets of all sizes and shapes they traded for with the local Quinault Tribe. Treasures! My parents have treasures, too, so along with ours (Stacie is just as bad as me), we'd sink a Clipper! *Sigh. Sigh.*

I share this to qualify my love of tradition. It's my favorite part of culture. However, as we all know, tradition can stand square in the way of innovation. I heard it said recently, "God is in the future pulling us forward." I believe this to be true. However, I also believe tradition is still valuable, and that God is there, too. Unfortunately, followers of Jesus have often allowed tradition to stand in the way of healthy progress and innovation. Fortunately, just as often, the church has been guilty of tremendous innovations and progress. So should we value tradition or embrace the future? Yes! And Yes!! Scripture agrees in one of my favorite verses:

> *Therefore every teacher of the law who has become a disciple in the kingdom of heaven is like the owner of a house who brings out of his storeroom new treasures as well as old. (Matthew 13:52, NIV)*

We can sing along with Tevia (The Fiddler on the Roof), lauding the value of tried-and-true tradition. But we can also enjoy and embrace the treasures of the new and improved. The empires of this world have their own "old" treasures of coins, shields, castles, and armor. Unfortunately, their "new" treasures are just recycled versions of the old. But the Kingdom of God has treasures, new and old, of eternal (past, present, and future) value, that won't rust, fade, crumble, or decay. In this verse, Jesus was specifically confirming the value of the old (law) and the new (kingdom). The ultimate treasure of the kingdom is Jesus himself, who the Old and New both point to and rejoice.

Argh!

Life in the Kingdom

> *They think their prosperity is of their own doing, but I will have nothing to do with that kind of thinking . . . The LORD gave me what I had, and the LORD has taken it away. Praise the name of the LORD! (Job 21:16, 1:21)*

Despite the clarifying rebuke from God, and the misguided rebukes of his buddies, Job was known as a righteous man. So much so he drew the attention of the Almighty and the attacks of the accuser. But Job continued to behave righteously despite *literally* losing everything, except four servants and his wife. The survivors didn't provide much comfort, however, delivering the worst possible news from every direction, and advising him to curse God and die. Perhaps he wished his wife was also . . . never mind. But Scripture says in the midst of all this, Job didn't sin. How is this possible? Because Job, like King David after him, had a heart after God's own heart. In a happy ending, Job's fortunes were restored. But his greatest treasure, of greater worth than gold, was never in jeopardy.

Treasure

Jesus consistently addressed matters of the heart. He also talked about money . . . a lot. Coincidence? I think not. In fact, nearly a third of the parables of Jesus address finances in some way. Jesus had more than a few awkwardly direct conversations with would be followers about their treasure (not just money). Here's a small sampling:

- *But God said to him, "You fool! This very night your life will be required of you. Then who will own what you have accumulated?" This is how it will be for anyone who stores up treasure for himself but is not rich toward God. (Luke 12:20–21, BSB)*
- *There is one thing you still lack: Go, sell everything you own and give to the poor, and you will have treasure in heaven. Then come, follow Me. (Mark 10:21, BSB)*
- *In fact, it is easier for a camel to go through the eye of a needle than for a rich person to enter the Kingdom of God! (Mark 10:25)*

We could continue for pages, but this should be enough to get our attention. Jesus wasn't messing around when he gave the "job description" of a follower. He might as well have said, "Come and die!" Wait, he did. Jesus doesn't want us to simply separate portions of our spices, crops, herds, or coins. He simply said *all*.

Kingdom Values of Great Weight

If you've been to merry old England, you'll find many oddities. Okay, that's true everywhere. But the English decided it was perfectly normal to drive on the left side of the road. They also come to a screeching halt in the afternoon in the name of tea. Stopping everything and overpaying for a hot beverage? That'll never catch on. They also name their currency after a measurement on the scale. The British *pound*. Of course, there is a good reason for this, in that scales were literally used in matters of trade and compensation. It wasn't just the British who weighed, but pretty much everybody. The English just continued to use the name, even for their paper currency. Odd. No wonder they lost the American Revolution. Sorry *cheap* (not many pounds) shot. God save the king.

But let's give the British Empire its due, because in the Kingdom of God there are also many values of great *weight*. Every culture has its core values. Many of these are universal, of course. Guess where the good ones trace back to? No, not to King George. Scripture warns against using inaccurate scales and cheating the poor. Scripture warns of trusting chariots and horses (and other implements of war), and riches. There isn't one king or political leader who has ever thought *that* will work. But in the upside-down and backwards kingdom, all *bets* are off. Too bad all wars aren't, either.

Here are a few more kingdom values of *great* weight:

Generosity over Selfishness

> *We are at our best when we give.*
> (Timothy Cardinal Dolan)

Name one kingdom in history that placed generosity over its own self interests. The Greeks and Romans would literally laugh you out of the room if you suggested such a thing. But in the Kingdom of God, according to Jesus, it is more blessed to give than to receive. He also said the love of money is the root of all kinds of evil. Why? Selfish interests. Yet, in every culture the love and pursuit of riches is *celebrated*. All except one. You heard it here first. No, we heard it from Jesus first.

Certainly, other teachers have echoed the value of generosity, in ancient and modern times. We also recognize the value of generosity seasonally, such as when the red kettles come out during the holidays. But where does the idea of generosity ultimately trace back to? As with every kingdom value, the very *heart of God*. We're called to be generous because God has been overwhelmingly generous to us. It is called grace and mercy. We not only don't receive the punishment we deserve (mercy) but are handsomely rewarded despite our previous and frequent unrighteousness (grace).

This is why Jesus told the parable of the unmerciful servant. A man who owed an overwhelming debt that could never be repaid by a lifetime of work was released from all obligation by a generous king. He responded to his unmerited freedom by grabbing a fellow slave by the collar and demanding he pay up immediately for a debt a fraction of what he'd been forgiven. All who originally heard this parable, and read it today, are outraged by this wicked ingrate! But not only have we *all* been guilty of this kind of behavior, but we live in a culture where it is expected, and yes, *celebrated*. Aren't you thankful we have been called to a kingdom that measures differently? Well... *aren't you*?

Treasure

Compassion over Success

> *Of course we'll be there.*
>
> (Convoy of Hope aid worker, on the border of Ukraine as war broke out with Russia in 2022)

Quick, give Jesus's definition of success . . .

Okay, what did you come up with? I've heard a lot of good ones. I've even come up with a few of my own. Though they seem to have slipped my mind. The question is, how similar is our definition to what we hear in our world? Because while these "empire slogans" may sound good, the reality is another story. Mostly a *bad* story.

The story might *start* out and *appear* to be good for a time. But appearances are deceiving, and the destination is destruction. In no area is this more visibly apparent than with money. A recent country song agrees money can't buy happiness, but nevertheless celebrates it can buy a boat. This is true, but where is said boat headed? Those who pursue money above all else are eventually going to run out of water, no matter how big the lake or how long the river. Unfortunately, not only do they lose their boat, but they shipwreck their lives. You've seen it. I've seen it. But are we currently leaving a wake as we pursue it? Are *we* launching out the front door into the wild blue seas of life with our compass set on that very same island of dead man's bones?

We must be honest with ourselves. The very air we breathe and waters we navigate in our culture loudly declare what success is, and we far too often breathe deep and navigate with a broken compass, just like everyone else. But Jesus came to declare and offer a *much better way!* The sobering words of Jesus bear repeating (see letter *A*):

> *You can enter God's kingdom only through the narrow gate. The highway to hell is broad, and its gate is wide for the many who choose that way. But the gateway to life is very narrow and the road is difficult, and only a few ever find it. (Matthew 7:13–14)*

This warning (and invitation) from Jesus refers specifically to his teaching. His teaching leads to life but the road is hard. Not only do few find it but fewer still *choose* it, though it is offered to all. Thus, we must hang on every word of Jesus because *each one* leads to either life or death. Jesus cares about all of our pursuits, especially as it relates to our treasure.

One area of our treasure Jesus doesn't mince words about is our ministry to the poor. Yes, Jesus said the poor would always be with us and we should prioritize worshipping him with our resources. However, the poor were *always* a priority of Jesus. He not only challenged his hearers with his teaching, but he *hung out with* the poor. Fishermen weren't in the upper class, to say the least. Nor shepherds, who *were* the least. Sure, he'd attend a party at a rich person's house, but it often didn't end well for the host.

If you want to be clear on Jesus's priority calling, we do well to turn and return to *Matthew 25*. The scene where the sheep and goats are separated at the final judgment. By the way, Brian Zahnd pointed out something I'd always missed in this story in one of his recent sermons. God isn't just talking to individuals; he's talking to empires! We might need to come back to that. For now, here is the king's *compassion calling*:

> Then the King will say to those on his right, "Come, you who are blessed by my Father, inherit the Kingdom prepared for you from the creation of the world. For I was hungry, and you fed me. I was thirsty, and you gave me a drink. I was a stranger, and you invited me into your home. I was naked, and you gave me clothing. I was sick, and you cared for me. I was in prison, and you visited me." (verses 34–36)

People over Stuff

> The greatest resource in the Kingdom of God is people.

Need I say more? We all love our stuff. But as I heard from a missionary who lost his entire household while overseas, "It's *just* stuff." It has been said, "Don't collect stuff; collect memories." I would make one *major* tweak: "Don't collect stuff; collect *people*." Relationships are the greatest treasure in the Kingdom of God. Actually, relationships are really the *only* treasure in the Kingdom of God. So we must fill our treasure chests to overflowing with friends and our Easter Baskets with *peeps*! When asked how many covenant relationships a person is capable of, Doug Coe answered simply: "Thousands." Let's go and do likewise.

The Upside-Down & Backwards Kingdom Economy

Here are a few more kingdom paradoxes I've collected relating to treasure:

- We are *not* in it to win it. We're called to lose it all, that we might gain everything.[1] (Andy Stanley)
- He is no fool who gives what he cannot keep to gain what he cannot lose. (Jim Elliot)
- The true measure of generosity is not how much you give but how much you have left. (Unknown)
- *People look at the outward appearance, but the LORD looks at the heart. (1 Samuel 16:7)*
- *But many who are the greatest now will be least important then, and those who seem least important now will be the greatest then. (Matthew 19:30)*

The Final Treasure Hunt

> *Now give me my horizon.*
>
> (Captain Jack Sparrow)

Speaking of boats, why is it that pirates get a pass in our world? These *filthy animals* were murdering thieves who raped and pillaged roughshod over the seven seas and all the unlucky souls in their paths. But now we celebrate these scurvy seadogs with the most popular ride at Disneyland, in movies, and by dressing up as them at Halloween. And, as Jim Gaffigan points out, "We think its adorable! It's so cute, he looks just like one of those sociopaths that terrorized the Caribbean."[2] I'm guilty on all charges. I loved my pirate costume back in the day. *Argh!*

But as we consider our primary life pursuit, let's remind ourselves of the destination of pirates of all persuasion. For those who avoided walking the plank, a hangman's noose was waiting for them upon capture. And those who avoided capture ended up with their bones mixed in with the treasure. But not for long, as the bones were left behind by the new

---

1. Stanley, *Not In It To Win It*.
2. Jim Gaffigan, Cinco, 2017 Comedy Dynamics. 06–13-2017.

owners of the *pieces of eight*. And the story repeats itself all the way to the present day. We never learn. But Paul did, so we'll give him the last word on our quest for real treasure:

> *Three things will last forever—faith, hope, and love—and the greatest of these is love. (1 Corinthians 13:13)*

Unexpected

When Israelites heard the phrase "kingdom of God,"... They thought about a day when God would crush Rome and give Israel their own king.[1]

(JOHN ORTBERG)

> To say that Jesus was not the Messiah the Jewish nation expected, or wanted, is a king-sized understatement.

Announcing the Kingdom

Israel wanted an end to Roman occupation . . . and the Romans. The Roman leaders most often led with cruelty and an iron fist, terribly oppressing the people of God, as the Egyptian Pharoah had done generations earlier. Only this time it was done in the land of promise. They grew up reading about Saul and David; thus they fully expected Messiah to be a warrior king with a giant sword (David carried Goliath's after all), and ready to wield it.

1. Ortberg, *Who Is This Man*, 503.

We now know God had other plans, that didn't require swords and spears. But it did require a hammer and nails. The people were ready to follow Jesus up the hill to watch him take over, not to watch him die. They had seen that story before, *many times,* with would be messiahs whose campaigns ended by being strung up by the Romans. That's why they were waving the palm branches (a sign of political rebellion), as they welcomed their king, who surely was coming to take charge and take names, starting with Caesar. They should have known when they watched Jesus ride into town on a young donkey.

> *You know that the rulers in this world lord it over their people, and officials flaunt their authority over those under them. But among you it will be different. Whoever wants to be a leader among you must be your servant, and whoever wants to be first among you must be the slave of everyone else. For even the Son of Man came not to be served but to serve others and to give his life as a ransom for many. (Mark 10:42–45)*

When Jesus told his followers leadership and authority in the Kingdom of God is *different* from the empires of this world, he wasn't kidding. Jesus was all about embracing the populace who were in the slave sector, not hobnobbing with the ruling class. He showed them the full extent of this on the cross, demonstrating his is a kingdom of *humility, sacrifice, mercy,* and *love*. The political oppressors had nothing but contempt for these values. The religious power mongers slunk back down the hill to their lairs, convinced they had executed another pretender, and that the *real* messiah was still on the way, sword in hand. Perhaps even Goliath's. Jesus was not their kind of king and therefore, most missed both the king and the kingdom. And so can we.

Picturing the Kingdom

Those who grew up in Sunday School probably remember the story of Gideon. It's yet another scriptural tale of Israel, as the overwhelming underdog, winning the day. Most have heard of the triumph of David over Goliath, Sunday School or not. David chose five smooth stones from the brook, but only needed one. David finished Goliath off with the giant's own sword, but the small stone was the ammunition of deliverance.

Unexpected

The story of Gideon's deliverance is a similar script, but with different "weapons." Both armies of Israel were vastly outnumbered. King Saul's army had faced and defeated the Philistine army, with their iron chariots, and their giant champion. But Gideon's army, numbering 32,000, looked down on the valley at a Midianite and Amalekite army spread out *"like a swarm of locusts,"* with camels *"as countless as the sand on the seashore."* (Judges 7:12, BSB) But no worries Gideon, for God was going to tip the scales. But unexpectedly, he turned the odds further in the favor of Israel's enemies by culling Gideon's army down to a mere 300! I don't want to ruin the story for you if you don't know the ending, but suffice to say, 300 was enough.

But what about Gideon's weapons? They were armed to the hilt and ready for battle, brandishing . . . *trumpets, jars,* and *torches!* Huh? You mean swords, spears, and catapults, right? Nope. A most unexpected twist for a God who won't share his glory with the armies of men, Israel or not. His *finger,* in the form of singing and shouting (Jericho), a donkey jaw (Samson), a brook stone, ram's horn, water jug, or staff *always* tips the scales. It violently tipped it in favor of the empire of Israel back in the Old days. Now it *lovingly* tips the kingdom scale, like a heavy hammer on a carnival game. *Tilt!*

Kingdom A, B, C's

Life in the Kingdom

The longing in Jesus's day was the longing for the kingdom of God. The question in Jesus's day was, 'How will it be brought to earth?'[2]

(JOHN ORTBERG)

Not only was the king unexpected, but so was everything surrounding him. His followers. His teaching. His actions. His intentions. His life. His death. But should it have been? The following are some of the biggest unexpecteds from the life of Jesus.

An Unexpected Plan

My favorite modern Christmas song, "A Strange Way to Save the World," tells the nativity story from the perspective of Joseph. Have you heard it? If not, stop where you are and get it playing on your iPod before you continue reading. Oh stop, where do you think *Pod*cast came from? Anyway, I recommend 4Him's version of the song. Yes, they even used electric instruments back then.

My point, along with my quartet of singers, is not only was this king unexpected, but so was his *unorthodox* plan (meditate on that irony for a moment). Joseph wasn't the only one thinking this, then and now. He just had a ringside seat for what seemed to be the worst plan of salvation for the world in the history of, well, *that*. Let there be no doubt the Kingdom of God Jesus is ushering in is not using the broken template of empire. And let the record show . . . it worked! But many still can't see it.

God's plan for your life and mine will be just as *strange*. If you haven't experienced this yet, just give it time. I was on the good ship *Will of God* for the first forty-five years of my life, shouting "Woohoo!" all the way. And then the bottom dropped out of my life for the next decade. Steven Curtis Chapman captured it perfectly when he sang about hitting the bottom, and then having it give way. Yeah, *that*. I'm now experiencing *that* today. Jesus wasn't kidding when he promised:

> Here on earth you will have many trials and sorrows. But take heart, because I have overcome the world. (John 16:33)

---

2. Ortberg, *Who Is This Man*, 507.

Unexpected

The question remains, then, why we're so surprised when the unexpected happens to us. It especially remains for me, as I don't relish a *different* script. *Are you listening God? It's me, Jay.* Sigh.

An Unexpected Announcement

Contrary to the protests of the religious elites of Jesus's day, and ours, Jesus the Messiah was *clearly* announced in the Old Testament. It's hard to believe they could possibly have missed it. Josh McDowell carefully catalogued the Old Testament prophecies made hundreds of years before the birth of Jesus, in his seminal apologetic book Evidence That Demands a Verdict. According to McDowell, there are sixty *major* Old Testament prophecies regarding the Messiah directly fulfilled in Jesus, including:

- His name (Immanuel)
- Where Messiah would be born (Bethlehem)
- Who Messiah would be born to (A virgin)
- The lineage of Messiah (Tribe of Judah, Line of David)
- Presented with gifts (Magi)
- Sold for thirty pieces of silver (Sanhedrin religious elites to Judas Iscariot)
- Side pierced, no bones broken (By a Roman soldier after crucifixion)
- And speaking of riding into town on a young donkey:

> *Rejoice greatly, Daughter Zion! Shout, Daughter Jerusalem! See, your king comes to you, righteous and victorious, lowly and riding on a donkey, on a colt, the foal of a donkey.* (Matthew 21, MSG)

You can't make this stuff up. You *literally* can't make this stuff up! I listed just eight of the sixty from McDowell's scholarship. McDowell states the probability of just these eight prophecies being fulfilled in one person is a probability of *1 in 10 to the 17th power*. Since I've already admitted to being a poor excuse of a mathematician, I'll let this unforgettable illustration that demands a verdict speak for itself:

> In order to help us comprehend the staggering probability, (Peter) Stoner illustrates it by supposing that we take 10^{17} silver dollars and lay them on the face of Texas. They will cover all of the

state two feet deep. Now mark one of these silver dollars and stir the whole mass thoroughly, all over the state. Blindfold a man and tell him that he can travel as far as he wishes, but he must pick up one silver dollar and say that this is the right one. Just the same chance that the prophets would have had of writing these eight prophecies and having them all come true in any one man, from their day to the present time, providing they wrote them according to their own wisdom.[3]

God is saying: "Let there be no doubt! It has happened just as the prophets announced and all should have expected." Despite the clarity of the Scriptures, they weren't *looking* for a Messiah like Jesus. We can miss it in *exactly* the same way. Mathematically speaking.

An Unexpected Invitation

I mentioned earlier the invitation to follow a Rabbi, in the time Jesus wore sandals, was akin to receiving news you'd been admitted to Harvard. The first followers of Jesus couldn't have been more shocked, nor could those who witnessed their calling. A rag-tag bunch if ever there was one. But unlike others who hesitated when Jesus invited, the twelve each said: "I'm in!" They weren't the first captive audience of Jesus (remember the temple when he was all of twelve years old?), but they became the *most* captivated.

Jesus continued to hand out unexpected invitations throughout his ministry. Zacchaeus. Nicodemus. Mary Magdalene. The woman at the well. The woman caught in adultery. Slaves. Prostitutes. Beggars. The list goes on and on to the present day. The invitation, of course, was to follow him. But Jesus illustrated and displayed it in the most compelling way imaginable. A banquet. But not just any banquet . . . *the* banquet. To an audience who spent most of their lives food insecure, this was an invitation not to be ignored. And this audience, who were largely the misfits from the margins of society, would end up entering the Kingdom of God *first*, just as Jesus said they would.

Jesus told the story of a rich man who prepared a great feast and sent his servants out to his important and worthy friends. They all responded with lame excuses. Let's pick up the parable right there:

---

3. Stoner, *Science Speaks*, quoted in McDowell, *The New Evidence That Demands a Verdict*, 193.

> *The servant returned and told his master what they had said. His master was furious and said, "Go quickly into the streets and alleys of the town and invite the poor, the crippled, the blind, and the lame." After the servant had done this, he reported, "There is still room for more." So his master said, "Go out into the country lanes and behind the hedges and urge anyone you find to come, so that the house will be full. For none of those I first invited will get even the smallest taste of my banquet." (Luke 14:21–24)*

Obviously, Jesus was talking about more than a table full of sumptuous food with quality entertainment. He was talking about the Kingdom of God. Those who should have been the first to enter, the Jews, and especially the religious leaders of the Jews, were those who made the lame excuses. The poor, the crippled, the blind, and the lame were literally those, but also represented the misfits and the marginalized of all mis-shapes, odd-sizes, and faded colors. And they came! And they're still coming.

The *primary* ministry of Jesus was to the marginalized and misfits. This was the good news for the poor the Scriptures promised. But unfortunately, it seems it is news to the western church that this is to be *our* primary ministry. Jesus could not have made that more clear, in fact just a few verses earlier in Luke's account. At one of the banquets Jesus had been invited to, he noticed the invited guests were jockeying for the best seats. Shocker. Then he shocked all present by advising people to select the lowest place at the table: *"For those who exalt themselves will be humbled, and those who humble themselves will be exalted." (verse 11)*

But he wasn't finished with the shock therapy. He went on to scold the host, and all would be hosts, for just inviting those who could repay the favor. There is no kingdom reward waiting for that (are we listening?). *"Instead, invite the poor, the crippled, the lame, and the blind." (verse 13)* We all (including me) must hear this again: Our *primary* ministry isn't to the important, the rich, the healthy, and the normal. It is to the misfits. To the marginalized. To the forgotten. To the broken. To the poor. In my beloved country music terms, our ministry is to the outcasts from the outskirts! We must always remember:

> *God chose the foolish things of the world to shame the wise; God chose the weak things of the world to shame the strong. (1 Corinthians 1:27, NIV)*

Hasn't God chosen the poor in this world to be rich in faith? Aren't they the ones who will inherit the Kingdom he promised to those who love him? (James 2:5)

An Unexpected Ending

Most of the stories of Jesus (parables and real life) had unexpected endings. They weren't just plot twists either. They were plot *cluster bombs*. Those of us who go to the movies expect we'll be treated to a happy ending, or at least a satisfying plot resolution. With Jesus you just never knew. A Samaritan the hero of the story? The widow who gave two copper coins gave the most? The prostitute who interrupted the banquet will be remembered and celebrated forever? Didn't see those coming. The religious leaders never did seem to see them coming, either, even when Jesus gave them hints their behavior was about to be the punchline. Little wonder the crowds so delighted in his teaching, even though they often returned home scratching their heads. Jesus must have had a sore mouth from smiling, or hiding his smile!

The crowds didn't expect the "ending" of the earthly ministry of Jesus to be on skull hill, ready to join the many others (skulls that is) who had been crucified, would be Messiah's or not. I heard recently that on *one day* the Romans crucified over 6,000 Jews. That's significantly more than the population of Nazareth. No wonder the crowds were waving the palm branches when Jesus entered Jerusalem for the "last time." Life under the Romans was *bloody awful* (to my readers from England, please excuse my French). Ha!

But there was one *accuser* who wasn't surprised by the death of Jesus on Golgotha hill. He had been plotting it all along, using the witless and the wicked alike (he still does). His plan worked out perfectly, with hardly a hitch during passion week (although Pilate's hesitation probably caused a bit of concern). But if you've heard Carman's classic song *The Champion,* you've laughed out loud when the Father began counting backward, instead of forward, after the "knockout blow" at the end of the fight. If you haven't, dear children, please humor me once again. It's a fantastic (and fun!) depiction of the unexpected *shock and aw*e experienced by the forces of hell when their brilliant plan led to their empire's ultimate destruction. And to the brilliant light of New Creation which exploded into the cosmos on that first Easter Sunday. What an ending! What a *beginning*.

As I close this letter, I must spoil the ending for you if you haven't read to the end of Scripture. No, I won't explain Revelation as there just isn't time. But I certainly understand all of it. I'm a doctor, remember. Actually, as your doctor, I must prescribe to you that if someone claims to have *the* interpretation of this book of symbols, *run!* Seriously. But one of the symbols I'm most fond of is . . . wait for it . . . *a banquet*. Shocker. But not just any banquet . . . *the* banquet. The Marriage Supper of the Lamb. It's the *best* symbol for the Kingdom of God. We've all been invited, but we must in faith RSVP. You have a reserved seat waiting for you and, spoiler alert, it's in the VIP section. So don't worry about where you're sitting at the feasts of the empires, or even if you're invited. Most of the royals will be *royally shocked* by this ending, anyway. But not the royal heirs of Jesus. The children of God can see it coming and, *surprise*, will be sitting at the big people table.

Woohoo!

Vessels

This looks like the humble cup of a carpenter.

(INDIANA JONES)

Announcing the Kingdom

Ahoy, fellow adventurers! We're back on the treasure hunt, but not for gold doubloons or jeweled goblets. We're seeking vessels—and surprise! We're not the hunters, but the hunted. God himself is seeking vessels of all shapes and sizes to fill with his divine treasure. Ready to embark on this quest? "I say, seadogs and scallywags, there are *vessels* on dem der islands. Hoist the main sail!"

We've already re-introduced Professor Indiana Jones as our ideal guide. He sure beats a rum-soaked, one-eyed captain who will make you walk the plank at the slightest provocation. Or "cut you out" of your share of the loot (You dig. You die. You dig?). Indy is smarter, more industrious, courageous, and trustworthy. He wasn't out for personal gain at any cost on his quests for the world's greatest treasures. That's why he was able to figure out the clues and make it past the saws, trapdoors, and faith bridge, into the sacred vestibule housing the Holy Grail (and the fakes). Say it with the ancient knight, "You must choose, wisely." And he did! Roll the credits.

Again, when it comes to the quest for vessels, we're the hunted. God himself has created, and is *today* pursuing, vessels of all colors, shapes, and sizes to fill (to overflowing) with his divine treasure. Jesus even tells us what that treasure is. *Water.* Huh?

> *Anyone who is thirsty may come to me! Anyone who believes in me may come and drink! For the Scriptures declare, "Rivers of living water will flow from his heart." (When he said "living water," he was speaking of the Spirit, who would be given to everyone believing in him.) (John 7:37–39)*

Living water. The Holy Spirit. Treasure beyond compare. All simply for the asking, seeking, and knocking. Jesus himself will even do the pouring.

So we must choose. Do we want to beat feet after coins, candlesticks, and crates, or do we want to *become* the vessels God has *designs* for, *dreams* for, and *desires* for? It's not much of a choice if we can overcome the glitter, glamour, and girth of those fakes that, like Indy's protagonist found out the hard way, will in the end *kill us*. It's true. So is this:

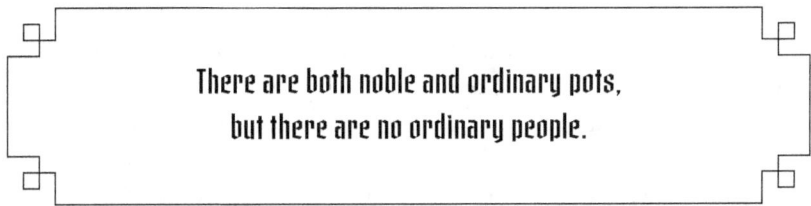

There are both noble and ordinary pots, but there are no ordinary people.

We'll get to more on the pots in a moment, but I must first stress the kingdom value of people. I'll say it again, the Kingdom of God is all about relationships. This is the true treasure of God's kingdom. He gives us the Holy Spirit so we can join the "divine dance" of the eternal community. The Trinity. So we can know and be known by the Father, Son, and Holy Spirit. So we can experience eternal relationship (life) with God himself.

But here's yet another kicker: We *all* become royals. Children born not just of natural descent but born of God. Therefore, there are no royals or commoners. No paupers or princes. No clergy or laity. No male or female. No Jew or Greek. No educated elites or illiterate peons. Oh, and no American citizens, or any others. We are all *one* in Christ Jesus, citizens of the kingdom, and each vessel has intrinsic and infinite worth. Not to mention the *one* vessel we form as the Body of Christ.

Speaking of *one* vessel, it must be noted that there is One who *is* the Holy Grail. When *he finds us,* the quest is over. The ultimate vessel, the ultimate human, the incarnate Christ himself overflows into each one of us the blessed and promised Holy Spirit. And what we end up with are vessels, and a vessel, filled and fit for a king!

The final kicker: Not just any vessels. *Holy grails.* The word Christian, which I'm not fond of (nor is most of the world), can be translated *little Christs.* It was originally meant as pejorative mockery, but it caught on with the early followers of *the Way.* It's a great image, actually. So if we are little Christs then it follows we are *little holy grails.* Yes, that's it!

Humble cups of the carpenter.

Picturing the Kingdom

Have you ever been smashed? No, not *that* kind of smashed. Perhaps it's better to ask if you've ever been smashed up? Smashed to pieces? Had a busted heart? I'll never forget the day, January 7, 2021 (the USA will never forget the day before). It was the worst day of my life. I hope this will remain true for my remaining days. On that day I was given, within quick succession, two pieces of awful personal news. The first was the results of an ultrasound of my first grandchild, showing significant and insurmountable physical realities for Caroline Joy. The second was legal papers delivered via email notifying me one of my best friends and mentors was threatening serious legal action against me. It was akin to two bunker busting bombs penetrating to the deepest parts of my heart and blowing it to pieces.

It wasn't until years later, with the help of a couple of therapists, medical doctors, and medications, along with the comfort and encouragement of close friends and family, that this Humpty Dumpty was slowly pieced back together again. *Years* later. But I also made a *cool* discovery. I learned about the Japanese art of Kintsugi. Literally translated as "join with gold," Kintsugi is the art of repairing broken objects, often ceramic pottery or glass, with liquid gold. What results is a vessel not only *more* beautiful, but stronger as well. I pray my busted heart will someday resemble the masterpiece you see pictured here. It is a slow work in progress.

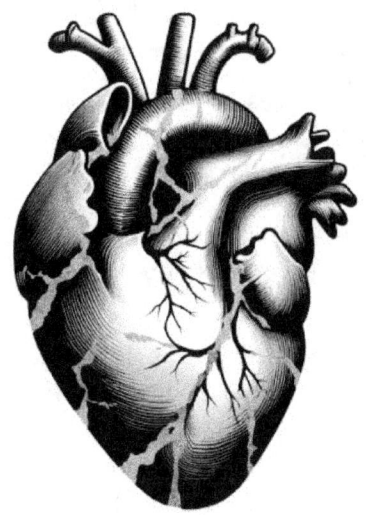

God is the master of repairing broken things. That is *all* he works on, after all. If you believe your heart is the only one that has been broken in two, or smashed to pieces, I have good news and bad news. The good news is you're *not alone*! The bad news is you're *not* alone. Our God doesn't just offer conversion to a religion. He offers transformation into a child of God. He doesn't just offer us a broom and dustpan to clean up our broken lives. He breathes on our shards and just like the bones in the valley of Ezekiel's vision, the pieces get put back in place and life is *fully* restored.

And not only does Jesus pour the living water of the Holy Spirit, but he also pours the *divine gold* of healing and his masterpiece is restored to even greater glory, strength, and usefulness. God transforms our brokenness into beauty. It is little wonder Paul, of badly broken body but vibrant spirit, says:

> *That's why I take pleasure in my weaknesses, and in the insults, hardships, persecutions, and troubles that I suffer for Christ. For when I am weak, then I am strong. (2 Corinthians 12:10)*

Life in the Kingdom

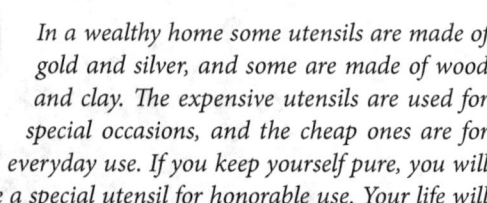

> *In a wealthy home some utensils are made of gold and silver, and some are made of wood and clay. The expensive utensils are used for special occasions, and the cheap ones are for everyday use. If you keep yourself pure, you will be a special utensil for honorable use. Your life will be clean, and you will be ready for the Master to use you for every good work. (2 Timothy 2:20–21)*

Now, before we put the pieces of this letter together, I need to address the elephant in the room. Poor elephants and monkeys, as it seems to always be a bad thing if they're in the room or on our backs. However, I must tell you just this past week I was in the same room as Lenny, my first grandson, and his blue stuffed elephant. It was *Horace,* of Dr. Seuss fame, and we played our first game of catch with this cuddly chap. But we were most gentle and didn't drop him once. Prodigy.

The big, bad, and blue elephant of which I speak is the misunderstanding and misapplication of the verse you see above. I allude to the inspired words of Paul:

> *There is no longer Jew or Gentile, slave or free, male and female. For you are all one in Christ Jesus. (Galations 3:28)*

The question is, do we *really* believe this? It's quite PC these days, *quite* unlike in the days of Paul and Jesus, so perhaps you were nodding your head in agreement. However, the reality in most institutions still eludes equality by a large margin. Dare I say especially in religion? Okay then, I will say it: *Especially in religion.* Culturally illiterate followers of all three branches of the trunk of Abraham (Jewish, Muslim, Christian) use these out of (cultural) context verses like a club.

I hope you winced, because we have *all* done it. So if you're a woman you simply haven't had the same access in the mosque, synagogue, or parish. And you still can't expect to be invited to train for rabbi, imam, or priest. And don't think you're off the hook as a protestant, because our history is also checkered in a black and white that Jesus (and Paul) don't subscribe to. We of all people, as people of faith, should get this right because Paul also put it in black and white, leading in to, and immediately after the verse above. I'll use an ellipse for the previous verse:

Vessels

For you are all Children of God through faith in Christ Jesus. And all who have been united with Christ in baptism have put on Christ, like putting on new clothes . . . And now that you belong to Christ, you are the true children of Abraham. You are his heirs, and God's promise to Abraham belongs to you. (Galations 3:27, 29)

Religious elites sit in the choir of the cathedral, right in front of the altar, while the commoners sit in the back behind a dividing wall? Just wrong. Churches are led by the "gold and silver vessels" while those of wood and clay do the commoners work? Come on. A large chasm between the most spiritual and the ragamuffins based on works? *Heresy.* I must stop or I'll be jumping out of my seat and screaming at the unsuspecting patrons in my favorite coffeehouse. For we are *all* children of God through faith in Jesus, of intrinsic and infinite worth, *none* ordinary among us!

There is, however, a difference in *pots*. Some are noble. Some are ordinary. This is not a contradiction to my recently completed rant. Here's how I see it: *Pots* refer to lives that are lived. Yours. Mine. Everyone. Yes, God does have a unique calling on each of our lives. He has good works in mind for *all of us* we can either obey and lean in to, or rebel and run away from (like Jonah, with rather slimy results). And like Jesus, he may have a "cup" of suffering for us. But that doesn't equate to the one in charge, the one in robes, or the one with the fanciest degree having greater *value* than the others. Quite the opposite, according to Jesus. So how do we embrace God's unique and ultimate calling on our lives?

God's Design For us is *Purity*

The difference in the utensils noted above is first their *purity.* By this I don't mean, nor does Paul, strict adherence to the law. Paul is flat out arguing against this in the letter to the Galations, who were being "bewitched" by religious legalists. I wish that crowd wasn't still with us, but they are. Pick your religion. Pick your culture. Pick your brand. Yes, God is calling us to a righteous life. But that life is characterized by faithfulness, love, and peace (See *2 Timothy 2:22*). It is characterized by making things right. It is ultimately characterized by love (See, well, the entire New Testament). *That*, my friends and fellow followers, is what purity is all about. And it is well within reach of all.

God's Dream For us is *Wholeness*

The religious among us also demand *holiness*. Yes, Paul too. However, holiness is less about moral perfection and much more about being "set apart" for the exclusive joy and use of the Creator (honorable and prepared for all manner of good works). But as our wonderful master, he knows we need to be whole. *Wholey,* if you will. Not only without a spot or wrinkle, but ultimately without a shard out of place or a bone missing. Thus was one of the primary works of Jesus on earth to bring healing. Physical. Emotional. Social. Mental. Soul. Spirit. That is also *still* one of our primary callings. God wants to heal us. *First.*

God also wants us to be healthy. Certainly, in our self-help world that worships youthful energy and bodily perfection, this can be elevated to wildly inappropriate levels. Lesson learned. But I also don't believe God's good, pleasing, and perfect will means we do our level best to rush our arrival in heaven by our poor habits, lack of discipline, or outright stupidity. Again, we're *all* guilty at one time or another, so I'm not throwing stones. I'm just saying being healthy, *truly* healthy, isn't just an empire value. It is a kingdom value, with much happier ends (and means). Yes, despite our best efforts, our bodies will break down. Our hearts will get broken, busted, and shattered. Our minds will eventually slip and then stop. We *will* be persecuted, suffer, and die. Scripture promises. But our king stands with a humble pitcher filled with liquid gold, ready to fill in the cracks and crevices. He stands ready to breathe life into our bones so we might really live. Healed. Healthy. Noble. *Now.*

God's Desire For us is to be *Useful, Purposeful*, and Just Plain *Full*

Finally, God's purpose is to transform us, that the world might be transformed through us. He wants to make things right, and he desires to use you and me. Broken vessels in the slow process of being made whole. Noble *people* living honorable *pots!* Ha! Yes, it is possible, through the ongoing work of the Holy Spirit. We *can* be useful. We *can* be purposeful. We *can* be full. It starts there, actually. Full of living water. Healed by gold. Fully inflated by the breath of God. Vessels holy and honorable, ready to make things right.

Humble cups of the carpenter. Little holy grails. Useful pots. Vessels filled to overflowing with purpose. Prepared for any and every good work. The hunt is over. The treasure overflows. Now let's choose wisely, live righteously, and be *wholey*. Here's the mic-drop from St. Paul:

> *But we have this treasure in jars of clay to show that this all-surpassing power is from God and not from us. (2 Corinthians 4:7, NIV)*

Wonder

> *Wonder is a simple virtue. Like childhood, it's grounded in innocence, taken for granted until it's impossible to reclaim.*[1]
>
> (TIMOTHY EGAN)

Announcing the Kingdom

Childhood is a time of wonder, where every day holds the potential for magic. Whether it's exploring creeks, conquering playgrounds, or dreaming of adventure, we're born with an innate capacity for awe. But as we grow, that sense of wonder often fades. Let's explore how to recapture childlike marvel, especially in our spiritual lives.

You've probably picked up on this already, but I had a *magical* childhood. I was the real-life inspiration behind the TV show The Wonder Years. I had world-class friends in small-town America where we ruled middle-class neighborhoods! We reigned from our bikes with banana seats or on the black-top basketball courts with our red and black rubber balls (Rip City!). We routinely emptied the creek of crawdads and Tastee Treat of its Tangy Taffy. And girls? Not in *our* fort!

I realize not everyone was as fortunate as me in their early years. I had the best of families, and we made the best of memories. But regardless

---

1. Egan, *A Pilgrimage to Eternity*, 161.

of how idyllic your childhood was, we were all created with an onboard and standard capacity for wonder. Somewhere along the way we tend to lose it, however, like our love for school. Like how the spontaneous experiments in the woods with unsuspecting critters somehow gives way to loud yawns in the science lab. What a tragedy.

Equally tragic and equally true is our loss of divine wonder. Sure, we may wonder what God is like or what he's up to from time to time. But to stand in awe at his wonderful works and mysterious ways? To puzzle and scratch our heads he not only knows our name and address, but the running total of hairs on our head (not hard in my case)? To run out of words as we praise him in the sanctuary, lift our hands in our bedroom, or venture a shout from a mountaintop vista? All this and more should be our default reality. Ah, but the cares of this life. The routines. The seemingly brass heavens as we pour out our hearts to a God we're told is listening (he is). Or making the greatest story ever told as dry and lifeless as a dollar store novel. Or reducing it to a simple equation. Or believing we have God, and our theology wrapped up with a bow. *Tragedy.* My friend Sean Silveri recently said, "We cannot worship someone we can fully understand." But we often insist on it and then are shocked when God doesn't do for us what we impossibly expect, or when he seemingly expects the impossible from us. Am I right? I know I am. I have the tattered t-shirt.

There is a much better way, and here it is: *Never lose your childlike wonder. Never. Never. Never.* Some of you fellow history nerds no doubt recognized the words of the most memorable speech given by Sir Winston Churchill, during the Second World War. *Never give in, never give in, never, never, never . . .* England listened, and because of their resolve, they are still speaking English. This was despite the overwhelming odds and overwhelming force of Germany's Third Reich who nearly bombed London into oblivion. I don't like military metaphors for kingdom values, but in the case of Churchill I'll make an exception. England's hero had a backbone of steel.

We must protect our childlike wonder in the same way. The world *will* attempt to press us into its mold, and part of its mold is *certainty* and *control*. Resist! Unfortunately, the world includes religious institutions. We build infallible theologies (they're not) and print boxes of God's promises (many out of context), so we can be *certain in our faith.* Think of the fallacy of that statement. Here's the truth:

> **Having faith requires us to sacrifice our certainty and control on the altar of wonder.**

Don't let any preacher, professor, or politician convince you otherwise. Resist!

And then worship the God of wonder we will never fully understand.

Picturing the Kingdom

Oh Christmas Tree

For most kids, the very thought of going to the forest, the farm, or the Wal-Mart lot to pick out the perfect tree is enough reason to get out of bed early on a day off. When I was a (smaller) kid, I have the fondest memories of going out to the Ochoco Mountains of Central Oregon to find our tree. It was a full day excursion, filled with snow, sledding, indecision, a campfire, hot chocolate, and freezing cold feet. And a long drive home. But we always came home happy! At least us kids did. Ah, the wonder of the season.

I love Brian Zahnd because he is a kingdom guy. He's also a childlike guy. I can give no two greater compliments. Here's another sample:

> The tragedy of growing up is not that we put aside childishness, but that we lose the capacity for *childlike wonder* . . . The simple act of growing up and leaving childhood behind shouldn't be such a catastrophe for our ability to wonder and be enchanted by mystery and beauty . . . Wonder is an essential ingredient if life is to be made livable. Wonder is the cure—the cure for life-killing boredom.[2]

When we grow up, Christmas loses a lot of its wonder. This is not only a tragedy but in Brian's words, a *catastrophe*. It doesn't have to be this way. We can still have an advent calendar where we get to eat a chocolate everyday leading up to Christmas. We can still dream of sugar plums and then wake up early and bound downstairs Christmas morning to open

---

2. Zahnd, *Beauty Will Save the World*, 34, 36–37.

our gifts. And we can still believe in Santa Claus. He was a real person, you know. And maybe, just maybe . . .

I gave a short devotional recently on the *incarnation*. I reminded everyone this is one of the central doctrines of our faith. But Brian puts it another way. He calls it *the greatest wonder of all*. That sounds like a much better devotional. And it surely must be true. How is it possible the only God of the universe, enthroned in glory, would become flesh and *"move into the neighborhood"*? How could Jesus set aside the rights of divinity, without losing it, to become a humble and suffering servant and die at the hands of his creation? How is it possible Jesus could be at the same time both *fully God* and *fully man*? That is the mystery of mysteries . . . the wonder of all wonders!

How is it possible we could lose the wonder of the incarnation . . . the wonder of Christmas? It could be because well-meaning preachers are giving holiday devotionals on central doctrines. Maybe. Or maybe we've just gotten so "grown up" or have heard the story read so many times we've lost the wonder of it all. It is still the greatest story ever told. The greatest wonder. And I still contend it's our greatest doctrine!

Don't lose your sense of wonder, kids, whatever the season. Life is full of it. We must intentionally look for it, pursue it, and believe.

Now go find that perfect tree.

Life in the Kingdom

Waterfalls

Other than Stacie, there are few things I'd rather stare at than a waterfall. Fortunately, for Jay the tour guide in western Oregon, they're everywhere! At the spring runoff there are over two hundred in the Columbia Gorge alone. It just never gets old, especially at the base of Multnomah Falls feeling the spray, with an extra hot latte in hand. That's living, kids. And looking up at the full 620-foot drop? That's *wonder*, kids!

For me the waterfall has become my favorite metaphor for a flourishing life. There are a lot of ways to describe the flourishing life. I introduced theologians Miroslav and Volf and their flourishing triangle, who see it as the ongoing continuum of "life led well, life going well, and life feeling as it should." This continuum is based on Paul's tripartite definition of the kingdom *"righteousness and peace and joy in the Holy Spirit." (Romans 14:17, NIV)* They continue, "What does it mean for life to be led well? It is righteous. What does it mean for life to go well? It is peaceful. And what does it mean for life to feel as it should? It is full of joy." And here is their mic-drop summary: "In Jesus's preaching, the answer to the question of flourishing life was the kingdom of God."[3] Yeah, baby!

God has a flourishing life full of wonder in store and in mind for everyone. No, not everyone can live in the Pacific Northwest. Sorry. But everyone can experience the refreshing of being under the waterfall of God's favor. The rushing stream of his mercy. The cool, clear water of his grace. The sparkling waves of the blessing of God. *Everyone.* That very fact should fill us all with unbridled wonder, because we certainly don't deserve it, child of God or not. The dam of God's love is constantly overflowing. Nothing can hold it back. And he desires, oh how he desires, to *soak* each and every one of his children. A divine super-soaker! Uncontainable dams of love overflowing into our parched world. Unstoppable streams of refreshing flowing into a dry and weary land. Waterfalls of the favor of God pouring over all. This is the will of the Father.

---

3. Volf and Croasmun, *For the Life of the World*, 150, 153, 164.

Mystery

The riddles of God are more satisfying than the solutions of man.

(G.K. Chesterton)

My favorite professor in Bible college was Dennis Leggett. He was the youth ministry guru, so as a YM major that makes sense. However, before I had declared said major, I had Professor Leggett for freshman Bible Survey. Think of a stuffed pantry, with barely room for one more bag of flour, and then pushing hard on the door to get it shut. That was Bible Survey. Then he opened the door and let it all come cascading out. That was the Bible Survey final. Ack! But our dear professor, along with many others, brought the Scriptures to life! But what I respected the most about Dennis (I can call him that now), is when asked a question he didn't know the answer to, he didn't try to fake it. He said the three words all of us would be scholars didn't want to hear; "I don't know." What, you're the BS professor (Ha!) at a Bible college and you don't know the answer to everything? *Get used to it, kids.*

In our Google, and now Chat GPT, culture we still don't like to hear that. Surely *someone* must know the answer. Yes, someOne does. But he doesn't give us all the answers on this side of the thin veil. Not even in the Scriptures. What? It's true. Never forget this: *The Bible isn't meant to resolve all divine mysteries. It is meant to introduce the Divine Mystery to us.* There *are* answers in Scripture, just not *all* the answers. So if your theology has to be airtight and fist on the table certain, then you are one hard-ball question away from a crisis of faith. We *must* be willing to embrace the mystery of faith. We *must* be willing to live with uncertainty. We *must* be willing to allow our faith and doubt to dance.

Everyone loves a good mystery. Some of us grew up with Nancy Drew and the Hardy Boys. We have all watched at least one of the twenty versions of Law & Order (just admit it). And many, like my wife, are hopelessly hooked on true crime shows like Dateline or one of the thousands of podcasts. So why is it when it comes to our faith we cringe, like Dracula at sunrise, at the very thought of there being divine mystery? I know, most end with the crime being solved and the perp doing the time. But not all. If we live our lives demanding answers and living in a small bubble of certainty, then we will certainly miss out. Brian McClaren says it perfectly when he reminds us we are called to live in "a world of wonders versus a world of answers."[4] Don't resist the mystery of faith . . . *embrace it!*

Magic

Everybody also loves a good magic trick. I remember watching master magicians and thinking to myself, "That person has made a deal with the devil!" There is no way to explain what I have just witnessed. Like David Copperfield miraculously getting out of chains in a boat before it plunged off Niagara Falls. He *didn't* . . . the camera didn't lie. Yet, there he was on a ladder hanging off a helicopter, safe and sound as it buzzed the falls. Or some of the America's Got Talent up and comers that literally did tricks right in front of the judges' noses, and our eyes. There is no explanation! Yet, there is. It's *magic*. Yet, it's not. But what great fun the unexplained and impossible is. How did they do that? No way.

But magic comes in more forms than the unexplained. Sometimes there is an explanation, but the reality is too good to be true. Like the moment my oldest son was on my shoulders on Mainstreet USA in Disneyland while we watched the fireworks exploding over the castle. It was the Christmas season, and the Magic Kingdom was decked out for the holidays. The Merriest Place on Earth didn't disappoint, with the daytime holiday parade and the evening electric parade. The Disney characters were at their jolliest, and did I see Donald in a Santa hat? I could've sworn. But the highlight was the snow falling on us as the Christmas music played and the fireworks boomed. It felt like real snow, even though it had been sixty degrees and sunny in Southern California that day. *Magic*. It was. It was a moment neither of us will forget. An animated Tinkerbell somehow flying over Sleeping Beauty Castle. And pyrotechnic stars with golden twinkling tails. How in the world? You know the answer. I have happily had a lot of magic moments in my life. Few compare to that night with Kyle. And where were Calvin and Stacie? Taking another look at the treasure trove in the creepy cave of Pirates of the Caribbean. *Argh!*

Jesus gave his audiences a lot of magic moments, too. His words left them aghast at the end of the Sermon on the Mount, causing them to ask, "Who is this guy?" His first miracle, turning Cana well water into wine, was missed by most at the wedding who had too much to drink already. But the servants didn't. *Magic*. The crippled man who was let down

---

4. McClaren, *Faith After Doubt*, 1172, iBooks.

through the roof to a waiting Jesus who not only healed him in front of a packed house (perhaps Jesus's own house?), but announced his sins were forgiven, too. The cripple in another town who had waited for a miracle by the edge of a pool for *thirty-eight years!* A demoniac filled with a *legion* of demons who got delivered, dressed, and then took the neighborhoods of the Decapolis by storm on *his* bike with the banana seat! Oh, how I hope we can watch the Tik-Tok of that someday. And the day that pigs could fly . . . into the bay. Perhaps the greatest childlike story of them all! Come on now, how do you explain all that? *Magic incarnate.*

Perhaps the most staggering verse in all of Scripture was this promise of Jesus. If you haven't heard it before, you'll need to read it more than once:

> *I tell you the truth, anyone who believes in me will do the same works I have done, and even greater works, because I am going to be with the Father. (John 14:12)*

Jesus wants *us* to be in on the magic. No, not the sleight of hand of the charlatans out for a buck. No, not the smoke and mirrors of the religious elites. And no, not the shift of direction of an amateur imitator. He calls us to *greater works.* How the . . . ? The Holy Spirit, that's how. If you want a life of certainty you can control, then you will surely miss out on the magic God wants you to witness . . . and assist in. Don't miss the boat, and the magic, by getting on the wrong ship (Pirates are everywhere). Or by your lack of faith. He is *still* the God of both the explained and especially the unexplained. The possible and especially the impossible. The ministry and especially the magic!

Where the Wild Things Are

One of my favorite childhood books was this very title. I can't remember a word of it, but I remember the unforgettable images of the monsters. So cool! Cool, too, were the pajamas of the boy who boldly left his room for the moonlit woods and discovered those monsters for himself. It turns out they were friendly. Who knew? He never saw the world the same again. Neither did we.

The *wonderful* question I leave you with is this: Do you want to live an ordinary pot (life), or do you want in on the magic? As I said, we were *all* created to experience divine mystery and unexplained wonder. We were all wired to stand in awe and worship. The magic and the wonder aren't reserved for the experts and the professionals. Remember, there are *no ordinary people*. It begins with a decision to trust. It continues with an ongoing heart of faith, and hands ready to assist. It ends with leaving our bedrooms in our favorite jammies and discovering Where the Wild Things Are.

They've been expecting you.

X

X marks the spot.[1]

(ROBERT LOUIS STEVENSON)

Announcing the Kingdom

What to do with the letter X? There aren't too many good words in the English dictionary to choose from for our kingdom alphabet. Xerox? Xylophone?? Xenodocheionology??? Yes that's a word, though my spellcheck doesn't agree. So instead of trying to shoehorn a word in just to say we've done it, let's go another route. Let's just use the letter. This letter, perhaps more than any other, is itself a word. Multiple words in fact. And multiple images perfect for our childlike purposes. Ironically, X stands for *multiply*, too.

So where to begin? Just there actually . . . at the beginning. At the first square on the Monopoly board. *Go. Start Here.* I stated earlier it really matters where you start, because this largely determines how and where you finish. We discussed already the most significant starting place being Jesus himself. Martin Luther would stress starting with and basing all truth claims on the Scriptures (sola scriptura). Scripture itself assumes

---

1. *Treasure Island* by Robert Louis Stevenson was originally published in 1883 and is now public domain.

the existence of God in the first four verses, "*In the beginning, God.*" If we don't have enough sense to start with this foundational belief, then things get squirrely fast. More on that in a moment.

Of all the images and words X can stand for, there is one that far outweighs them all. Some of you know where I'm going. *Shhh!* But first, have you ever noticed how often Jesus followers get outraged at the world? Unfortunately, *quite* often. I remember when the movie The Last Temptation of Christ was released and the firestorm of protest that ensued. I didn't see the movie, but most every critic believed it was awful (despite what they might have said publicly). Unfortunately, the outrage gave it far more press and revenue than it deserved. There is also outrage about abortion, border security, gay marriage, guns, taxes, and vaccines. Some of it is warranted, certainly. But I wonder if Jesus always shares our outrage. He probably *is* outraged, but perhaps not in the way everyone assumes.

One largely shared outrage in Christendom is taking Christ out of Christmas. You can't spell it without *Christ* after all! He is the reason for the season!! Don't say Happy Holidays . . . it's *Merry Christmas!!!* Some of you are nodding your heads right along, even though we Christ-followers actually commandeered this holiday from the pagans. By the way, you know Jesus wasn't actually born on December 25th, right? Sorry if I just told you there wasn't a Santa Claus. Most scholars believe it was in the spring. Which kind of messes up the calendar. So never mind. But what *really* galled me growing up, was when people had the audacity to use X-Mas instead of Christmas. That's the last straw! Well . . . Language Arts (English & History) to the rescue.

Those with a bit more education than my younger self, realize my outrage was a bit misguided. It turns out X is the symbol for the Greek letter "chi" and thus the first letter in the Greek word for . . . wait for it . . . *Christ*. There's your language lesson. Regarding history, it also turns out the early Christians used X as a secret symbol to indicate their membership in the church of Jesus Christ. That's also where the sign of the fish came from. Well, that's an animal of a different color! I guess I'll have to get a new cause to protest. And new signs. But Christmas is still way too commercialized, so there!

Here is what I'm trying to say in the simplest terms I can. X doesn't just mark the spot:

 X marks the Messiah.

Christ becomes part of a name when it follows *that* name. Jesus Christ. However, Christ alone is a title derived from the Greek word Christos, which translates the Hebrew term *meshiah* (Messiah), meaning "the anointed one." John the Baptist's followers were sent to Jesus with the express instruction of asking, *"Are you the Messiah we've been expecting, or should we keep looking for someone else?" (Matthew 11:3)* Scripture records Jesus told them to look around them at the signs of the kingdom. He saved. He delivered. He healed. What it doesn't record is Jesus reaching down and drawing in the sand, like he did with the woman caught in adultery. Scholars speculate about what he wrote on that occasion. But in this case, I believe he wrote one word. X. And he drew a circle around it.

And then he stepped into the middle of the circle.

Picturing the Kingdom

From secret symbols of early Christians to imperial banners, X has a long history of representing Christ. Let's look at one of its most famous incarnations.

In the early fourth century, Constantine the Great, Roman Emperor from 306–37, popularized this shorthand for Christ. According to legend, on the eve of his great battle against Maxentius, Constantine had a vision that led him to create a military banner emblazoned with the first two letters of Christ on it: chi and rho. These two letters, then, became a sort of shorthand for Jesus Christ.[2]

Unfortunately, this super cool symbol started out as a military image. But I say we commandeer this, too, and take out the camo colors. The emperor Constantine is a glaring enigma in the history of Christianity. On the one hand, when he declared it the state religion of the Roman Empire, the bloody killings of the

2. vox.com

faithful, from crucifixions to colosseums, immediately ceased. *Hallelujah!* said the fourth century saints. Understandably so. For Constantine it was a political move, certainly. It was also a strategic military move to claim to have a deity on the side of your empire.

But it also recognized the incredible influence and social value Christianity had and was continuing to express throughout the empire, despite incredible persecution. But be careful what you wish for because religion and politics *never* mix well. As the saying goes, "power tends to corrupt, and absolute power corrupts absolutely." (Lord John Dalberg-Acton) Marrying political and religious power is a one-way ticket to absolute power, and a temptation too great for *any* to endure. Like the ring of power in Tolkien's Lord of the Rings. *Exactly* like that.

But as a purveyor of semiotics, my tribe of Issachar contends for (re)signing the images and metaphors of yesteryear to serve a much higher purpose in our day. And any symbol that turns our attention to Jesus the Christ is one worth baptizing. So connect the hose and fill the tank. But while you're at it, drop the swords and shields, and let's tattoo this sign of the Christ on our *hearts*. Feel free to put it in ink anywhere else you want if it helps. But as with circumcision, a cut or a tattoo on the heart has *much* greater value. May this symbol remind us, whatever we do, or not do, be . . .

. . . *for the King and his Kingdom!*

Life in the Kingdom

Start Here . . . X

I'll never forget seeing the full page spread in the local newspaper of two groups visiting the Grand Canyon. The first was a group of creationists who see this canyon of canyons as one of the best creation labs in the world. The second was a group of evolutionists who believed the same thing. So how is it two groups, led and filled with ostensibly smart people, could look at the same evidence and arrive at two opposite conclusions? It *really* matters where you start. If you start with a belief in the existence of God, the inspiration of the Scriptures, and the divinity of Jesus Christ, well, your conclusions look drastically different than what is taught in most university Biology, Bible, and Philosophy classes.

This is not to say we ignore evidence from creation or do our best ostrich in the sand imitation. Quite the opposite. Josh McDowell had a video series years ago I showed to my students entitled, Don't Check Your Brains at the Door. Yes, church history is replete with examples of believers doing just that. Galileo comes immediately to mind. However, historically the church has largely led the charge in education, medicine, and yes (gasp!), science. Where would all of these be without the influence of the church? Light years behind, despite what the so-called experts in lab coats say. There are just as many lab-coated experts who are filled with faith and followers of Jesus. Science and Scripture are *compatible*, after all. But if you start by believing there is not a God who has created, you can make the evidence sing your song. But just because you're singing doesn't mean you're in tune. Start with Jesus, Scripture, and the ongoing work of the Holy Spirit, and then raise your voice!

You Are Here . . . X

If you're in a shopping mall, on a long hike, or in a strange city, a reader board with a map used to be your best friend (pre iPhone). And to help you get your bearings, there is always the friendly X showing right where you're standing. *Ah, now I see!* And off you go to Eddie Bauer to get that new quarter zip and beanie. You've got a long hike coming up.

I wish Scripture had a sixty-seventh book, just for me, entitled *The Account of God's Will for Jay*. At the beginning of the book there would be a map with that friendly X in bright red showing me right where I am. Oh, and then a green dotted line showing the precise course for me from A-Z. Of course, all the lines would be the shortest possible between points. It would be just like Candyland, with rainbow trails and gumdrop passes but no molasses swamps or getting lost in lollipop woods on the way to the Candy Castle! But what fun would that be, right? Sigh.

However, Scripture *does* help us get our bearings. It does help us realize where we are and where God wants us to be. We have all started somewhere, but it is never too late to change our thinking and direction (repent), even if it means we must go back several spaces on the board. It's more about direction than speed in the Kingdom of God, anyway. And making the course corrections to stay on the right (rainbow) path. We need the illumination of Scripture and the Holy Spirit to help us know where we are. We're given a divine lamp for our journey, the most powerful of flashlights . . . batteries included:

> *Your word is a lamp to guide my feet and a light for my path. (Psalm 119:105)*

Now tie your Gore Tex boots and let's go, kids. It's adventure time!

What a Difference a Letter Makes

A little "birdie" told me there is even a new company called X.

When I was a senior in college, my dorm mailbox often had a love letter waiting for me. I fell in love with Montana girl during an internship at my home church over the summer prior. She was the youth secretary. I was the youth intern. We ran off together. It was scandalous! And I'd do it all again a hundred times over. So much for repentance. We didn't get far, however, as I was hired there right after graduation. Stacie, however, refused to be my secretary anymore.

I was looking through my memory boxes the other day and found those sweet and sacred missives. Oh my! Stacie was *really* in love with me. How do I know? Because the letters, and envelopes, were full of Xs. and Os. Put those letters together and what do you get? Hugs and kisses. Scandalous! Or sometimes there was just an X. Does that mean a hug or a kiss? I still don't know. But *both* please. However, if there was only space for three letters, pre-marital Stacie had to make sure there was an O in the middle of the Xs. *That* truly would have been a scandal. But she was careful in her communications. I know. I double checked. So how did XXX, or X-rated come to have such a negative connotation? Hmm. I'll let someone else write that book. All I know is one letter can make a big difference. Especially if it is signed by Stacie. *Especially* if it has a circle around it and Jesus is standing in the middle!

So you see, X is a letter that's more than just a placeholder in our alphabet. It's a symbol rich with meaning, from marking treasure on maps to love on letters. But no purpose is more significant, for a letter or a child of God, than representing Christ himself.

X marks the Messiah.

Yield

I will neither yield to the song of the siren nor the voice of the hyena, the tears of the crocodile nor the howling of the wolf.[1]

(GEORGE CHAPMAN)

Announcing the Kingdom

You dream about a lot of things as a kid. Childhood dreams are a kaleidoscope of possibilities. From hitting the winning shot at the buzzer or the home run at the bottom of the 9th inning, our young hearts yearn for greatness. Then our heart's attention turns elsewhere, to beauty and connection. For me, it was a Montana girl. So what do little Montana girls dream of? I'm still not sure I can say for sure. A rodeo buckle? A barn wedding? Somewhere along the way it became an Oregon boy, though. Woohoo! But as the days progressed from slugs, snails, and puppy dog tails to sugar, spice and, *wow nice* (!) . . . there was the opportunity to drive. Which is kinda important if you want the girl. But driving mom & dad's baby blue diesel station wagon? Well, at least I knew she was falling for *me*.

In order for the dream of automotive freedom, and a blonde in shotgun, to become reality there were two big tests that loomed like dark

---

1. Chapman in *Bartlett's Familiar Quotations*, 177:2.

thunderclouds. The written and driving tests. To prepare for that day was high school driver's ed and Mr. Schimpf. After him, the DMV lady was a piece of cake. I even passed both tests on my first try! Well, I had to go home for another piece of ID first, but still.

Of the many lessons to learn, chief among them was learning the signs. Red octagons (hold it!). Orange and black rectangles (take the *long* way). Green (take *that* way), brown (there's something cool ahead), and blue (better stop for gas) squares. Oh, and the black and white rectangle (no, not *that* way!). But perhaps the hardest sign of all to obey, for kids of all ages and driving experience, are the yellow (or red and white) triangles. *Yield*. It's a nice way of saying, "You must give way," or "Don't even think about it"! For those who are control freaks it is the most optional of all signs. Well, I guess there are also the speed limit signs. At least, I think they have those. Moving right along (fast) . . .

We talked all the way back in the beginning about living *fully surrendered* lives. A couple of lines bear repeating (those of Jesus always do):

> But more than anything else, put God's kingship first and do what he wants. Full surrender doesn't stop after we've put down our sword. It has just begun. Because fully surrendered living equals abundant life in the kingdom. When we seek first his kingdom and his righteousness, the upside-down and backwards kingdom kicks in. *(See Matthew 6)*

There is something else that must kick in, as well. *Humility*. Oh, that again. Yeah, sorry. But only if we truly desire the Childlike Kingdom to fully kick in. Otherwise, knock yourselves out, and everyone who dares to get in your way. But Jesus has a much better way in mind for you, me, and those around us. These childlike words are also worth repeating:

> *You must have the same attitude that Christ Jesus had. Though he was God, he did not think of equality with God as something to cling to. Instead, he gave up his divine privileges, he took the humble position of a slave and was born as a human being. When he appeared in human form, he humbled himself in obedience to God and died a criminal's death on a cross. (See Philippians 2)*

We must *continue* to choose wisely. Choosing humility is *always* the wisest option available. However, be advised choosing humility always involves heeding the yellow triangle, on the highway or on any way. Because:

Yield

> The way of childlike humility requires we yield.

Picturing the Kingdom

There is a Childlike Kingdom sign you won't see on the road in your Tesla or Toyota. It is purple, of course. We're on the *royal* highway, after all. And it's shape? It could have been shaped like the simple chalice of a carpenter. Or the foot-washing basin of a slave. Or even a cross. But we wouldn't want anyone to think someone has died, so *that* won't do. Ha! But the yellow triangle is the universal sign for yield, whether there are those words on it or not. So let's keep the triangle, and we can even add more color. Like royal gold. Is that a color? It is now. Whenever you see this Childlike Kingdom sign, let it remind you to *yield*. But in the way of the upside-down and backwards kingdom, here's what it means:

- It means we take the *narrow* road, not the wide.
- It means we take the *low* road, not the high.
- It means we take the *slow* lane, not the fast.
- It means we let *others* go first.
- It might even mean we drive a Ford or Fiat instead of the Tesla or Toyota.

If I'm honest, I'm not sure I like these rules of the kingdom road. If I'm honest, I'm *sure* I don't. It's one thing to read a list of ideals, such as those above, or especially the Beatitudes, and nod assent. Good ideas to consider. Bravo for your good heart. But the kingdom way isn't paved with good intentions, either. It is paved by the resolve of Jesus followers who are intentionally obeying his command to love. To be little. To be last. To be humble. To drive like a child. *That* is the most beautiful, good, and true way. Just look for the purple and gold sign.

See ya on the road!

Life in the Kingdom

We also talked earlier about full surrender being the point where we access the kingdom. When we lay down our sword, when we lay down our very *lives*, life truly begins in the Kingdom of God. But what does a fully surrendered life look like? It begins by losing something.

The Illusion of Control

To get to heaven you must give up control.

(Overheard)

There are myriad illusions in our world, from the hand of the master magician to the desert mirage. But what takes most people a lifetime to discover is control is the ultimate illusion. At the end of the day and the end of our lives, we really don't control *anything* but our responses. Power hungry politicians and kings steal, kill, and destroy their way to power only to find in the end they have only a pile of sand to show for it (including their own). Money hungry bankers, brokers, and hedgers believe they have it all figured out, and then a pandemic strikes. Or a Ponzi-schemer rides off into the sunset with the retirement of thousands.

But it's not just the politicians and money grubbers who are hungry for control. We *all* are. We're hungry for certainty. We're hungry for security. And we're hungry for *more*. All of us. J.D. Rockefeller famously answered, when asked how much money is enough, "Just a little bit more." But if we're wise, we'll realize our tireless efforts for all the above is nothing but a fool's errand. Jesus even asked what it profits a man to obtain all the above and lose his soul. But when we finally come to our senses, and sadly most don't, cease striving and fully surrender, *yield*, we find life eternal, abundant, and out of (our) control!

I Am Second

What does true humility look like? Unfortunately, not much like our religious defaults, machinations, and history. Yet, we're called to follow the example of Jesus (see above). Sigh. How can we keep missing something so critical, so badly? Part of the reason, I believe, is our obsession with winning. But that is *not* our calling. Andy Stanley, the fantastic pastor from north Atlanta, has a book titled *Not* in it to Win it. A-men, Andy. The NBA, NFL, NHL, and MLB can be indulged and enjoyed. But we dare not share their values or role models (in most cases). Sorry, it's just true. But in most cases, we do.

Perhaps another reason is a total misunderstanding of what humility really is and looks like. Well-meaning believers will sometimes say, "I'm a nothing and a nobody from nowhere." Is that what God creates, nothings and nobody's? *No*. We are made in the image of God (imago Dei). We are children of the king. We know humility is not seeing yourself and showing off as higher than you ought. However, it also means we don't see ourselves as worm eaters and lower than we ought. When it comes to humility, we must let Goldilocks be our guide: Not too hot. Not too cold. Not too big. Not too small. Not too hard. Not too soft. *Just right.*

Walking in humility means we put Jesus first. There is a new initiative *started* by the founder of Interstate Batteries (get it?), called I Am Second. You can find it online and it features the stories of those from all walks of life, famous and not, who have learned to put Jesus first and themselves second. That's the perfect way to start. But there must be more to the story. Because living yielded to Jesus also means we live yielded to one another, especially in the body of Christ. We don't just put ourselves in the second chair when Jesus is in the room. We put ourselves in the second chair when *anyone* is in the room. Seriously? That's what Paul means when he says:

> Do nothing out of selfish ambition or vain conceit. Rather, in humility value others above yourselves, not looking to your own interests but each of you to the interests of others. (Philippians 2:3–4, NIV)

In fact, all of Paul's letters are a call to humility in the body of Christ. *This* is how we live as God's children . . . *together*. He who has ears to hear, *yield*.

What a Yoke!

Finally, what does *true* freedom look like? It doesn't look like doing whatever I want, with whoever I want, whenever I want, the exact way I want. In fact, I just heard my new favorite definition of sin: "Meeting my needs in my own way."[2] (Tyler Staton) That sure sounds like freedom, but in the end, we are led away in chains. Here is the good news of the Kingdom of God: *All other kingdoms lead to oppression & slavery.* We are slaves no more! All that is required is taking on the light yoke of the teaching and life of Jesus. *Then* we are free to love, serve, and follow. The "freedom" the empires of this world offer are simply the joke of a court jester. But the freedom of the Kingdom of God is the yoke of a king! A good, beautiful, and true king. And all we must do?

Yield. Yoke. And live second.

---

2. Tyler Staton, sermon November, 2024, delivered in Portland, OR.

Zeal

Do all the good you can, in all the ways you can, to all the souls you can, in every place you can, at all the times you can, with all the zeal you can, as long as ever you can.

(JOHN WESLEY)

> Our compassion must always outweigh
> and outpace our passion.

Announcing the Kingdom

Since you've made it this far you deserve a medal. Or a participation trophy. Remember those schoolhouse reading awards? I still cherish (and have) mine from Crooked River Elementary School. Welcome to our own Roaring Readers club! That certificate sparked my zeal for reading, though I suspect my parents played a bigger role. Isn't it funny how small moments can shape our passions?

Every one of us is passionate about something. Those whose passion burns extra hot are often referred to as zealots. Unfortunately, the religions of the world have more than their share of these. The religious experts and elites of Jesus's day believed their righteous obedience would usher in God's kingdom and throw off the yoke of the Romans. They were zealous for righteousness, but their zeal often dwarfed their love.

All of us have been well-meaning religious experts and elites at one time or another. We don't mean to be, but we can get carried away by our righteous zeal. We want to honor God. We want to serve God. We want to be holy. We believe we're right and others are wrong. Perhaps we've even joined a cause, and we're convinced it is just, and is *just* what the world needs. This all too often becomes a deadly brew.

We love being around people with passion, who are ardent in their pursuits and full of fervor. We are drawn to follow people who burn with passion, even to the death. There are scores of examples from history; good, bad and ugly. Washington? Good. Lenin? Bad. Hitler? *Ugly.* We could all make a list of heroes and villains whose zeal changed the world.

No one who has walked the planet possessed more zeal than Jesus. The clearing of the temple is top of mind. He brandished a whip and turned over tables and called the merchants a pack of thieves? Now we're talking! Indiana Jones, eat your heart out. But it is telling the first followers were as surprised as anyone with this outburst. As they were trying to make sense of it, *"His disciples remembered that it is written: Zeal for your house will consume me." (John 2:17, NIV)* Oh, got it. Unlike Indy, it doesn't sound like Jesus carried the whip around with him. The zeal of Jesus led to all manner of miracles, clashes with the religious establishment, and ultimately to a horrific death he could have called off with a single utterance. Now *that* is zeal!

There is also no question the compassion of Jesus far outweighed and outpaced his passion. Consider again the woman caught in adultery. There were plenty of zealous religious people with rocks in their hands on that occasion. Jesus wasn't one of them. How about the woman at the well? The twelve were rather shocked on this occasion, as well. They had been steeped in animosity toward the Samaritans and were likely less than pleased when they returned from town to find Jesus with *her.* Jesus didn't care. Actually, he did! Jesus healed recklessly, regardless of race, politics, or religion. Jesus loved recklessly, including thieves on surrounding crosses, soldiers pounding nails, or a woman six husbands in. Or was it seven?

How about us? We can be full of zeal, but why is there a rock in *our* hands? We say we love each other, but then we kill (or banish) our own.

Zeal

We are full of passion to worship, to serve, to help, but only on our mountain, in our building, in our organization. But does our passion outweigh our compassion? If it does, Jesus is *not* impressed. We can sing or yell at the top of our voices, give until it hurts, call out the sin and the sinner, and lead the company and the crowds to a brighter future. We can burn with passion, but everything we do *will* burn without love.

Just ask Paul, who wrote the famous love chapter *(1 Corinthians 13)*. There is no question as to *his* zeal, either. Just ask Stephen, whose stoning execution Paul witnessed and approved. He probably had a rock in his hand, too. Fortunately, Jesus got ahold of him before he got to Damascus, or you could add those believers to Paul's tally. Full of zeal he was on his way, with the papers in order, to throw those dangerously misguided Jesus freaks in jail where they belonged, or worse. He believed he was doing God a favor. Jesus begged to differ, saying he was *persecuting* him. But zealously, of course.

Paul makes it clear, in his writing and living, zeal for God isn't a bad thing. But he also makes it abundantly clear it isn't enough. And he serves as an example of how completely evil zeal can become when terribly misguided. It must have the proper *foundation* (love), and the proper *focus* (love), in order to have the proper *fruit* (love). If we're going to be zealous about *anything*, let it be love! I strongly believe when we do:

Our compassion will greatly outweigh and outpace our passion.
Jesus will be pleased.

Picturing the Kingdom

Let's return to the idea of the deadly brew, which comes from our misguided zeal—our whole-hearted pursuit of God based on our righteous acts alone. Obviously, a whole-hearted pursuit of God and his righteousness is a good thing. The question is, why do religious people always seem to want to kill each other? Seriously. How many times does Scripture record the religious experts and elites concluding killing Jesus was the best option? *Seriously.* And these are the religious *leaders*? But they are hardly alone in the scriptural record, as prophet after prophet and follower after follower is killed by the religious establishment of their day.

All the while they believed they were doing God a favor. Fortunately, the worst examples are all recorded in Scripture, right?

Wrong. *Dead* wrong. The killing continued and continues to this day. Holy wars have been waged off and mostly *on* since records have been kept. If you are a religious type, studying history can be downright depressing. The Crusades get most of the press, but they are hardly the exception. Every major religion has blood on its hands. *Buckets* of blood. Obviously, the deities of the Aztecs and Incas weren't the only bloodthirsty ones. Catholics and Protestants killing each other for generations across Europe. Jews and Palestinians killing each other in the Middle East. Christians and Muslims killing each other pretty much everywhere. Jews being exterminated in the name of gods and men, also pretty much everywhere. And we haven't even made our way to the far-east. It is enough to make grown men and women (and God himself) cry. And we zealously believe we're doing God a favor.

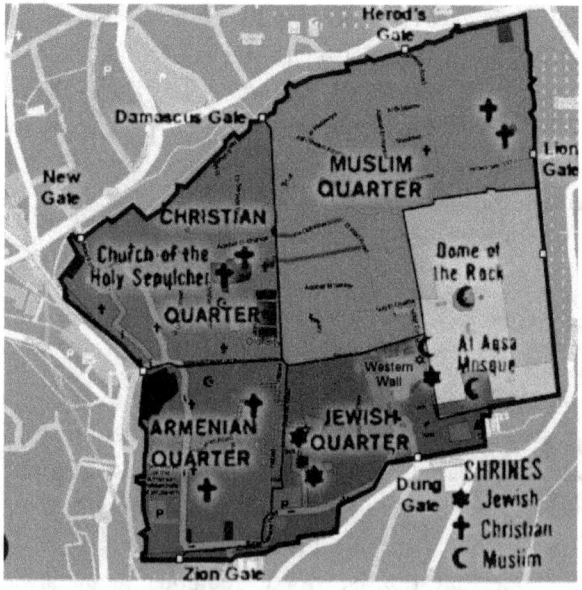

The three religions of Abraham (Jews, Muslims, Christians) all lay claim to the holy city of Jerusalem. For Muslims the Temple Mount, featuring the al-Aqsa Mosque and Dome of the Rock is their third holiest site. For Jews, no site in the world is more holy than where the temples of Solomon and Zerubbabel once stood. For Christians there are many sites in Jerusalem, in addition to the Temple Mount, considered sacred. But how sad, how unbelievably sad, the old city of Jerusalem has been carved up into a Muslim Quarter (including the Temple Mount), a Christian Quarter (including the Church of the Holy Sepulchre), a Jewish Quarter (including the Western Wall), and an Armenian Quarter (including the Citadel). And we all zealously believe we're doing God a favor.

So the next time you see pictures of the Temple Mount, the holy site in the most holy city, let's stop and ask ourselves again, "Why do we religious people keep killing each other?"

Jesus said:

> *I have told you these things so that you won't abandon your faith. For you will be expelled from the synagogues, and the time is coming when those who kill you will think they are doing a holy service for God. This is because they have never known the Father or me. (John 16:1–3)*

He also said:

> *Believe me, dear woman, the time is coming when it will no longer matter whether you worship the Father on this mountain or in Jerusalem . . . But the time is coming—indeed it's here now—when the true worshipers will worship the Father in spirit and in truth. The Father is looking for those who will worship him that way. (John 4:21, 23)*

Or we can keep killing each other.

Life in the Kingdom

A Scriptural Snapshot of Zeal God's Way

If killing in the name of God isn't an acceptable form of worship, what do the Scriptures say we should be zealous about? The following are but a few examples. Please hang on *every* word:

- *This is what the LORD Almighty said: "Administer true justice; show mercy and compassion to one another. Do not oppress the widow or the fatherless, the foreigner or the poor. Do not plot evil against each other." (Zechariah 7:9–10, NIV)*

- *No, O people, the LORD has told you what is good, and this is what he requires of you: to do what is right, to love mercy, and to walk humbly with your God. (Micah 6:8)*

- *Greater love has no one than this: to lay down one's life for one's friends. (John 15:13, NIV)*

- *Dear friends, let us continue to love one another, for love comes from God. Anyone who loves is a child of God and knows God. But anyone who does not love does not know God, for God is love. (1 John 4:7–8)*

- *Love must be sincere. Hate what is evil; cling to what is good. Be devoted to one another in love. Never be lacking in zeal, but keep your spiritual fervor, serving the LORD. Be joyful in hope, patient in affliction, faithful in prayer. Share with the LORD's people who are in need. Practice hospitality. Bless those who persecute you; bless and do not curse. Rejoice with those who rejoice; mourn with those who mourn. Live in harmony with one another. Do not be proud, but be willing to associate with people of low position. Do not be conceited. Do not repay anyone evil for evil. Be careful to do what is right in the eyes of everybody. If it is possible, as far as it depends on you, live at peace with everyone. Do not take revenge, my friends, but leave room for God's wrath, for it is written: "It is mine to avenge; I will repay," says the LORD. On the contrary: "If your enemy is hungry, feed him; if he is thirsty, give him something to drink. In doing this, you will heap burning coals on his head." Do not be overcome by evil, but overcome evil with good. (Romans 12:9–21, NIV)*

I had to keep the last passage fully intact as it gives us the perfect description of a perfect love which should be the hallmark of our faith communities. Perhaps we should read it again. It's not only a mouthful but a mission to be zealous about!

Speaking of killing each other, zeal without love manifests the grim reaper in all areas of life, including:

- **Our Bottom Line.** Do we value profit over people?
- **Our Charity/Cause.** Do we believe ours is the only important one?
- **Our Candidate.** Does it ultimately matter if our candidate or party wins?
- **Our Team.** Does it ultimately matter at all?

- **Our Country.** Does God love countries or people?
- **Our Success.** Is *my* success all that matters?
- **Our Issue.** What is *truly* a matter of life and death?

The question is, do the ends always justify the means? Zeal would say yes. Love would say no. It is not enough for us to be passionate about whatever it is that drives us. *Compassion driven by love and led with mercy must win the day.*

Zeal to Love > Zeal for Righteousness

As we prepare to close shop on this final letter, I want to make it clear what I am *not* saying. Zeal is not a bad thing. Scripture commends many for their zeal, including Jesus. However, when zeal for righteousness is elevated above our greatest life calling, love for God and neighbor, then it is a recipe for disaster. There are many who believe their righteous zeal is justified as an expression of love to God. Yes, and no. But if our zeal for righteousness means we become judgmental, hateful, arrogant, rude, or violent to our neighbors then we are most decidedly *out* of the will of God. There is simply no justification, as God's loving ambassadors, for us to represent him as a cranky and impossible to please father who is ready to throw a lightning bolt at the slightest provocation. That is Zeus, by the way, *not* our benevolent, compassionate, and righteous king.

Yes, Scripture is full of injunctions, commands, and pleas for us to live holy and righteous lives. Be zealous about that! But we do it because we *love* our triune God and desire to please and glorify him, not in a vain attempt to be saved from an angry God or gain favor from a hard to please tyrant. We'll reserve that for the emperors and other politicians who are more passionate for power than zealous for righteousness. Remember, righteousness is less about achieving perfection and more about putting things *right*, in our hearts and especially in our world. *That* will be worth reading (and roaring) about. *That* will be beautiful, true, and good.

A-men.

The Final Bridge

London's Tower Bridge (1886)

I need to plug in my book.

(3RD GRADE STUDENT)

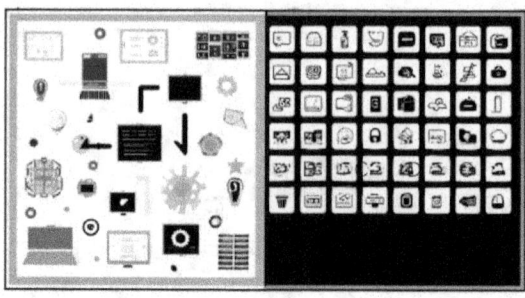

Application   Operating System

There is a big difference between an *app* and an *operating system*. To be sure, apps (digital applications) have revolutionized the way we get information and efficiently function in an increasingly digital world. There is an app for everything under the sun with scores being added daily to the thousands currently available. But as helpful and genius as these cool new tools are filling our digital boxes, they can't replace the Internal Operating System (IOS). The operating system controls everything on the laptop, tablet, or smartphone. It allows programs to talk to each other, data to flow smoothly across platforms, and keeps everything neat, tidy, and available with just a few clicks.

Imagine the Kingdom of God not as just another app on your spiritual smartphone, but as an entirely new operating system. It's not an add-on; it's a complete overhaul of how we process, well, *everything*. The words of Jesus aren't something we click in and out of. When Jesus came to declare and offer the Kingdom of God, he was offering a whole new way of thinking, living, and loving. He offers us a *Kingdom Internal Operating System (KIOS)*. It was never meant as an add-on but rather a find and replace. You won't need to install any updates.

This is the repentance—the change of thinking about everything—Jesus is talking about. This is the life Jesus is calling us to. This is the kingdom Jesus wants *all* to enter, experience and enjoy forever . . . beginning *now*. He doesn't want us to simply be informed. He wants us, like a butterfly breaking out of its pupae, to be *transformed*. This transformation includes our head, heart, and hands:

> *Therefore, I urge you, brothers and sisters, in view of God's mercy, to offer your bodies as a living sacrifice, holy and pleasing to God—this is your true and proper worship. Do not conform to*

The Final Bridge

> *the pattern of this world, but be transformed by the renewing of your mind. Then you will be able to test and approve what God's will is—his good, pleasing and perfect will. (Romans 12:1-2, NIV)*

Don't miss the wondrous result of repentance in the last sentence. We all want to know God's will and to accomplish it in the fleeting moments of our life. Clearly, we can. But the access point, according to Jesus, is to heed his clarion call:

> *Repent, for the kingdom of heaven has come near. (Matthew 4:17, NIV)*

It all goes back to the bottom line we began with:

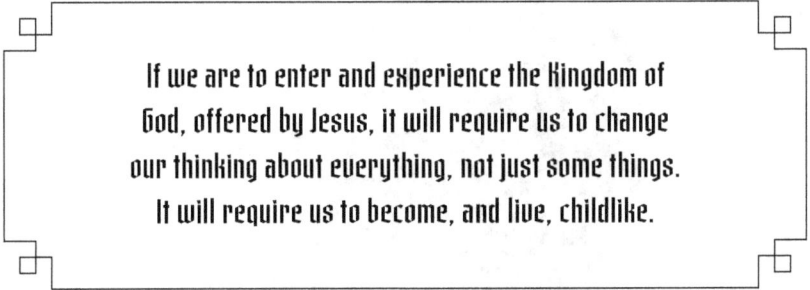

> *I tell you the truth, anyone who doesn't receive the Kingdom of God like a child will never enter it. (Mark 10:15)*

Following Jesus requires us to change our thinking. It requires we become childlike. It involves a new operating system. It involves learning to read. The good news is, we don't (and can't) do it alone. We have been given divine resources, beginning with the Holy Spirit. You see, flesh and blood can never reveal Jesus to us. It is a work of the Spirit. You and I can only testify of him. I hope The Childlike Kingdom will be yet another helpful resource to add to your backpack.

One of the last *proverbs* I heard from Doug Coe before his passing was, "Following Jesus isn't an exact science." I have found this to be true and imagine you have, too. There is no formula, equation, or theorem to quantify it. There are not enough letters in the alphabet to describe it. It is sometimes (usually) a messy experiment. It is sometimes a muddy path. It is impossible to fully articulate or sketch. But it is amazing how Jesus can use even the simplest of tools (teaching, writing, drawing) to point us to transformation, whether using pencil, crayon or paint. Or a smartphone. Or even AI? Perhaps in the next book.

Yet, we *can* learn to follow. We can learn to think and live according to King Jesus. And we will, until our final birthday or Christmas morning gives way to a whole new kingdom reality . . . still complete with castles and schoolrooms.

The bell is ringing but class *isn't* dismissed. The gate is open and kingdom adventures await. But more than anything, kids . . . *the King himself awaits!*

For Yours is the kingdom and the power and the glory forever.

Amen.

And we will all live happily ever . . . forever!

Appendix

CLK Main Takeaways

> If we are to enter and experience the Kingdom of God offered by Jesus, it will require us to change our thinking about everything, not just some things. It will require us to become, and live, childlike.

1. Eternal Life Through Jesus (Only Him)
   The Divinity of Jesus (He's God)
   The Incarnation of Jesus (Fully God. Fully Man)
   The Crucifixion of Jesus (He Died)
   The Resurrection of Jesus (He Rose From The Dead)
   The Return of Jesus (He's Coming Again)
   The Image of Jesus (The imago Dei)
   The Inspired Word of God (The Scriptures)
   The Bride of Jesus (The Divine Community)
   The Trinity (One God . . . Three Persons)

2. But more than anything else, put God's kingship first and do what he wants.

3. Be Less. Be Little. Be Last. Be Least.

A	In God's Childlike Kingdom, the king is always available, fully accessible, and is actively seeking us . . . first!
B	Everything in the Kingdom of God is transcendental.
C	The Kingdom of God is best (re)signed as a childlike kingdom.
D	Death is a reality in the empires of this world, and painfully felt by all who are currently inhabiting the Kingdom of God on earth. So are dungeons. And dragons. Fear not!
E	Eternal Life is a relationship.
F	Hey kids, c'mon . . . let's follow Rabbi Jesus and get his dust all over us.
G	The Kingdom of God is a perfect smash-up . . . a Gardencity.
H	The greatest journey home is from a place to a person.
I	I identify as an adopted child of God: created by a loving Father; redeemed by a benevolent king; animated by a Holy Spirit. We identify as the adopted family of God, the very bride and body of Christ: created by a loving Father to be a chosen generation; redeemed by a benevolent king to be a royal priesthood; animated by the Spirit to be a holy nation.
J	"Hey!"
K	When we compare the Kingdom of God with the empires of this world, we quickly realize there is nothing but contrast, and the kingdom Jesus offers is beyond compare.
L	Love is over everything!
M	A kingdom and king whose time has come.
N	New creation begins at the resurrection of Jesus.
O	In the Kingdom of God, there is only One.
P	Lasting peace is only found in the Prince of Peace.
Q	What is the gospel? Where do I start each day? Why am I here? How do I navigate this life? Who do you say Jesus is?
R	The principal work of our Messiah, King Jesus, is rescue.

Appendix

S   *Scripture is not an owner's manual or rule book. Scripture is God's story; the greatest story ever lived.*

T   *According to Jesus, true righteousness always begins with the heart.*

U   *To say that Jesus was not the Messiah the Jewish nation expected, or wanted, is a king-sized understatement.*

V   *There are both noble and ordinary pots, but there are no ordinary people.*

W   *Having faith requires us to sacrifice our certainty and control on the altar of wonder.*

X   *X marks the Messiah.*

Y   *The way of childlike humility requires we yield.*

Z   *Our compassion must always outweigh and outpace our passion.*

Coming Spring 2026
The second book in the Childlike Kingdom series
by Dr. Jay J. Anderson

About the Author

Dr. Jay J. Anderson is a Jesus follower, writer, teacher, and pastor and plans to spend his remaining days doing all four with all his heart. Jay is the favorite son of Don & Marianne, husband and best friend of Stacie, father of the best two boys *ever* (Kyle & Calvin), and their surprisingly cute and talented girls (Claudia & Annie), as well as two twin grandkids (London & Lenny), and one already in our heavenly home (Caroline Joy). He can't wait to meet her! In addition to his kingdom musings, Jay also writes love stories for Stacie, and adventure stories for his boys, all of which he dreams of being published someday. Jay has degrees from Northwest University (BA), Evangel University (MA), and Portland Seminary of George Fox University (DMin). He has been a pastor, adjunct professor, academic advisor, school superintendent, chaplain, tour guide, shuttle driver, and furniture salesman. In addition to writing Jay loves to read, hike, kayak, travel, and drink coffee in cool Pacific Northwest shops. He currently resides in the Willamette Valley of Oregon.

Connect With Jay

Join The Childlike Kingdom Facebook Group for Jay's weekly blogs:
https://www.facebook.com/groups/730479421099974

About the Author

Several years ago, after reading Bob Goff's most inspiring book, *Love Does*, he was surprised to find Bob's personal number in the back of the book, with an encouragement to call him if so desired. Jay did and amazingly Bob picked up! Jay is honored to extend the same invitation. His personal cell is 503-858-4090 and email jjajesusfollower@gmail.com.

Bibliography

Bartlett, John. *Familiar Quotations: A collection of passages, phrases and proverbs traced to their sources in ancient and modern literature.* Boston: Little, Brown and Company, 1980.

Batterson, Mark. *Soul Print.* Colorado Springs, Multnomah Books, 2011.

Calvin, John. *Institutes of the Christian Religion.* ed. John T. McNeill; trans. For Lewis Battles; 2 vols; Philadelphia, Westminster 1960.

Cambridge Dictionary. Cambridge, UK: Cambridge University Press, 2024.

Comer, John Mark. *Garden City: Work, Rest, and the Art of Being Human.* Grand Rapids: Zondervan, 2015.

———. *Practicing the Way: Be with Jesus. Become like him. Do as he did.* Colorado Springs: WaterBrook, 2024.

Dickens, Charles. *Great Expectations.* Originally published in 1861 and is now public domain.

Downing, Crystal. *Changing Signs of Truth: A Christian Introduction to the Semiotics of Communication.* Downers Grove: InterVarsity, 2012.

Egan, Timothy. *A Pilgrimage to Eternity: From Canterbury to Rome in Search of a Faith.* New York: Viking, 2019.

Goff, Bob. *Everybody Always: Becoming Love in a World Full of Setbacks and Difficult People.* Nashville: Thomas Nelson, 2018.

———. *Love Does: Discover a Secretly Incredible Life in an Ordinary World.* Nashville: Thomas Nelson, 2012.

Ladd, George Eldon. *The Gospel of the Kingdom: Scriptural Studies in the Kingdom of God.* Grand Rapids: Wm. B. Eerdmans, 1959.

Lewis, C.S. *The Magician's Nephew.* New York: HarperCollins, 1955.

Lucado, Max. *Just Like Jesus.* Nashville: Word, 1998.

Luther, Martin. *A Mighty Fortress is Our God,* Public Domain, 1529.

McDowell, Josh. *More Than a Carpenter.* Carol Stream: Tyndale House, 1977.

———. *The New Evidence That Demands a Verdict.* Nashville: Thomas Nelson, 1999.

McDowell, Josh and Geisler, Norm. *Love is Always Right: A Defense of the One Moral Absolute.* Dallas: Word, 1996.

McDowell, Dottie & Josh, with David Nathan Weiss. *The Topsy Turvy Kingdom.* Mexico: Tyndale for Kids, 1996.

McClaren, Brian. *Faith After Doubt: Why Your Beliefs Stopped Working and What to Do About it.* New York: St. Martin's Group, 2021, iBooks.

———. *A New Kind of Christianity: Ten Questions That Are Transforming the Faith.* New York: HarperCollins, 2010, iBooks.

McKnight, Scot. *The King Jesus Gospel: The Original Good News Revisited.* Grand Rapids: Zondervan, 2011.

———. *Kingdom Conspiracy: Returning to the Radical Mission of the Local Church.* Grand Rapids: Brazos, 2014.

Milne, A.A. *The Complete Tales of Winnie-the-Pooh.* New York: Dutton Children's Books an imprint of Penguin Random House, 1992.

Moore, Beth. *John: 90 Days With the Beloved Disciple.* Nashville: B&H Group, 2008.

Ortberg, John. *The Life You've Always Wanted: Spiritual Disciplines For Ordinary People.* Grand Rapids: Zondervan, 1997.

———. *Who Is This Man? The Unpredictable Impact of the Inescapable Jesus.* Grand Rapids: Zondervan, 2012.

Oxford English Dictionary. Oxford, UK: Oxford University Press, 2024.

Prince Harry. *Spare.* New York: Random House, 2023.

Saltzman, Royce. *Growing Up Good: Reflections of a Boy From Kansas.* Amazon Digital Services, 2019.

Smith, James Bryan. *The Magnificent Story: Uncovering a Gospel of Beauty, Goodness & Truth.* Downers Grove: InterVarsity, 2017.

Stanley, Andy. *Not In It To Win It: Why Choosing Sides Sidelines the Church.* Grand Rapids: Zondervan, 2022.

Stevenson, Robert Louis. *Treasure Island.* Originally published in 1883 and is now public domain.

The Story: The Bible as One Continuing Story of God and His People. Grand Rapids: Zondervan, 2021.

Sweet, Leonard. *Jesus Human: Primer for a Common Humanity.* Absecon: The Salish Sea Press, 2023.

Sweet, Leonard, and Frank Viola. *Jesus Manifesto: Restoring the Supremacy and Sovereignty of Jesus Christ.* Nashville: Thomas Nelson, 2010.

———. *Jesus: A Theography.* Nashville: Thomas Nelson, 2012.

———. *Jesus Speaks: Learning To Recognize & Respond To The Lord's Voice.* Nashville: W Group, 2016.

Timmons, Tim. *Jesus Plus Nothing.* Newport Beach: Embers, 2012.

Tverberg, Lois. *Walking in the Dust of Rabbi Jesus.* Grand Rapids: Zondervan, 2012.

Van Der Kolk, Bessel. *The Body Keeps the Score: Brain, Mind, and Body in the Healing of Trauma.* New York: Penguin, 2014.

Volf, Miroslav, and Croasmun, Matthew. *For The Life of the World: Theology That Makes A Difference.* Grand Rapids: Brazos, 2019.

Wright, N.T. *Simply Christian: Why Christianity Makes Sense.* San Francisco: HarperCollins, 2006.

———. *Simply Jesus: A New Vision of Who He Was, What He Did, and Why He Matters.* New York: HarperOne, 2011.

———. *Surprised By Hope.* London: Society for Promoting Christian Knowledge, 2007.

Yancey, Philip. *The Jesus I Never Knew.* Grand Rapids: Zondervan, 1995.

Zahnd, Brian. *Beauty Will Save the World.* Lake Mary: Charisma House, 2012.

www.ingramcontent.com/pod-product-compliance
Lightning Source LLC
Chambersburg PA
CBHW060556230426
43670CB00011B/1846